POSTTRAUMATIC STRESS INTERVENTION

POSTTRAUMATIC STRESS INTERVENTION

Challenges, Issues, and Perspectives

Edited by

JOHN M. VIOLANTI, Ph.D.

Department of Criminal Justice
Rochester Institute of Technology
Rochester, New York
Department of Social and Preventive Medicine
School of Medicine and Biomedical Sciences
State University of New York at Buffalo

DOUGLAS PATON, Ph.D., C.PSYCHOL.

School of Psychology, Massey University
Palmerston North, New Zealand

CHRISTINE DUNNING, Ph.D.

Department of Governmental Affairs
University of Wisconsin-Milwaukee, Wisconsin

Charles C Thomas
PUBLISHER • LTD.
SPRINGFIELD • ILLINOIS • U.S.A.

Published and Distributed Throughout the World by

CHARLES C THOMAS • PUBLISHER, LTD.
2600 South First Street
Springfield, Illinois 62704

ISBN 0-398-07066-0 (cloth)
ISBN 0-398-07067-9 (paper)

Library of Congress Catalog Card Number: 00-025323

With THOMAS BOOKS *careful attention is given to all details of manufacturing
and design. It is the Publisher's desire to present books that are satisfactory as to their
physical qualities and artistic possibilities and appropriate for their particular use.
THOMAS BOOKS will be true to those laws of quality that assure a good name
and good will.*

Printed in the United States of America
SR-R-3

Library of Congress Cataloging-in-Publication Data

Posttraumatic stress intervention : challenges, issues, and perspectives / edited by
John M. Violanti, Douglas Paton, Christine Dunning.
    p. cm.
Includes bibliographical references and index
ISBN 0-398-07066-0 (cloth) — ISBN 0-398-07067-9 (paper)
1. Post-traumatic stress disorder—Prevention. 2. Crisis intervention (Mental
health services). I. Violanti, John M. II. Paton, Douglas. III. Dunning, Christine,
1948–

RC552.P67 P675 2000
616.85'21—dc21
                                                           00-025323

CONTRIBUTORS

Paul T. Bartone, Ph.D., received his Ph.D. in Psychology/Human Development from the University of Chicago in 1984. Since 1985, he has served as a research psychologist for the U.S. Army, first at the Walter Reed Army Institute of Research (WRAIR) in Washington, D.C., then as Director of the WRAIR psychology field unit in Heidelberg, Germany, to his current position as research scientist, Department of Behavioral Sciences and Leadership, United States Military Academy, West Point. He has conducted numerous studies of stress, health and adaptation among military personnel and their families. He is a member of the American Psychological Association, American Psychological Society, American Public Health Association, International Society for Traumatic Stress Studies, the European Research Group on Military and Society, and the Inter-University Seminar on Armed Forces and Society. He serves as member-at-large for the Military Psychology Division (19) of APA, and also chairs that division's Committee on International Military Psychology.

Lawrence G. Calhoun, Ph.D., is a professor of psychology at the University of North Carolina at Charlotte. He is a clinical psychologist whose work focuses on trauma, posttraumatic growth, and the aftermath of suicide. He is the co-author of *Dealing with crisis* (1976), *Trauma and Transformation: Growing in the aftermath of suffering* (1995), *Facilitating posttraumatic growth: A clinician's guide* (1999), and co-editor of *Posttraumatic growth: Positive changes in the aftermath of crisis* (1998).

Ingrid V.E. Carlier, Psy.D., Ph.D., is a clinical and social psychologist. Since 1991, she has headed the Psychotrauma Section, Department of Psychiatry, Academic Medical Center of the University of Amsterdam. She leads the diagnostics and treatment of traumatized clients, and the research on prevention and treatment of posttraumatic stress disorders.

Christine Dunning, Ph.D., is a professor and Chair of the Department of Governmental Affairs at the University of Wisconsin- Milwaukee. She received her Ph.D. in Criminal Justice/Social Science from Michigan State University with a joint major in Public Administration and Organizational Sociology. In addition, she attended Marquette University Law School. Dr. Dunning formerly served as Associate Director–Police at the Des Moines, Iowa Criminal Justice Center and as director of In-Service Police Training for Southeastern Wisconsin Police Academy. She has published extensively on police stress and trauma, disaster stress management, and in numerous areas of police administration. A three-term board member and former vice-president of the International Society for Traumatic Stress Studies, she has consulted with officials responsible for mitigation in a large number of catastrophic events annually.

Liisa Eränen, Ph.D. Cand., is a social psychologist. She is a founding board member of the European Society for Traumatic Stress Studies and has published several articles and book chapters on trauma and disaster psychology. Since 1985, she has worked as a researcher for the Ministry of Interior and as a researcher and assistant professor at University of Helsinki, Department of Social Psychology where she created a new research tradition through her empirical research studies in trauma psychology. With Clay Foreman, and in cooperation with the Finnish Ministry of Interior, she initiated and supervised the research project on UN civilian police duty. Recently, she was appointed to be the (first female) Head of Social Services in the Finnish Navy.

Berthold P. R. Gersons, M.D., Ph.D., is professor of psychiatry and chair of the Department of Psychiatry of the AMC/University of Amsterdam. He has been involved in the traumatic stress field since the 1980s when he set up the first self-help team within the Amsterdam police force. Together with Dr. Ingrid Carlier, he performed a number of studies on critical incidents in the police force, debriefing and treatment, and the Bijlmer air crash disaster. He published many papers and chapters on these topics in international literature. He developed a 16-sessions short treatment protocol for PTSD. He was chair of the first World Conference on Traumatic Stress in 1992 and member of the Editorial Board on the *Journal of Traumatic Stress*. He was a member of the Board of Directors of the International Society of Traumatic Stress Studies. He is currently a member of the Board of Directors of the European Society of Traumatic Stress Studies.

Richard Gist, Ph.D., is Principal Assistant to the Director of the Kansas City, Missouri Fire Department and Associate Professor of Psychology at the University of Missouri-Kansas City. He had prior service as Director of Social Sciences and Social Services for Johnson County (Kansas) Community College, one of the top ten two-year institutions in the United States, and concurrently as Consulting Community Psychologist for the Health and Fire Departments in Kansas City. He has assisted a great variety of public safety and social facilitation agencies throughout the United States and Canada in developing programs to address organizational and community needs. A widely known author and lecturer, he edited (with Bernard Lubin) the acclaimed 1989 volume, *Psychosocial aspects of disaster* from John Wiley & Sons, and the recent *Response to disaster: Psychosocial, ecological, and community approaches* from Brunner/ Mazel.

Gisela Perrin-Klingler, Dr. Med. Dr. Perrin-Klingler's interests are: (1) in response to her occupation with torture victims: The connection between basic mental health and human rights, mental health and political/judicial responses to violations of human rights and the participation/limitations and ethical tasks of psychotherapy in this process; (2) Prevention of violence at a primary and secondary level, peace education (schools); (3) Transcultural approaches in mental health, combination of traditional (religious, non-medical) and modern (medical and mental health) interventions for victims of torture and other violence; (4) Mental Health as an occupational problem in professions exposed to violence: (police, firemen etc., medical and paramedical professions, international aid workers); (5) Mental health in marginalized populations (migrants, refugees, detainees, foreigners, adolescents, drug addicts, HIV persons); (6) Self empowerment of marginalized groups; and (7) Networking between North/South professional groups and different human rights groups.

Malcolm D. MacLeod, Ph.D., is a lecturer in social and forensic psychology in the School of Psychology at the University of St. Andrews, Scotland. He has published widely in the field of eyewitness testimony, person identification and criminal victimization. His current research focuses on the social cognition mechanisms by which people adjust to, and recover from, victimization episodes, illness, and other traumatic events.

Douglas Paton Ph.D., C.Psychol., is an Associate Professor at Massey University, New Zealand and an Honorary Senior Lecturer at

St. Andrews University, Scotland. He is a foundation member of the Australasian Society for Traumatic Stress Studies and the founding editor of the *Australasian Journal of Disaster and Trauma Studies*. He is currently involved in a longitudinal study of occupational and traumatic stress in New Zealand police officers.

James W. Pennebaker, Ph.D., is Professor of Psychology in the social and clinical areas of the Department of Psychology at the University of Texas at Austin, where he received his Ph.D. in 1977. He has been on the faculty at the University of Virginia, Southern Methodist University, and, since 1997, The University of Texas. He and his students are exploring the links between traumatic experiences and physical and mental health. His studies find that physician use, medical costs, and alcohol use can be reduced and work performance increased by simple writing and/or talking exercises. His most recent research focuses on the nature of language and emotion in the real world. Author or editor of 7 books and over 100 articles, Pennebaker has received numerous awards and honors.

Leigh M. Smith, Ph.D., is Head of the School of Psychology at Curtin University of Technology in Perth, Western Australia. His main research foci are the development and application of research techniques and data analyses in applied settings, measurement theory and the construction of psychological response scales. He is interested in psychological well-being in work, and in particular the relation between organizational practices and the mental health of workers.

Cynthia M. Stuhlmiller, Ph.D., is Professor and foundation clinical chair for the Academic Department of Mental Health Nursing—a joint venture between the University of Technology, Sydney and South Eastern Sydney Area Health Service. Her clinical background includes over a decade of work with Vietnam Veterans and other people exposed to extreme circumstances and has worked in a variety of inpatient and outpatient acute and chronic mental health settings. She has held academic appointments at The University of San Francisco, The University of Tromsoe, Norway, and Massey University in New Zealand. Her publications and research interests include: disaster response, narrative picturing, action-based therapy, seasonal variation, and the dangers of diagnostic disordering.

Richard G. Tedeschi, Ph.D., is a professor of Psychology at the University of North Carolina at Charlotte. He is a Clinical Psychologist whose work focuses on traumatic loss, bereavement, and posttraumatic growth. He is the co-author of *Trauma and Transformation: Growing in the aftermath of suffering* (1995), *Facilitating posttraumatic growth: A clinician's guide* (1999), and co-editor of *Posttraumatic growth: Positive changes in the aftermath of crisis* (1998).

John M. Violanti, Ph.D., is an associate professor at the Rochester Institute of Technology (RIT) Rochester, New York, and an assistant clinical professor at the University of Buffalo School of Medicine and Biomedical Sciences, Department of Social and Preventive Medicine. Dr. Violanti has focused the majority of his work on police trauma and suicide. He is the author and co-author of numerous journal articles and four other books on those topics.

S. Joseph Woodall, Ph.D., holds a Ph.D. in Human and Organizational Systems, and a Master of Education and Arts in Professional Clinical Counseling. He is a seventeen-year veteran of the professionals fire service, currently serving as Captain on Ladder Company 193, Peoria Fire Department, Peoria, Arizona. In addition to his duties as company officer, he serves on the Phoenix Fire Department's Juvenile Setter Provider panel, providing counseling services for juvenile fire setters. As a National Board Certified Clinical Professional Counselor, Joe frequently works with the St. Luke's Employee Assistance Program as an instructor and counselor therapist. The majority of his off-duty time is spent as the Associate Dean of Graduate Studies within the College of Continuing Studies at Grand Canyon University, Phoenix, Arizona. Dr. Woodall is in the process of co-authoring *Chicken Soup for the Lifesaving Soul,* with Jack Canfield, Rick Canfield, and Mark Victor Hansen. This compilation of lifesaving stories gathered from fire fighters, police officers, nurses, doctors, military veterans, paramedics, and everyday heroes will likely be another best seller in this long line of best sellers.

PREFACE

IN THE BEGINNING there was nothing. Decades ago, the mental health profession was unexpectedly faced with a new problem called "Posttraumatic Stress Disorder" (PTSD). Fortunately, pioneers in various academic and research disciplines stepped forward to deal with the problem. We owe them a debt of gratitude for first addressing PTSD intervention, and for establishing contemporary intervention techniques.

Change, however, is the product of time and scientific progress. This book examines an evolving consensus that we must now profit from our past and present knowledge and explore new ideas about intervention. Since the 1980s, posttraumatic stress intervention has focused primarily on "psychological debriefings" to help prevent PTSD. Debriefings involve individual or group meetings with a psychologist or trained peer after a traumatic event. While debriefing is said to be important in preventing PTSD, mental health professionals are uncertain about outcomes. Indeed, researchers are surprised at the high levels of incidence and chronicity of PTSD reported by those participating in debriefs. There is agreement that debriefing may be somewhat hindered by its pathogenic nature (an automatic assumption of PTSD pathology) rather than being a positive method for preventing trauma stress.

As the efficacy of debriefing remains empirically questionable and its protocol unchanged with advancing scientific knowledge, alternatives to the approach have been suggested. One suggestion is a salutogenic model, which focuses on the ability of individuals themselves to psychologically withstand fatigue, hardship, and horrific conditions. Individual inner strength appears to foster courage and fortitude in the face of the overwhelming demands occasioned by the traumatic event. Individual hardiness or resiliency is thought to represent the manner in which a person approaches and interprets an experience. These attributes may influence how people successfully process and cope with traumatic event, with or without intervention from others.

Ideas about trauma intervention may thus be moving away from the negative slant of pathogenic models and towards the strength of the individual. The individual is now seen as an *active agent* who generates resistance to PTSD, positively reinterprets a negative traumatic incident, and may personally grow from the experience.

Since trauma intervention is practiced across different situations and persons in need, the ideas expressed in this book may be useful for mental health professionals, disaster workers, emergency worker counselors, police counselors, relief workers, and any group or individual that works with persons exposed to trauma. It is hoped that the ideas described herein will add to the repertoire of those who seek to help others.

John M. Violanti
Douglas Paton
Christine Dunning

CONTENTS

POSTTRAUMATIC STRESS
INTERVENTION

Chapter 1

POSTTRAUMATIC STRESS INTERVENTION: CHALLENGES, ISSUES, AND PERSPECTIVES

Douglas Paton, John M. Violanti, and Chris Dunning

THIS BOOK IS ABOUT ALTERNATIVES in posttraumatic stress intervention. Not just alternatives for doing things, but also for ways of thinking and accomplishing goals. To explore these issues, we have brought together contributions from international experts who discuss existing practices and seek to define the emerging evolution in posttraumatic stress intervention.

Although posttrauma intervention has a history dating back some 60 years, the practice of formalized intervention has grown exponentially since the early 1980s. While this growth may be attributed to helping people cope with adversity, often competing political, economic and sociolegal pressures can influence current thinking.

For work-related populations, the growth in intervention has focused primarily on one modality: Critical Incident Stress Debriefing (CISD) (Mitchell, 1983). In their respective chapters, Stuhlmiller and Dunning and Gist and Woodall comment on the phenomenal growth of CISD, presently labeled Critical Incident Stress Management (CISM), and the almost evangelical level of support evident for this practice from its adherents.

Despite the popularity of this approach for posttrauma intervention, concerns are increasingly being expressed regarding its ability to achieve its aim of mitigating traumatic symptomatology. Carlier and Gersons and Gist and Woodall review recent evaluative studies of debriefing, and CISM in particular, and conclude that not only is the ability of CISM to mitigate symptoms questionable, evidence increasingly points to it having iatrogenic properties. Rather than mitigating symptoms, debriefing may actually contribute to the development of posttrauma pathology.

These findings raise several questions. For example, it is pertinent to inquire into the reasons for the growth and popularity of CISM and why such concerns are emerging long after the protocol was introduced. In addition, it is not enough to describe the effectiveness of an intervention. We must also define, in empirically testable ways, why an intervention is ineffective, why it might contribute to iatrogenic effects, and be able to describe the mechanism(s) by which protocols attain their efficacy. In this text, we examine the paradigm upon which most contemporary posttrauma intervention is based and discuss implications for future research and intervention.

Why has debriefing achieved its enduring popularity and why, despite increasing concern about possible harmful effects, has it retained such popularity? Two lines of inquiry cast light on this issue. One relates to the prevailing paradigm underpinning its origins and the other to the evaluation methodology adopted.

The debriefing concept emerged in its current form at a time when the diagnostic criteria for posttraumatic stress disorder encompassed by the Diagnostic Statistical Manual of the American Psychiatric Association (DSM III/IV–1980/1994) had only recently formally established the existence of posttraumatic stress disorder as a psychiatric disorder. Stuhlmiller and Dunning argue that the mental health community were presented with a problem, but not the solution. They discuss how the inclusion of posttraumatic stress disorder within the psychiatric diagnostic scheme increased the incidence of traumatized individuals seeking financial redress, usually against an employer, and created pressure for a low-cost means of eliminating or minimizing this threat to organizations. CISD emerged to fit the latter gap and thus fitted neatly into a ready-made niche, even though little theoretical work had been done to define the nature of posttrauma stress. CISD represented a convenient solution to a human resource problem of containing spiralling litigation and compensation costs. In their respective chapters, Stuhlmiller and Dunning and Gist and Woodall describe the subsequent growth of this protocol.

Violanti offers a different perspective. Using a medical analogy, the sick role, Violanti describes how attempting to manage a poorly defined problem can "script" the expectations of organizations and personnel alike into accepting the need for a specific procedure. Violanti draws attention to the fact that critical incident stress represents a social construct or script which acts to preclude discussing, let alone using, alternatives, including those that require doing nothing or which require organizational action to facilitate well-being. Paton, Smith, Violanti and Eränen describe how another social cognitive process, the "social amplification of risk," provides an alternative mechanism of explaining the adoption of CISD in the absence of an understanding of the phenomena under consideration or empirical evidence of its effectiveness.

Hence, there exists several paradigmatic, social psychological, and organizational mechanisms that can be invoked to explain commitment to a protocol in the absence of demonstrable effectiveness, or even when empirical analyses argue against the use of such protocol.

While the original authors of the debriefing protocol, and others, did indeed seek to evaluate their intervention, the outcome measure(s) adopted may have confounded this process. Carlier and Gersons draw a distinction between studies that focus on satisfaction and those that constitute more rigorous attempts to evaluate outcomes over time. They point out that while perceived satisfaction (the basis for several conclusions regarding the efficacy of CISM) with debriefing is generally described as high, high satisfaction is rarely associated with lowered symptomology or beneficial changes in other possible indices of effectiveness such as time to return to work or a reduction in sick leave.

While debriefing protocols have remained largely unchanged since their inception, the same is not true of our knowledge of stress and traumatic stress processes. The contributions to this text draw upon recent advances in psychological, sociological, anthropological and organizational theory and analyses to substantiate concerns regarding the efficacy of debriefing.

As described above, it is not sufficient to demonstrate the ineffectiveness of any protocol, we must also establish the substance of our concerns and critiques and express them as theoretically sound and testable proposals. It is only by this process, and their testing and evaluation in methodologically rigorous ways, that we can establish an objective and comprehensive understanding of posttrauma stress intervention. In their respective chapters, Stuhlmiller and Dunning, Gist and Woodall, Carlier and Gersons and MacLeod all discuss reasons for the lack of debriefing effectiveness. The problems they identify include: inadequate definition of the nature of critical incidents; over-representation of a need for acute intervention; inadequate articulation of the relationship between critical incidents and trauma; confusion between physiologically discrete stress and traumatic stress processes; failure to develop a process that is consistent with the ecology of survivors; inadequate research into determining who should administer it; the timing and content of intervention; and the ethics of intervention. These critiques are substantive, theoretically rooted and provide a base for the development of testable hypotheses regarding the development of effective posttrauma intervention.

Critical reviews, such as those described here, have also provided the foundation for the development of alternative approaches to this issue. Carlier and Gersons, Gist and Woodall, Calhoun and Tedeschi, and Pennebaker describe several posttrauma interventions that are theoretically rigorous, derived from the empirical analysis of the nature of posttrauma processes, and developed to cater for the specific professional and organizational contexts of those they are intended to assist offer more than protocols that are rigid in both design and application. These not only accommodate some or all of these concerns, they also represent protocols that are more flexible and capable of being adapted to the needs of individuals and organizations, and are more amenable to change in response to developments in theory and knowledge.

In the present text, we additionally seek to demonstrate how we can use our knowledge to explore the development of organizational/environmental capabilities which serve to protect individuals from the impact of adversity, allow natural resilience resources to operate, and facilitate the capability of individuals to grow as a consequence of adversity. Accomplishing this goal requires that we question the paradigm that has dominated how we define problems and develop the means to resolve them. Stuhlmiller and Dunning open this debate by calling into question the validity of a paradigm that orientates problem definition, and thus the means by which we seek to resolve problems, towards pathology. They demonstrate how the extension of the medical model into the area of mental health, or more accurately, mental ill-health, drove the use of the pathological paradigm. Perren-Klingler, approaching the issue from a psychiatric perspective, reaches the same conclusion. Both advocate a need to reframe the way in which we think about traumatic stress and adopt a salutogenic approach that focuses attention on encouraging people to use natural coping and resilience resources to deal with adversity.

Pursuing this course of action requires that we define what a shift to a salutogenic paradigm means for posttrauma intervention. The pathologically-oriented paradigm of debriefing defines exposure to trauma in terms of a set of negative reactions which, if not dealt with immediately by mental health practitioners, could result in the development of a psychiatric disorder. According to Stuhlmiller and Dunning, facilitating a paradigm shift requires that we address the following issues. First, we must identify the natural coping strategies and the social and psychological mechanisms that facilitate resilience. Secondly, we must accept that rather than inevitably leading to negative outcomes, coping with trauma and adversity may constitute a growth experience. We therefore must understand the processes which act to protect psychological well-being when faced with adversity; that is, the mechanisms which facilitate resilience.

Resilience describes an active process of self-righting, learned resourcefulness and growth; the ability to function psychologically at a level far greater than expected given the individual's capabilities and previous experiences (Dunning, 1999). Resilience is not a unidimensional phenomenon. Rather it represents the action of factors that operate at dispositional, cognitive and environmental levels (Dunning, 1999). In Chapter 7, Bartone presents an empirical analysis of United States soldiers exposed to stressful circumstances during the Gulf War and demonstrates not only that ill-effects are not an automatic consequence of exposure to high and multiple stress circumstances, but also that a psychological construct, hardiness, can be invoked to explain this outcome. Bartone also discusses possible mechanisms to explain the operation of this construct as a protective factor and the means by which it can be developed and enhanced through training.

MacLeod, in Chapter 10, argues that an understanding of coping is essential to the task of gaining a full understanding of resilience. MacLeod asks what we mean by coping and, importantly, draws a distinction between describing coping mechanisms and understanding how people actually achieve psychological adjustment following trauma. He draws upon social cognition processes to explore how people adjust to adverse experience and how such processes can promote resilience. He also introduces a temporal orientation as a basis for clarifying the complex relationship between resilience and social cognition processes such as counterfactuals, rumination, social comparisons and temporal disintegration, and for intervention development. In Chapter 9, Violanti provides an empirical illustration of how coping with military style training can constitute a personal protective factor in police officers and increase the likelihood of traumatic work experiences providing opportunities for growth.

In their respective chapters, Gist and Woodall and Paton, Smith, Violanti and Eränen discuss how cognitive resilience can be enhanced through training and through interventions designed to promote a better fit between operational requirements and personal well-being. These contributions also describe how the organizational environment can be designed to facilitate and sustain resilience. Perren-Klingler also discusses environmental determinants of resilience. She describes the role of culture in this context and argues for the need to accommodate cultural diversity and resources when conceptualizing traumatic stress reactions and intervention to ensure that the rich personal and spiritual resources of those affected are utilized to assist their recovery.

Resilience thus describes how people, when faced with trauma and adversity, are capable of drawing upon social and psychological resources that act to protect them from harm and facilitate their ability to "recoil" from a negative experience. This is only one facet of a shift to a salutogenic paradigm. The adoption of the latter also allows us to think of traumatic experiences in terms of their ability to facilitate growth.

Calhoun and Tedeschi discuss how being faced with trauma and adversity can be a growth experience. They make the important point that growth does not automatically imply freedom from the potentially negative consequences of traumatic events. In the past, these have been conflated, artificially emphasizing the possible negative consequences of trauma and lessening the likelihood of alternatives even being considered. Consequently, as several contributors, notably Stuhlmiller and Dunning, Calhoun and Tedeschi, and Bartone note, important growth outcomes and mechanisms were ignored or, if noticed, dismissed as interesting but insignificant curios. We can also speculate that the anecdotal nature of most growth observations illustrates another consequence of the operation of a pathological paradigm. A focus on negative symptomatology results in the development of assessment instrument and protocol content capable only of picking up the anticipated negative outcomes. Moreover, their use by professionals "scripted" to identify and treat symptoms further confounds this state of affairs. Consequently, given a predisposition to find negative symptoms, and the use of procedures designed to assess only negative consequences, it is not surprising that the realization and acceptance of the incidence and importance of positive outcomes and growth has lagged behind its pathologically-orientated counterpart.

The adoption of a salutogenic paradigm directs us to look at natural coping resources and encourages us to consider how other protective resources can be instilled in individuals. It also affords opportunities to consider outcomes radically different from those anticipated by a pathological orientation. However, as Calhoun and Tedeschi point out, growth does not automatically imply the absence of negative consequences. Recognition of the possible coexistence of negative symptoms and growth suggests a need to develop a framework for conceptualizing traumatic stress within a salutogenic paradigm, but which accommodates the possibility of a range of outcomes; from growth to distress. In the final chapter, Paton, Smith, Violanti, and Eränen discuss the use of a risk management framework to accomplish this goal.

Throughout the remainder of the text, there are further discussions of paradigmatic, conceptual and practical problems associated with dominant protocols in intervention, and an alternative framework based on salutogenesis and growth.

REFERENCES

American Psychiatric Association: *Diagnostic and statistical manual of mental disorders,* (3rd ed.), Washington, DC: American Psychiatric Press, 1980. (Fourth edition current, 1994).

Dunning, C.: Postintervention strategies to reduce police trauma: A paradigm shift. In J.M. Violanti and D. Paton (Eds.): *Police trauma: Psychological aftermath of civilian combat.* Springfield, IL: Charles C Thomas, 1999.

Mitchell, J.T.: When disaster strikes. The critical incident stress debriefing process. *Journal of Emergency Medical Services, 8,* 36–39, 1983.

Chapter 2

CHALLENGING THE MAINSTREAM: FROM PATHOGENIC TO SALUTOGENIC MODELS OF POSTTRAUMA INTERVENTION

CINDY STUHLMILLER AND CHRIS DUNNING

INTRODUCTION

PSYCHOLOGICAL DEBRIEFING FOLLOWING disastrous events has become a widespread and popular trend over the past two decades. Despite concerns regarding its efficacy, psychological debriefing currently stands as the panacea organizational response for stressful conditions. Here we argue that its derivation from a pathogenically-oriented diagnostic framework overshadows positive outcomes and may undermine individual and collective responsibility and resilience. A critical rethinking is called for to incorporate a balanced perspective that includes self-reliance, resilience, and the positive utilization of everyday occupational and personal connections for recovery.

POSTTRAUMA INTERVENTION AND THE MEDICAL MODEL

For millennia, people have experienced, adapted to or recovered from, life-threatening and traumatic events. Why, then, have these basic facts of human existence become a medical condition demanding psychological intervention? In part, this reflects a medical concept of life which has resulted in a litany of disorders to evolve, with corresponding rises in professional disciplines devoted to serving the needs they themselves created (Illich, 1974). Based in the medical model and logical positivistic foundations of science, medical diagnoses support the notion that there is objective reality that can be measured, remains consistent over time and place, and which can be generalized across populations. The ensuing framework prescribed strict definitions, rules, and standardized perspectives that shaped both professional and lay understandings and interventions. Posttraumatic stress disorder (PTSD) is one product of this medicalization process (Stuhlmiller, 1995). By definition, the person exposed to a traumatic event (abnormal situation) risks developing negative psychological symptoms (normal reaction). However, a pathogenic orientation within psychiatry, and the corresponding development of methods to assess DSM-III-R/DSM IV (American Psychiatric Association, 1998; 1994) criteria for PTSD fueled professional perceptions of a need for psychological intervention. Specialists are now dispatched to treat this pathological norm in all situations defined as being traumatic.

DEBRIEFING: MEETING A HUMAN RESOURCE NEED

Where once rendered by family, friends, or other community members, the contemporary solution for dealing with the psychological aftermath of traumatic situations is to get help from experts who intervene with strategies of response known as demobilization, defusing, and debriefing. Various protocols labeled Critical Incident Stress Debriefing (CISD), the Australian Debrief Model, and the Multistressor Debrief Model have been described (Mitchell, 1983, Raphael, 1986; Armstrong, O'Callahan, & Marmar, 1994). If one looks at the history of debriefing, it is important to note that the modality had its genesis in attempting to address stress, not trauma (Wagner, 1979; Dunning, 1999). First utilized in combat to address battle fatigue, the modality has progressively been transplanted to serve the profession of law enforcement as well as other emergency services (Kroes & Hurrell, 1975; Blakemore, 1975). Served by the rising field of police psychology, former military psychologists used the rubric of debriefing to introduce mental health counseling in emergency and critical incident situations. Their ministrations were embraced as these professions accepted that the duties performed by those in the emergency services produced a high incidence of stress in personnel. The dramatic increase in the number of stress claims for workers compensation substantially drove the trend to develop formal organizational responses to stress. Stress management training and reduction programs flourished in the 1970s in response to the need to mitigate stress to improve officer performance and health. The physiological reaction called stress or "fight or flight" was well understood and its presence easily identified and monitored by both officer and administration.

Programs that offered low cost solutions and minimized operational disruption were highly valued. Debriefing to mitigate stress had been supported by Roberts (1975) and Davidson (1979) in relation to the professional response to postshooting, air and train crash, and civilian massacre incidents. Roberts utilized the psychological debrief as a mechanism to reduce stress and anxiety levels and facilitate return to service for police officers involved in a variety of incidents, predominantly shootings and riots. The military debrief technique was further extended by Dunning and colleagues to address the emotional stress associated with police work in rescue, recovery, and disaster mitigation incidents. While the seminal article entitled *Disaster-Induced Trauma in Rescue Workers* (Dunning & Silva, 1980) spoke of stress debriefing, the word trauma was not meant to convey the development of PTSD, a diagnosis not in existence at the time of publication.

Once conducted as an individual intervention modality, the debrief as a group process gained popularity in response to the need to cover, with a minimum of intrusion and cost, a large group of responders to stressful assignments. Mantell (1991) examined the effects of group debriefing for stress following the 1978 PSA air crash and the 1982 San Ysidro McDonald's massacre, noting the drop in claims for disability rehabilitation and retirement. By early 1981, Michael Roberts and Marcia Wagner had traveled the country giving in-service training to police administrators and psychologists about the benefits of group intervention following significant operations as a mechanism to reduce stress (Wagner, 1979, 1981 a, b). The sessions were purported to provide two benefits: (1) the opportunity to talk about disaster recovery experience helped some police officers to avoid stress symptoms and to lessen the intensity of the symptoms that did occur; and (2) discussion of critical incidents and individual reactions of rescue personnel could be used to educate the participants about the nature of stress reactions and provide stress inoculation to prevent future stress. By 1984, debriefing had become the accepted modality to reduce stress in the police services as evidenced by FBI Training Keys, police magazine articles, and training presentations on the subject by the Consortium of Police Psychologists (COPS). No claims were made that the protocol had any effect on trauma which, by then, had been codified by the American Psychiatric Association (APA) as PTSD.

Despite the existence of several problems (Dunning, 1988), Mitchell (1983) argued that debriefing could mitigate trauma among emergency workers. The generic use of the word "trauma" led many to believe that debriefing represented a technological fix for the more serious and persistent effects of posttraumatic stress disorder. First presented as a psychological treatment (psychological debrief) by Mitchell for critical incident stress conceptualized as PTSD, criticism from Dunning (1988) regarding its efficacy for treating trauma led to the reformation of the CISD protocol to fit historic psychoeducational roots. What was not understood at that time, since PTSD had not been codified as a diagnosis until 1980, was that many different sequelae other than stress could emanate from traumatic experience. In this context it is doubtful whether a "one size fits all" rigid protocol could deal with all the issues raised by responders or those traumatized, increasing the likelihood that they would fail to address the true needs for recovery of trauma survivors.

During the 1980s traumatic stress research was enamored with conceptualizing the common pathway of trauma that led inevitably to PTSD and validating the existence of PTSD in those exposed to traumatic events. PTSD became the diagnosis of choice, with other manifestations of grief, loss, bereavement, worry, anxiety, phobia, and depression essentially ignored as they were not compensable under worker's compensation, insurance, or civil award. What the field was looking for was the "golden wound," an injury that can generate financial compensation of PTSD, for validation of the injury incurred by the survivor, thus making the issue of interest to the work organization as well. Yet, legal liability issues have caused concern for work-related trauma to ebb and flow over the last two decades. When debriefing resulted in large numbers of workers compensation, insurance, or civil claims, the modality was rejected by administration who perceived it as instigating malingering and secondary gain.

Some administrators perceived control of debriefing as a mechanism for controlling later access to treatment. Concurrently, unions picked up the protocol as a "safety program" for mental injuries and made its formalization as part of the organizational response mandatory as an employee benefit. Critical Incident Stress Debriefing (CISD–Mitchell, 1983) became the program of choice. Easily implemented due to the low cost of training, reliance on low level counselors, and the minimum of intrusion into the operation and culture of the work organization, CISD became the standard of care in human resource response to traumatic organizational experience. Hence, it became a solution to a human resource rather than a mental health problem.

THE POPULARIZATION AND GROWTH OF DEBRIEFING

The field of protective and emergency medical service personnel management has essentially been acculturated to believe that exposure to, or witnessing, an event that most people would consider as traumatic has potential to cause emotional harm in virtually anyone. This assumption, however, does not emanate from empirical evidence. Treatment of all exposed is excessive and ignores the healing effects of natural coping strategies.

Why has this phenomenon occurred? To a large extent it was driven by gratification that stress-related injury was being validated, and in fact normalized, thus lessening the stigma previously attached to it. For example, the medical director of American Airlines following the Flight 191 crash in 1979 stated: "These are professionals . . . from the sheriff, police, ambulance crew, and so forth. They've seen it all before.. this is what they are trained to do. If any of them need help dealing with a situation such as this, perhaps the worker really is not suited for this type of job" (Staver, 1979). Thus, the debrief movement has developed through its validation of risk rather than from any theoretical integrity, hypothesis testing and data analysis. However, legitimizing the experience of psychological stress is not the same as defining the underlying psychological constructs, the mechanisms of its operation, nor does it represent an appropriate basis for legitimizing a means for managing occupational stress.

Rather, proselytizing and identification replaced sound empirical and professional judgement as existing experience and research in mental health, cognitive psychology, and rehabilitation medicine were ignored. The standard of care became critical incident intervention. The basis upon which this standard evolved was that "everyone else had one" therefore debriefing must be a good thing. Dire warnings of the need for immediate intervention, within 24 to 48 hours, added extra burden on organizations who were pressured to accept the canned response, as to do nothing was perceived as unacceptable. Organizations who had never planned or prepared for the reality of a critical incident or traumatic event chose the critical incident management package as an acceptable alternative.

Additional momentum for the adoption of debriefing came from the inclusion in DSM-IV of Acute Stress Disorder (lasting from two days to one month) and new criteria for PTSD beyond one month. The emphasis on the use of debriefing to mitigate Acute Stress Disorder and PTSD rather than stress and anxiety became more compelling. This movement occurred despite empirical findings that most persons suffering acute trauma spontaneously remit in symptomatology within six months with or without any formal intervention (Breslau et al., 1991). Throughout this period, proponents continued to assert the efficacy of CISD in treating PTSD and trauma, yet describing stress in "critical incidents." With the adoption of the pathogenically-orientated debriefing model, the standard of care had shifted from survivors utilizing natural coping strategies and systems of support. Normal expectations of resiliency, hardiness, and strength gave way culturally to expectations of symptomatology and injury.

A more serious problem concerns the fact that a large percentage of those exposed suffered no long-term deleterious consequences and may even have benefited from their experience. It could well be that the success claimed by debriefers was, in fact, a natural phenomenon of individual resilience, coping strategies, and the operation of natural social support systems, of wait list or placebo effect, or the fact that PTSD was a rare response in reality.

WHAT ACTUALLY HAPPENS FOLLOWING
TRAUMATIC INCIDENTS?

While countless publications have documented the psychopathology that may result from traumatization, exposure does not inevitably lead to PTSD, and may even lead to positive outcomes and growth (Lyons, 1991; Tedeschi & Calhoun, 1996; Higgins, 1994; Stuhlmiller, 1992; Taylor, 1989). Such considerations are frequently overlooked in the mental health profession, as they do not fit with the medical model, which assumes a role of treatment following a recognized injury. It is too inconvenient, given the high incidence of events of a catastrophic, disastrous nature, to suggest that the mental health field take the time to consider what else may be going on in persons exposed.

An additional issue here is the possibility that those currently being debriefed may be experiencing co-morbid disorders due to their experience. Where is the research on, for example, substance use, dissociation, grief and loss, anxiety and panic, phobia, attachment and intimacy? We know that such sequelae are frequently connected to trauma exposure, yet no attempt has been made to document their existence or to determine the effect of debriefing under these circumstances. The obvious conclusion is that we really don't know much about what is going on in the population being served, nor what should be done. The adoption of the medical model allows us to skirt all that. But, is that wise?

As the protocols involved in helping victims of traumatic events increase, so, too, should the need to examine the ethics of research and clinical interventions. We must ask whether acute posttrauma interventions are truly in the best interest of those they are expected to benefit. This is especially important given that individuals experiencing trauma are in particularly vulnerable situations. Survivors are easily suggestible to the idea that some intervention is necessary following specific types of incidents. It is also interesting to note that the CISD model has remained relatively unchanged despite the proliferation of research to document PTSD and other sequelae in a variety of populations that has burgeoned since the models inception in the early eighties. This work has progressed from documenting the existence of PTSD to understanding what caused or exacerbated the disorder. Yet, the CISD/M model has not evolved to reflect this growing understanding.

Revisiting the literature on traumatized individuals following work-related events helps us understand what people experience during, and subsequent to, trauma and focus on the physiological and biochemical reactions that allow the body to respond to threat. Nor have we adequately considered the ecological impact of the environment on trauma survivors. Issues of self-fulfilling reaction, secondary wounding, and retraumatization have not been adequately explored to date. The debrief modality developed without consideration of the wealth of research and knowledge that exists about rumination, disclosure, and social sharing; about strengths, hardiness, resiliency, and psychological growth in trauma (see also MacLeod, Chapter 10). Nor has knowledge about the natural systems that have for centuries provided holistic healing to mentally injured trauma survivors been examined.

PROBLEMS WITH DEBRIEFING

Aside from adjustments made by Mitchell and others, several fundamental aspects of debriefing remain problematic. This can be illustrated by reference to the models of Tehrani and Westlake (1994), and Samter, Fitzgerald, Braudaway, Leeks, Padgett, Swartz, and Gary-Stephens (1993).

The common denominator between these models is a pathogenic framework. The basic assumption is that those who experience or witness events construed as traumatic need to be treated. The treatment of choice is "talk therapy." The therapeutic vehicle of choice is group, selected for its basic economy and its facilitation of disclosure and social sharing. The focus is on obtaining a directed chronicle of an incident from what happened (the facts) to how the person was affected (emotionally). Each model, however, varies in its emphasis on eliciting the negative aspects of the encounter, while positive experiences are minimized. An exception to this trend is Raphael's (1986) model.

As with all theoretical models and guidelines for intervention, the information solicited by the facilitator or debriefer is that which experts have identified as important. By using standardized context-free formats, the debriefer is actually helping co-construct experience by directing the narrative according to a predetermined set of concerns. In a group format, the pressure to conform and fulfill expectations such as following the line of inquiry of the group leader, will undoubtedly have a major impact on understandings and interpretations of the experience. Because each of these models has its roots in the theoretical orientations of learned helplessness, with an assumption of potential postincident difficulty, individuals become sensitized toward vulnerability while significantly less attention is paid to strengths, resilience, and positive outcomes. Moreover, there is a growing concern that debriefing may exercise iatrogenic effects (see Carlier & Gersons, Chapter 4 and Gist & Woodall, Chapter 5). Given that the efficacy of psychological debriefing following trauma remains uncertain and unsupported by research, it is puzzling that it continues to be a mainstream intervention.

It is argued here that interventions based on pathology, interfere with and undermine personal coping as well as the identification of positive outcomes, strengths, and resilience. Although researchers and clinicians are driven to gain generalized understandings of phenomena so that difficulties can be anticipated and mitigated, crisis situations are self-defined and do not transcend all people and cultures in the same way. As a result, there is often a gap between scientific expectations and actual experience. Narrative accounts of those debriefed following disastrous events reveal such discrepancies and concerns.

Between 1989 and 1995, research on the psychological impact of several major California disasters was conducted with several occupational groups (Stuhlmiller, 1992, 1994, 1995, 1996). Data was obtained from on-site participant observation at disaster scenes and an interpretative phenomenological approach asking people to describe their experiences at different points after the event. Psychological debriefing was one aspect of experience discussed in their narratives. Among their concerns were questions regarding: what is a critical incident; who should receive it voluntarily or involuntarily; who should facilitate it and when should it be done.

What is a Critical Incident?

A standard definition developed for occupational groups is, "any unplanned, unexpected, or unpleasant situation faced by service personnel which causes them to experience unusually strong emotional reactions and has the potential to interfere with their ability to function either at the scene or later" (Mitchell, 1983). Strong emotional reactions may not be shared by all people exposed to the same event. What is traumatic to one may not be to another. For example, on a medical call several responders may find the incident to be rather routine, while one responder may be shocked and upset by the sight of a victim who happens to be wearing the same pajamas as his own child, thus triggering specific significance. Even the most obvious stress events may be similarly experienced as threatening and disruptive but personal meanings and interpretations will vary from person to person and culture to culture.

As an example, the 1989 Loma Prieta earthquake in Northern California was considered by most traumatologists to be a highly stressful event, meeting the definitional criteria of a critical incident. Despite only 60 sixty deaths in the affected area of five million, debriefing services were deemed necessary and organized throughout the locale. While a member of a psychological team responding to a freeway collapse which resulted in 43 deaths, the first author heard a much different interpretation of the event than that expected. The quake had indeed been sudden, life-threatening, and challenged assumptions of life, death and personal invulnerability. For some, usual coping skills were rendered ineffective. However, those who helped in the highly dangerous rescue effort, generally found the experience to be rewarding because of the opportunity created by helping "undo the tragedy." So, while the event, by definition, met the criteria of a critical incident, mental health difficulties were, in part, mitigated by the fact that, for many, it was an opportunity to do what they practiced doing and found important and sustenance in their work. The following interview excerpt illustrates this: "The big events are more exciting, more memorable. You know, more of a challenge to do what you practice to do."

Further evidence to support the above claims was found by Marmar et al. (1996). They queried all research participants about aspects of the disaster that, as it turns out, only a few rescuers had been exposed to. As a result, those not exposed were given new information that they had not know about. In the end, their data failed to show symptoms and social functioning disturbances. Better knowledge of the disaster context would have enabled an approach that undoubtedly would have led to more meaningful results. This underscores the need for research designs to incorporate a better contextual understanding of specific events. Additionally, it highlights the conceptual flaws of traumatic stress studies that suggest that experiences can be defined, operationalized, generalized, and measured with consistency. It is important to ask "Stressful to whom?" and accept that events that cause stress can equally produce positive stress reactions that facilitate the physical response needed to respond to subsequent stresses.

Differentiating Traumatic and Critical Incident Stress

All fields of science evolve as theories are tested and reviewed as new paradigms emerge and new data come to light. In part, the defensive controversy surrounding debriefing reflects its failure to evolve in this way. Consequently, it becomes imperative to determine what is really happening to all participants, not to just the few who have later emerged in clinical or research populations with PTSD.

First, stress and traumatic stress are different phenomena, representing different physiological, neurobiological, and psychological responses. It is unfortunate that the word stress even exists in the diagnosis of PTSD. Many clinicians see stress and traumatic stress as existing on a continuum with traumatic stress being the most intense, severe form of stress, the ultimate "flight or fight" response. This is a misconception. While stress relates to anxiety and the adrenaline response of "fight or flight," traumatic stress involves the way in which the brains physical structures and chemistry takes in information, encodes it, stores it, and is able to retrieve it as memory. It is important for any clinician involved in the intervention of trauma subsequent to crisis to have a basic understanding of the neurobiological differences between stress and traumatic stress (Yehuda, 1998; Yehuda & McFarlane, 1997). This is especially true as the confusion as to whether critical incident stress comprises stress or traumatic stress causes an overstatement in support of the efficacy of debriefing.

Basically, stress results in an increase in HPA (hypothalamus, pituitary, and adrenal) function which increases the release of chemicals such as cortisol into the bloodstream. Those stressed by the event soon are able to resolve their anxiety and its physiological arousal and the body returns to homeostasis where cortisol levels stabilize. Traumatic stress appears to result in a reduction of HPA function as the cortisol, which in fact is released in great amount, is consumed at a significantly higher rate by glucocorticoid receptors. Traumatic stress is then characterized as increased cortisol production and consumption, thus resulting in low cortisol levels. Critical incident stress conceptualized as traumatic stress should then focus on the low cortisol, high glucocorticoid receptor response. Yet more effective psychopharmacological interventions, such as research suggesting the effectiveness of a "morning after" pill for trauma, propanalol, would appear more promising than debriefing in acting prophylactically to prevent trauma.

Secondly, since debriefing has also been viewed as a preventative or remedial protocol to address PTSD, it is important to examine studies undertaken to substantiate or refute such claims. Research suggesting a neutral or negative effect on PTSD among those debriefed are compelling (Bisson & Deahl, 1994). Further, debriefing may accentuate the stress response causing prolongation of the HPA reaction, thus fostering depression (sustained high cortisol) or PTSD (engagement of increased glucocorticoid reception) (Yehuda & McFarlane, 1997). It is also possible that debriefing exacerbates the traumatic stress response, further activating the physiological structures that result in acute stress and ultimately posttraumatic stress disorder (Herman, 1992; Dunning, 1995; Paton & Stephens, 1996). The traumatized person in a group debriefing may be triggered into the same neurobiological response as the traumatic event when confronted by the disclosure of others. As an officer stated: "You know, I didn't start feeling bad till we went over it in the group . . . I thought we had done a good job . . . should be proud. Now I guess I was wrong, and that bothers me a lot . . . I wish I hadn't gone."

In affective overload, the cognitions involving imagery, sensory-motor memory, and interpretative sense of meaning held by persons who experienced the event, the traumatized person may confabulate and bring such material into their trauma set. What would appear problematic, then, is when group debriefing exacerbates or intensifies the physiological process that causes stress or traumatic stress. One criticism of contemporary research in posttraumatic sequelae has been the reactionary bias in favor of identifying pathology resulting from traumatization in the move to validate negative consequences to victims. Hence, all research on debriefing centered on its efficacy in preventing or ameliorating the "golden wound" of PTSD.

It would appear that no research has looked at the effect of debriefing on anything other than PTSD. No studies examine stress, anxiety, depression, or grief, and research exploring the positive growth that might accompany traumatic experience is sparse. Numerous authors have concluded that subjects not disclosing negative symptomatology were "in denial," which in itself created the certitude of later pathology of "delayed stress or PTSD" (Dunning, 1988).

Should Disclosure be Encouraged?

In recent years, many agencies have been persuaded by professionals that debriefing is not only valuable, but necessary, following critical incidents. As a result, participation has been deemed mandatory in some settings. As evidence grows to suggest that debriefing may have iatrogenic effects, ethical and legal considerations became increasingly prominent. Interventions provided without informed consent could have serious ramifications. Yet, participants are rarely offered a choice of formal interventions. Intervention is seen as all or nothing, either you participate in the debrief or there will be no other offer of formal intervention. While the option of natural coping strategies and systems still remains, the door is shut to consideration of other types of prevention and treatment modalities. The only offer, at least of a formal nature, is to seek assistance in the framework of a group exercise. Based on the assumption that ventilation is healthy, and that social sharing is cathartic, debriefing has institutionalized myths and assumptions that may not be valid.

The intrusive nature of debriefing requires a reconsideration of the research on the effectiveness of disclosure, especially in identifying its underlying mechanisms. While disclosure is most often thought of as verbalization, traumatized individuals might use other expressive methods such as writing, art, kinesthetic movement, role-playing, stress inoculation rehearsal, or other experiential therapies. An insistence on verbalization is to ignore and devalue other effective coping modalities. "You know, I really didn't like being put on the spot like that . . . it was like show and tell, show me your trauma and I'll get the chief to lay-off. . . Either they accuse you of not being tough enough or being a cry-baby. Am I supposed to get these symptoms or what? If I do, is that good or bad? The old-timers say they had it worse and they never had problems. But it seems you're supposed to. . . ."

Furthermore, several studies have shown that self-focused attention or rumination is associated with more severe and long-lasting periods of distressed mood and subsequent depression (Lybomirsky & Nolen-Hoeksema, 1993). Persons induced to ruminatively self-focus on their feelings and personal characteristics endorse more negative, biased interpretations, are more pessimistic about positive events in their future and generate less effective solutions (Lybomirsky & Nolen-Hoeksema, 1993; see also Macleod, Chapter 10). Why, then, would one consider debrief with its parallel focus to be restorative.

We know that ruminative thought characterized by a focus on personal problems combined with a negative tone, self-criticism, and self-blame for problems, as well as reduced self-confidence, optimism, and general perceived control are found to be counterproductive to trauma recovery. Ruminators, as compared with distraction, rate their problems as severe and unsolvable, but did not reduce their confidence in the effectiveness of their solutions. However, ruminators reported a low likelihood of actually implementing their solutions. This finding suggests that rumination in the presence of a depressed mood may deplete motivation to solve one's problems. Lybomirsky and Nolen-Hoeksema (1993) found that activities of active distraction which interfere with rumination have been found to be strongly positive in terms of avoiding or reducing the psychological impact of trauma on cognitive dysfunction. It would appear that activities to distract would prove just as useful as disclosure and social sharing in preventing or ameliorating the deleterious effects of trauma.

Research of Pennebaker and colleagues (see Chapter 6) suggest it is the nature of the sharing that is significant. For example, they documented a natural process of disclosure following traumatic events which found that individuals were not reticent, in fact were spontaneously and naturally disclosing up to eight to twelve times a day in the first three weeks following the event. Attributes of completed attempts of processing involving emotional rehearsal and social sharing seemed to be met, and indicators of distress suggested that people actually coped quite well. Note that natural spontaneous social sharing is not the same as guided reflection imposed by professionals. Pennebaker and colleagues have also repeatedly shown that verbal elicitation of negative emotion and cognitions frequently does little to alleviate traumatic sequelae and in fact leads to rumination, subsequent depression, and traumatic decline. Instead the elicitation of positive disclosures, in writing or verbally, is strongly associated with positive mental and physical health following traumatic experience.

The self-reflective group approach required by debriefing may be antithetical to occupational groups (e.g., emergency and law enforcement professionals) who are socialized into developing positive illusions of invincibility in order to transcend the dangers that they face, and whose work depends on lack of reflection and confidence in team strength. Rehashing can create anxiety about future situations, question others' ability to respond, inhibit performance, and undermine occupational values. Debriefing which increases self-consciousness and vulnerability may thus lessen performance effectiveness in these groups. In addition, if team strength depends on not publicly admitting weakness, the group forum may not be appropriate. As a fire fighter commented:

> People don't want to muck around in that because they have to go right back out there again. . . . I think you can overdo it. You can over-dwell. If you're having trouble coping with it, I'd say it is great to have it available but I don't think it should be mandatory. You're not going to spill your guts in front of the guys you work with that you feel emotional, that you felt drained. No, Man, I'm ready to go. You want that feeling.

Emergency personnel are often involved in different aspects of a rescue operation. Thus not all are exposed to the same things at the scene, or even there at the same time. For example, some may be involved in live rescues, while others are performing extrication of dead bodies. The thrill of saving a life can thus be reduced when forced to listen to others not involved in successful rescue efforts. As a fire fighter indicated:

> I think it was a joke. I think it's good and it should be available for those who need it. But after an accident, to have someone tell you that you have to do it, direct orders, that's bull, because here our adrenaline was going over something positive, and they wanted us to sit there and listen to all of this negativity. I thought it was garbage. I think I would have resentment or hesitation if someone would force me to wait a minute, you saw some bad stuff. You have to go through this. Some guys weren't even in an incident and they were debriefed. There was an engineer at the hydrant, three blocks away and at 3.00 am in the morning they're debriefing. Well, I want to go to bed. No, you have to be debriefed. What are we doing here. You know, debriefing has lost it's point. So the whole crew had to stay up and they had to debrief.

Confounding Effects on Effectiveness

Debriefing protocols are oriented to disclosing the worst fear, sight, experience, or meaning. In addition, the educational component typically dwells on the emergence of pathological symptomatology associated with traumatic events. When the inevitable does not happen, no nightmares and flashbacks, it would be easy to tout the efficacy of the healing rate of a modality, especially if it cannot be verified that disorder ever existed. Finding no trauma subsequently could then be construed as effectiveness. Finding trauma brings a response that without treatment, the rate would have been much higher. It is a win-win situation, the lack of documentation that the problem ever existed, or to what extent it existed, allows the purveyors of the protocol to claim success. To treat those who are mildly stressed to extremely stressed, and those who are traumatized as the same, will eventually result in some success stories. As one police officer reported: "They said I had to do this or I would have nightmares. I haven't had nightmares so maybe its working. But, you know, I've seen worse–extricated mangled babies from under dashboards at traffic accident scenes and I never had nightmares before."

In this context, high spontaneous remission rates among trauma survivors who receive no treatment and placebo effects surely account for some of the success reported by many participants. The debriefers just have to sit back and let "nature" prove their product. They support the efficacy of the protocol based on the "number served" rather than on positive results. By overwhelming participants with the detrimental aspects of adding gruesome and horrific imagery, negative emotion and sense of utility, as well as adding to interpretations of lack of meaning and negative outcome thus confabulating other's stories and insights into their own trauma set, the harm is ignored. A deputy sheriff who conducted rescue operations following an airplane crash stated: "We all got a hoot out of the media. They showed us carrying out a body bag from the crash site while the voice-over talked about the emotional crisis we were supposed to be experiencing. It was all very solemn . . . and we roared with laughter because we knew that the bag contained a dead deer caught in the fire."

Can Traumatized Individuals Effectively
Participate in Debriefing?

Lacking an understanding of the most basic tenets of the psychobiology of trauma, the debrief protocol ignores the need for a higher
level of abstraction and cognitive reasoning that is not generally found
in the dissociative and concrete mental processing of the traumatized
person. The debrief process fails to recognize that the reflective
approach it requires only adds to the fears and frustrations of traumatically impaired individuals who may become anxious, confused, or
"shut down" in the debrief process. The demand to "let go" or vent
when a traumatized person desperately is trying to maintain a sense of
composure is in itself mechanisms reinforced. It would appear that
debriefing reinforces a sense of lack of control, of vulnerability, of damage. Since there is no evidence that a cathartic recounting of one's trauma story brings psychological relief or comfort, one wonders why
individuals utilizing concrete reasoning, emotional numbing, and techniques of dissociation would benefit by the forced ventilation. In fact,
the traumatized individual with acute stress disorder may dissociate
during the debrief. Or, the use of dissociative coping to avoid loss of
control may be reinforced An individual required to attend and participate may have their sense of identity as a "mentally injured" individual reinforced. Following a major air disaster in which over 300
persons were killed, a police officer complained: "What are they (the
debriefers) trying to do to me . . . cause another heart attack? I've
already had one the last time, at the fire. They put me through this and
make me go through that all over again. I don't need this level of
stress!"

The use of conventional techniques such as "breaking down denial"
and "labeling" have often proved to be counterproductive and ineffective in engaging persons in treatment. Why then would we believe that
the process provided by debriefing would produce a motivated and
compliant client? Given the circumstances of traumatized individuals
in crisis and their perceptions of their problems which do not generally focus on psychological injuries, many are not ready to undergo the
rigorous demands of the debrief or meet the expectations of the group
to participate. Trying to avoid the victim label and the entire stigma
and shame attached, the traumatized person is hardly likely to embrace

demarcation into the "inner circle" of trauma experience. It is common to hear, from those compelled to participate in debrief, that the process is "fine for the others that need it, but not me. I don't!"

This process is compounded by employing agencies who want to cover themselves and meet the "standard of reasonable care" and so compel this treatment modality so that the courts cannot find them negligent in consideration of employee safety. In fact, we use the argument that traumatized individuals would resist or forego treatment if not otherwise compelled. It is "in their best interest" to have an external support system "look out for their injury and recovery" by compelling attendance as a function of work assignment or fitness for employment assessment. In "covering their butts," what the employee agency accomplishes is creating the second group of coerced clients to be treated in a mental health system. Mandatory, inescapable mental health treatment is generally only associated with those found criminally insane or in need of protection of self or society. To refuse to participate, even when voluntary, creates problems associated with the recovery of civil or workers compensation damages. It is inconceivable that the traumatized person is placed in a position of being compelled to receive a therapeutic modality that the provider cannot even guarantee has benign, at best, or positive results.

Group Versus Individual Participation

What needs to be changed in our attempt to resolve the potential deleterious impact of traumatic exposure is to better understand how a group mitigates individuals' experience of trauma reaction. It is clear that debrief modalities have ignored long-held tenets of group, especially of group dynamics. Since debrief protocols were developed in an environment where the groups under consideration were of long standing, being members of an employment organization, it was assumed that the stages of "forming, storming, norming, and performing" were already accomplished. Issues of safety in a group, the existence of trust and expectation of helpful assistance and of group norms about the value of the individual and the group was assumed to be positively established. This need not be the case. Just because a work group has existed over a period of time, the mental health professional cannot assume that all members feel safe, trust other group members, or believe that membership in the group will have positive results. A work group cannot be construed as a therapeutic community. Nor can most work groups be transformed into functioning task groups in one session. Group process formation is not accomplished simply because the group shares a common employer, organization, or event.

Far from enhancing recovery, the group debrief model can perpetuate pathology. It fosters dependence on the mental health system rather than in natural coping strategies and supports. It allows the individual to reject ownership of problematic sequelae as it sets "the event" up as the culprit. Rather than engaging in optimizing and prioritizing steps to be taken to effect change of whatever is bothersome to the individual, group members are focused on a narrow set of expectations and responses associated with negative traumatic events.

Is Acute Intervention Necessary?

In incorporating definitions of events construed to be traumatic or critical incidents, and in using the threshold of the occurrence of the event as the impetus for treatment, the mental health field has failed to follow steps to even consider whether their services are necessary. Using the occasion of the event as the instigating decision point for initiating treatment, the debriefing is relieved of the need to conduct an assessment of whether any mental injury has occurred. Rather than following a parsimonious, or least intrusive, approach when none is needed, the field of acute intervention has rushed in and enveloped a whole population of normal people who might not ever need their service. What has ensued has been the carving out of turf. Having established themselves as a necessary and integral component to the critical incident event experience, mental health professionals seem reluctant to give up participation. Clearly, the proponents of debriefing have failed to consider and determine the needs of the client. By hiding behind the disease model, trauma is considered a progressive disorder and the course of the illness is expected to worsen unless treated. Starting where the client is at and what they want to accomplish in the debrief does not seem to be a consideration.

Practitioners have failed to keep pace with research on the psychobiology of trauma and on changing paradigms for conceptualizing and treating traumatic stress. Consequently, professional perceptions of those touched by trauma are incompatible with the clients' own perceptions of issues they associate with their experience. Individuals possessing a high degree of self-efficacy are able to recognize and resolve their trauma, to take the necessary action steps to change their present condition without the assistance of a mental health professional.

Increasing attention is being given to individuals with varying responses to trauma, emphasizing wellness over illness. To accommodate this diversity, greater emphasis needs to be placed on a variety of intervention approaches reflecting the continuum of symptoms, behaviors, coping capacities, and needs of the diverse client group. Rather than reinforcing notions of illness, dependency, and the need for immediate and possible long-term treatment, we suggest another paradigm. Brief intervention should convey the optimistic message that with the support of significant others, the individual has the inherent coping resources to deal with what "trauma has wrought in their perception, what it means to them personally."

An approach that involves brief non-therapeutic intervention is based on the expectation that potential for growth and recovery is possible for those exposed to traumatic events without the interventions of a mental health therapist. This approach is aimed at enhancing self-directed efforts to resolve the traumatic event as a self-efficacy experience rather than reinforcing the notion that the ultimate outcome will be illness and the need for treatment. By conveying the optimistic message that with the support of others, the individual has the inherent coping resources to find meaning in the event and recovery from the mental injuries it inflicts, the focus changes to the positive aspects of trauma experience. The brief intervention approach is grounded in the principle of natural recovery. Underlying this assumption is that individuals have the inherent coping resources to initiate and maintain growth and health with minimal involvement of mental health professionals. Change of this sort must be initiated through interventions that involve individual control.

Who Should Administer the Debriefing?

Mental health professionals in many settings suffer from a lack of status and recognition (Deahl, Ernshaw, & Jones, 1994). Peer counselors who have not yet achieved sufficient respect by their peers have also been found to be problematic (Stuhlmiller, 1992).This case often leads to group sabotage. It is the common belief that the debriefer should be a mental health professional, someone who is able to facilitate disclosure and discussion of sensitive issues. Lazavik (1995) provides a strong argument that a person who is trusted and respected in terms of professional integrity and competence, is sufficient. A major criticism of the group debrief is that it can generate secondary wounds when it occurs in an environment in which the participant does not feel safe. This creates additional pressure for a facilitator, often a stranger to the group, to ensure safety and support. The debrief frequently occurs without the necessary development of a therapeutic alliance between the facilitator and group members.

The Timing of Intervention

Debriefing is often seen as an acknowledgment of someone's experience as both important and potentially stressful. Persons or groups excluded from debriefing sessions begin to question whether their participation was of value or even stressful. Often, the responsiveness of the debriefing team is based on work load and logistics. In situations that involve large numbers of personnel, it may not be possible to conduct group debriefings in a timely manner. This can have extremely detrimental effects for persons who begin to interpret the lack of acknowledgement as a significant message.

It is not uncommon to find debriefers at disaster scenes, who insist on keeping to the Mitchell model, which advises that intervention be provided between 24 to 48 hours after an incident. Clock-watching and demanding response coordinators to provide them with people to debrief can create more stress than the incident itself. As Everstine and Everstine (1993) posited, it is not conducive to recovery to encourage a traumatized person to "let go" of or "vent" feelings at a time when the person is struggling to regain composure and to make sense of chaos, horror, or loss. They pointed out that emotions may be the only thing that the traumatized person feels they can control. Any cathartic response elicited–crying, screaming, storytelling–may not produce psychological relief to the person. Koval (1986) reported that one respondent to a mailed survey of police officers assigned to an air crash noted that he was passed over for promotion to senior rank for crying at the debrief. His superiors felt that: "He can't be trusted to assume a command position. Look at the way he broke down."

Prolonged Needs and Consequences

Body recovery after the Pan Am Lockerbie crash continued for seven months. Persons conducting acute intervention need to be sensitive to the unfolding nature of rescue and mitigation operations. Common sense should overrule procedural dogma regarding timing. The reality is that workers often have to repeatedly return to the same site or situation, not only to continue with recovery efforts but also to conduct normal work operations. Since the magical 24 to 48 hour time period is not supported anywhere in the literature, other than as opinion, it doesn't make sense to interrupt the normal defenses that allow the individual or group to continue to perform their duties. To intervene to achieve some sort of psychological processing is premature, at best, and harmful at worst. Reacting to being informed of potential dangers that existed at an oil refinery fire, one police officer said: "I've got to go back out there. I didn't need to hear about all the danger that I hadn't considered. Now I'm really stressed out."

The Need for Professional Involvement

As crises become part of our every day reality, efforts to control and cope with situations that fall outside of human command will undoubtedly increase. Creating specific technologies for widespread application is also part of progress. Striving to conquer the unconquerable may be a way to defend against a shared vulnerability that tragedy brings out and binds us to one another. We are compelled to want to do something, to want something in place, to feel that all bases have been covered to deal with mental, as well as physical, injuries.

Because we live in times where social contact has been replaced by coaxial cable, it is perhaps good news that people do help each other in emotionally difficult times. "And counselors were called" seems to be the tag ending of just about every media story dealing with mass catastrophe. Depending upon the event, there can even be a surplus of willing helpers. We seem to have forgotten, though, that on an everyday basis individual personal traumas occur that go unnoticed and unaided. For example, a recent major landslide in New South Wales, Australia which took the life of 18 people, attracted truckloads of debriefers, some of whom spent 24 hours up to 3 months on-scene supporting the survivors. That same weekend, survivors of eleven fatal vehicular accidents in a nearby city received no mental health attention. Yet, it is important to recognize that debriefing is a growth industry in affluent societies and has largely ignored the more insidious, yet every bit as tragic, events that befall people.

Whether debriefing is helpful or not, open debate is a crucial professional responsibility because organizational response systems are guided by social and scientific constructions of psychological risk and illness. As a result, the ideologies of professional experts affect the lives and activities of hundreds of thousands of human beings who have come to be identified as at risk. These representations, when applied to other populations and societies, can seriously undermine restorative capabilities especially in situations where they do not accommodate local understandings. In order to broaden posttrauma understanding, reduce iatrogenic concerns, and create the everyday caring culture, a paradigmatic shift is called for and, certainly, our professional ethics further compels us.

Ethical Concerns

The ancient medical motto, *Primum non nocere* (First, do no harm), does not seem to have permeated the mental health profession as we inundate clients with modalities and protocols that stand no rigor of testing to determine if the benefits of treatment outweigh hidden risks. Unlike the stringent scrutiny of the Federal Drug Administration in relation to psychopharmacological treatment, our profession has subjected suffering, and non-suffering clients presumed to have psychological wounds with all manner of intrusive treatment protocols. As a discipline, we seem to have forgotten the most basic tenets of the helping profession. That is, in an age where the urge to do something, anything, often overpowers prudence, we seemed to have forgotten that oftentimes it is better to do nothing.

The trend toward professional updating in training that can best be described as "edubites" has caused professionals not to avail themselves of traditional sources of validation of treatment efficacy. The sentiment that it's better than doing nothing has seemed to replace a professional concern to intervene only when it is readily apparent that mental health intervention can and will make a difference. It is appropriate that the media has begun to pick up on this issue and portray mental health professionals following disasters, accidents, and violent acts as "ambulance chasers." If the professional has achieved that level of consideration by the public, we would think that they would be concerned enough to question their own intentions. Where have the professional values associated with the constant search for truth, for verification, for validation gone?

Maybe its time to regain some common sense and go back to support what we are doing with acutely traumatized individuals with sound empirical and theoretical consideration. It's time to return to caution and common sense, to figure out what has been going right all these centuries, rather than to run in with a quick fix. It may well be our need as professionals to have an active role, to be seen as players, and to be helpers that has driven our rush to treat trauma survivors before ascertaining whether they need assistance. The second author, in particular, is guided by memories of responding to her first tornado in 1971 where a client asked: "Can you restore my home, my children's baby pictures, my wedding dress? Then, what good are you?"

It is difficult to achieve a sense of virtue in defending a modality that does not address the first needs of the traumatized for safety, for restoration, for acknowledgment of strength. Instead, we point out the nobility of our provision of validation and normalization to support our role in the recovery process.

FROM PATHOGENESIS TO SALUTOGENESIS: A PARADIGM SHIFT

The issues identified by emergency workers underscore a need to modify current strategies and to rethink the tenets of debriefing. There is no question that some people find value in talking, sharing, and expressing emotions. This is inevitably what debriefing is intended to accomplish. There is disagreement that it is necessary for all people and that the guided group format focusing on emotional content is helpful. The problem lies in assumptions from which debriefing models have been derived which suggest to individuals that they should have a certain amount of anxiety following a critical incident and that there are some standardized normal responses that if identified and disclosed, will reduce negative after-effects.

Integration of experience occurs according to a combination of individual, group, and societal meanings that can't always be readily identified or teased out. To achieve greater understanding, the framework must enable identification of sources of hope, courage, and recovery, which would require a shift away from a disease to a health-oriented conceptualization. The framework for such investigation was developed by Antonovsky (1987) in his salutogenic model. The central concern in salutogenesis is on how people manage to stay healthy following stressful encounters in contrast to why people get sick (pathogenesis). It is believed that the differences between health breakdown and wellness may depend more upon one's outlook on life than upon the avoidance of stress. According to Antonovsky, stress is omnipresent. A person's coping ability and sense of health or well-being is connected to the degree of the person's "sense of coherence" (SOC) or to what extent stress is experienced as coherent, manageable, and meaningful (Antonovsky, 1990 a,b,c). This is similar to the treatise of Janoff-Bulman in *Shattered Assumptions* (1992) and the meaning discussed by Herman in *Trauma and Recovery* (1992). Antonovsky has demonstrated that the stronger the person's SOC, the more likely the person will be able to successfully deal with life stressors.

By adopting the salutogenic model, many of the concerns raised by emergency workers are dealt with. Instead of the assumption that stress, traumatic stress, and critical incidents cause or put people at risk to develop negative outcomes, a salutogenic perspective acknowledges the ubiquitous nature of stress and that consequences are not necessarily pathological but possibly salutary. This idea affirms what we already know that even people who experience extreme stress survive and do well.

By adopting this perspective, debriefing strategies would include not only illness-susceptibility factors (sources of stress) but resistance factors such as sense of coherence. By enhancing or strengthening the resources of the person, resistance is maximized. A strengthened sense of coherence during periods of crisis may result in improved ability to withstand future stress as well as modify the deleterious effects of the immediate crisis.

By shifting the paradigm, mental health professionals are asked to consider the wealth of research that documents the positive aspects of trauma incident experience. In changing from the perception of experience as injurious to facilitating growth, the potential protocols for acute intervention that do not exacerbate traumatization widen considerably. Research compels us to take action to reconsider our orientation to our role as mental health professionals in the lives of individuals exposed to trauma. Rather than support the efficacy of the protocol based on the number served, we have an ethical responsibility to achieve positive results.

Positive Aspects of Trauma Experience

We seem to have forgotten that research conducted on community or group-experienced disaster also consistently documents how survivors support one another and enhance a collective sense of strength. That strength could be found not only in what people had just experienced but also in relation to their future ability to control and respond to the demands occasioned by the event (Dynes, 1970) and led to recognition of the importance of interventions that would support the group in its strengths and acknowledge survivorship in facing and recovering from "what God or man has wrought." Higgins (1994) suggested that resilience best captures the active process of self-righting and growth. By viewing resilience as a process in which the person experiences learned resourcefulness, the worker contributes internal strengths, which are validated by the natural honeymoon process of the group. Lyons (1991) supported this orientation in suggesting that it is imperative that we do not err in the opposite direction of attempting to identify pathology resulting from traumatization.

While they may have differing core resilient capacities, all persons possess a capability to learn and grow from traumatic experience. Lyons (1991) suggested that there are "natural holding environments" that promote the growth of these capacities. In order to facilitate the maximization of these capabilities, the holding environment must attend to the culture and climate that surrounds the event. Just as individual characteristics influence outcome, so, too, do group norms, values, interpretations, and meanings that are communicated to its members. Yalom (1975) and others have long noted the impact of the group as a source of healing and recovery or of exacerbation and decline. What is done in the group has not been as widely examined, although benefits of the group for protective service personnel have been suggested (Paton & Stephens, 1996). Maybe what we should be focusing on is learning to create positive "holding environments" after traumatic incidents, paying attention to organizational culture and behavior rather than on turning our attention to the individual as patient.

It is important that any formal response subsequent to a traumatic event build upon the strengths and capabilities of those affected. Most individuals who experience traumatic events are normal people who are generally capable of functioning in an effective manner, both physically and emotionally. They have been subjected to severe stress and it is not unusual for them to show signs of emotional strain. This transitory disturbance is to be expected and does not necessarily imply mental illness or posttraumatic reaction. In fact, while the literature gives brief mention to hardiness and resiliency little attention has been paid to the assessment of positive outcome from traumatic experience. The author has repeatedly heard from police officers that: The (shooting, disaster, tornado) . . . was the greatest thing that happened to me. I proved to myself that I could do it, that my training worked. I feel more confident now about my ability to respond to emergency situations. I know what I'm made of . . . I've got the right stuff.

The possibility of positive impact of negative events and the potential, and possible prophylaxis, of resilient factors that can lead to posttraumatic growth is becoming increasingly evident (Burt & Katz, 1987; Kahane, 1992; Silver, Boon, & Stones, 1983; Sledge, Boydstun, & Rahe, 1980; Stuhlmiller, 1992; Tedeschi & Calhoun, 1996; Thompson, 1985; Veronen & Kilpatrick, 1983). Tedeschi and Calhoun (1996) found at least three categories of perceived benefit that individuals have identified in connection with traumatic experience: changes in self-perception, changes in interpersonal relationship, and a changed philosophy of life (Table 2.1).

People who have experienced horrific traumatic events have extolled the importance of consequent positive growth benefits, identification of meaning, and of connection with others as a salutary consequence of their sorrow (Frankl, 1963). It would appear that the

Table 2.1
CHANGES IN THOSE TRAUMATIZED ASSOCIATED WITH
POSTTRAUMATIC GROWTH

Perceived Change in Self

Emotional Growth	Affleck et al., 1985a, b
Made Them a Better Person	Andreasson & Norris, 1972
Feel More Experienced About Life	Joseph, Williams, & Yule, 1993
Feel Stronger and More Self-Assured	Collins et al., 1990
Improved Self-Evaluation of Competence	Tedeschi & Calhoun, 1996
Newfound Skills and Confidence	Stuhlmiller, 1992
Conclusion That They are Stronger, More Confident	Thomas, DiGiulio, & Sheehan, 1991

Changed Sense of Relationships With Others

Closer Family Relationships	Affleck et al., 1985
Importance of Child/Children/Parent	Malinek, Hoyt, & Patterson, 1979
Fostered Deepening in Relationships	Stuhlmiller, 1992
Must Make Decisions in Own Best Interests	Veronen & Kilpatrick, 1983
Increase in Self-Disclosure and New Behaviors	Dakof & Taylor, 1990
Recognition of Vulnerability Led to More Emotional Expressiveness	Collins et al., 1990
Willingness to Accept Help and Utilize Social Supports	Collins et al., 1990
Increased Sensitivity to Other People	Collins et al., 1990
Increased Efforts Directed at Improving Relationships	Collins et al., 1990

Change in Philosophy of Life

Increased Appreciation for Own Existence	Malinek et al., 1979
Better Perspective on Life	Affleck et al., 1985
Positive Changes in Priorities, Such as Taking Life Easier and Enjoying It More	Taylor, Lichtman, & Wood, 1984
No Longer Taking Life for Granted	Stuhlmiller, 1992
Preciousness of Life	Stuhlmiller, 1992
Live Each Day to the Fullest	Joseph et al., 1993
Spiritual Beliefs Strengthened	Pangament, Royster & Wood, 1990
Increased Sense of Control, Intimacy, and Finding Meaning	Pangament et al., 1990

identification of benefits and measurement of growth add significantly to the perception of meaning that survivors derive from their trauma experience. What is significant, according to Higgins (1994), is that resilience can be cultivated and that the group can influence the individual: "good company" can change the course of individual reaction from traumatic decline to traumatic growth. Ursano, et al. (1986) and Sledge (1986) also suggested that coping style and social cohesion can act to cognitively integrate the traumatic experience. The salutogenic effects of resilience and social perception inform us that the group can facilitate the active process of self-righting and growth. Interestingly, the Raphael Australian Debrief protocol (1986) contained many of the same positive-directed questions to be asked by the debriefer. Yet, subsequent iterations of debriefing have retained the negative, worst case, worst outcome orientation. We need to revisit the building block of human cognition, disastrous experience, and recovery in an ecological environment. It is here that the work of Antonovsky and others has much to offer.

The views expressed in this chapter are not intended to undermine the goodwill or intentions of those striving to find ways to assist humankind in understanding, living through, and integrating horrific memories and experiences of extraordinary events. Rather, our objective is to open up and spur along a long overdue and necessary debate in challenging mainstream views by drawing upon a wider range of research, literature, and experience. Our perspective is driven by the disciplinary understandings of nursing and social psychology that offer a broader framework for inquiry which includes salutogenesis. We believe that the disturbing trend and focus on widespread psychopathological risk has overshadowed the discovery and advancement of the personal and cultural meanings and strategies that enable individuals, families, and communities to cope with crisis in constructive self-enhancing ways.

REFERENCES

Affleck, G., Allen, D., Tennen, H., McGrade, N., and Ratzan, S.: Causal and control cognitions in parents' coping with chronically ill children. *Journal of Social and Clinical Psychology, 3:* 367–377, 1985.

Affleck, G., Tennen, H., and Gershman, K.: Cognitive adaptations to high-risk infants: The search for mastery, meaning, and protection from future harm. *American Journal of Mental Deficiency, 89:* 653–656, 1985.

American Psychiatric Association: *Diagnostic and statistical manual of mental disorders,* (3rd ed.), Washington, DC: American Psychiatric Press, 1980. (4th ed. current, 1994).

Andreason, N.C., and Norris, A.S.: Long-term adjustment and adaptation in severely burned adults. *Journal of Nervous and Mental Disease, 154:* 352–362, 1972.

Antonovsky, A.: *Health, stress, and coping.* San Francisco: Jossey-Bass, 1979.

Antonovsky, A.: *Unravelling the mystery of health how people manage stress and stay well.* San Francisco: Jossey-Bass, 1987.

Antonovsky, A.: Pathways leading to successful coping and health. In Rosenbaum, M. (Ed.): *Learned resourcefulness: On coping skills, self-control, and adaptive behavior.* New York: Springer, 1990a.

Antonovsky, A.: Personality and health: Testing the sense of coherence model. In Friedman, H. (Ed.): *Personality and disease.* New York: Wiley, 1990b.

Antonovsky, A.: The salutogenic model of health. In Ornstein, R., and Swencionis, C. (Eds.): *The healing brain: A scientific reader.* New York: Guilford Press, 1990c.

Antonovsky, A.: The structural sources of salutogenic strengths. In Cooper, C., and Payne, R. (Eds): *Personality and stress: Individual differences in the stress process.* London: Wiley, 1991.

Antonovsky, A.: The implications of salutogenesis: An outsider's view. In Turnbull, A., Patterson, J., Behr, S., and Murphy, D., et al. (Eds.): *Cognitive coping, families, and disability.* Baltimore, MD: Paul H. Brookes, 1993.

Armstrong, K., O'Callahan, W., and Marmar, C. R.: Debriefing Red Cross disaster personnel: The multiple stressor debriefing model. *Journal of Traumatic Stress, 4,* 518–593, 1991.

Bisson, J.I., and Deahl, M.P.: Psychological debriefing and prevention of Post-Traumatic Stress: More research is needed. *British Journal of Psychiatry, 165:* 717–720, 1994.

Blakemore, J.: Are police allowed to have problems of their own? *Police Magazine, March:* 47–55, 1975.

Breslau, N.G., Davis, P., Andreski, R.N., and Peterson, E.: Traumatic events and post-traumatic stress disorder in an urban population in young adults. *Archives of General Psychiatry, 48:* 216-222, 1991.

Burt, M.R., and Katz, B.K.: Dimensions of recovery from rape: Focus on growth outcomes. *Journal of Interpersonal Violence, 2:* 57–81, 1987.

Collins, R.L., Taylor, S.E., and Skokan, L.A.: A better world or shattered vision? Changes in life perspectives following victimization. *Social Cognition, 8:* 263–285, 1990.

Dakof, G.A., and Taylor, S. E.: Victim's perceptions of social support: What is helpful to whom? *Journal of Personality and Social Psychology, 58:* 80–89, 1990.

Davidson, A.: Air disaster: Coping with stress–A program that worked. *Police Stress, 1:* 20–22, 1979.

Deahl, M., Earnshaw, N., and Jones, N.: Psychiatry and war: Lessons learned from the former Yugoslavia. *British Journal of Psychiatry, 164:* 441–442, 1994.

Deahl, M.P., Gillham, A.B., Thomas, J., Searle, M., and Srinivason, M.: Psychological sequelae following the Gulf War: Factors associated with subsequent morbidity and the effectiveness of psychological debriefing. *British Journal of Psychiatry, 165:* 60–65, 1994.

Dunning, C.M.: Intervention strategies for emergency workers. In Lystad, M. (Ed.): *Mental health response in mass emergencies.* New York: Brunner/Mazel, 1988.

Dunning, C.M.: Fostering resiliency in rescue workers. In Kalayjian, A.S.: *Disaster and mass trauma: Global perspectives on post disaster mental health management.* Long Branch, NJ: Vista Press, 1995.

Dunning, C. (1999) Postintervention strategies to reduce police trauma: A paradigm shift. In J.M. Violanti, and D. Paton (Eds.): *Police trauma: Psychological aftermath of civilian combat.* Springfield, IL: Charles C Thomas, 1999.

Dunning, C.M., and Silva, M.: Disaster-induced stress in rescue workers. *Victimology: An international journal, 5:* 287–297, 1980.

Dynes, R.: *Organized behavior in disasters.* Lexington, KY: Heath-Lexington, 1970.

Everstine, D., and Everstine, L.: *The trauma response.* New York: Norton. 1993.

Frankl, V.E.: *In search of meaning.* New York: Washington Square Press, 1963.

Herman, J.: *Trauma and recovery: Aftermath of violence from domestic abuse to political terror.* New York: Basic Books, 1992.

Higgins, G.O.: *Resilient adults: Overcoming a cruel past.* San Francisco: Jossey-Bass, 1994.

Illich, I.: *Limits to medicine. Medical nemesis: The appropriation of health.* Harmondsworth, UK: Penguin Books, 1976.

Janoff-Bulman, R.: *Shattered assumptions: Toward a new psychology of trauma.* New York: The Free Press, 1992.

Joseph, S., Williams, R., and Yule, W.: Changes in outlook following disaster: The preliminary development of a measure to assess positive and negative responses. *Journal of Traumatic Stress, 6:* 271–279, 1993.

Kahane, B.: Late-life adaptation in the aftermath of extreme stress. In Wykel, M., Kahene, E., and Kowal, J. (Eds.): *Stress and health among the elderly.* New York: Springer, 1992.

Kobasa, S., Maddi, S., and Cahn, S.: Hardiness and health: A prospective study. *Journal of Personality and Social Psychology, 42:* 168–177, 1982.

Koval, S.: Midwest Flight 160: Air crash trauma in rescue workers, Master's thesis. Cardinal Stritch University, 1986.

Kroes, W., and Hurrell, J., Jr.: *Job stress and the police officer-identifying stress reduction techniques.* Washington, DC: U.S. Government Printing Office, 1975.

Kroes, W.H.: *Society's victim, The policeman: An analysis of job stress in policing.* Springfield, IL, Charles C Thomas, 1976, 2nd ed., 1985.

Lazavik, J.: Remembering how to stay well: A regenerative tool for counseling center staff. *Journal of College Student Psychotherapy, 9:* 57-77, 1995.

Lyons, J.A.: Strategies for assessing the potential for positive readjustment following trauma. *Journal of Traumatic Stress, 4:* 93–112, 1991.

Lyubomirsky, S., and Nolen-Hoeksema, S.: Effects of self-focused rumination on negative thinking and interpersonal problem solving. *Journal of Personality and Social Psychology, 69:* 176–189, 1995.

Lyubomirsky, S., and Nolen-Hoeksema, S.: Self-perpetuating properties of dysphoric rumination. *Journal of Personality and Social Psychology, 65:* 339–349, 1993.

Malinek, D.E., Hoyt, M.E., and Patterson, V.: Adults reaction to the death of a parent. *American Journal of Psychiatry, 136:* 1152–1156, 1979.

Mantell, M.: When the badge turns blue: The San Ysidro massacre. In Goldstein, H., Reese, J., and Horn, J. (Eds.) *Psychological Services for Law Enforcement.* Washington, DC: U. S. Government Press, 1991.

Marmar, C.R., Weiss, D.S., Metzler, T.J., Ronfeldt, H.M., and Foreman, C.: Stress responses of emergency services personnel to the Loma Preita Earthquake interstate 880 freeway collapse and control traumatic incidents. *Journal of Traumatic Stress, 9:* 63–85, 1996.

Mitchell, J.T.: When disaster strikes: The critical incident stress debriefing process. *Journal of Emergency Medical Services, 8:* 35–39, 1983.

Mitchell, J.T., and Everly, G.S.: *Critical incident stress debriefing: An operations manual for the prevention of traumatic stress among emergency service workers.* Ellicott City, MD: Chevron, 1995.

Pangement, K.I., Royster, B.J., and Wood, M.: *A qualitative approach to the study of religion and coping: Four tentative conclusions.* Paper presented at the annual meeting of the American Psychological Association, Boston, MA, August, 1990.

Paton, D., and Stephens, C.: Training and support for emergency responders. In Paton, D. and Violanti, J. (Eds.) *Traumatic stress in critical occupations: Recognition, consequences, and treatment.* Springfield, IL, Charles C Thomas, 1996.

Raphael, B.: *When disaster strikes.* London: Century Hutchinson, 1986.

Roberts, M.: Debriefing and peer counseling of police officers subsequent to shootings and crises. *FBI Training Key,* 1975.

Samter, J., Fitzgerald, M., Braudaway, C., Leeks, D., Padgett, C., Swartz, A., Gary-Stephens, M., and Dellinger, N. (1993). Debriefing: From military origin to therapeutic application. *Journal of Psychosocial Nursing, 31:* 23–27.

Silver, R.L., Boon, C., and Stoves, M. (1983). Searching for meaning in misfortune: Making sense of incest. *Journal of Social Issues, 39:* 81–102.

Sledge, W.H., Boydstun, J.A., and Rahe, A.J.: Self-concept changes related to war captitivity. *Archives of General Psychiatry, 37:* 430–443, 1980.

Staver, S.: Victim's relatives ignored, M.D. Claims. *American Medical News, June 15:* 7–8, 1979.

Stuhlmiller, C.M.: *An interpretive study of appraisal and coping of rescue workers in an earthquake disaster: The Cypress Collapse.* Dissertation Abstracts International, 52, 09B p. 4671. (University Microfilms No. 9205240), 1992.

Stuhlmiller, C.M.: Rescuers of Cypress: Work meanings and practices that guided appraisal and coping. *Western Journal of Nursing Research, 16:* 268–287, 1994.

Stuhlmiller, C.M.: Narrative methodology in disaster studies: Rescuers of Cypress. In P. Benner (Ed.): *Interpretive phenomenology: Embodiment, caring and ethics in health and illness* (pp. 323–349). CA: Sage, 1994.

Stuhlmiller, C.M.: The construction of disorders: Exploring the growth of PTSD and SAD. *Journal of Psychosocial Nursing and Mental Health Services, 33:* 20–23, 1995.

Stuhlmiller, C.M.: Rescuers of Cypress: Learning from disaster. (Book #2 of the International Healthcare Ethics Series). New York: Peter Lang Publishing, 1996.

Stuhlmiller, C.M.: Studying the rescuers. *Sigma Theta Tau International Reflections, 22:* 18–19, 1996.

Stuhlmiller, C.M.: (in revision). Bonds of commonality in the experience of disaster and rescue work.

Taylor, S.E.: Positive illusions: *Creative deception and the healthy mind.* New York: Basic Books, 1989.

Taylor, S.E., Lichtman, R.R., and Wood, J.V.: Attributions, beliefs in control, and adjustment to breast cancer. *Journal of Personality and Social Psychology 46:* 489–502, 1984.

Tedeschi, R., and Calhoun, L: Posttraumatic growth inventory: Measuring the positive legacy of trauma. *Journal of Traumatic Stress, 9:* 455–471, 1996.

Tehrani, N., and Wastlake, R.: Debriefing individuals affected by violence. *Counseling Psychology Quarterly, 7:* 251–259, 1994.

Thomas, L., DiGiulio, R., and Sheehan, N.: Identifying loss and psychological crisis in widowhood. *International Journal of Aging and Human Development, 26:* 279–295, 1991.

Thompson, S.C.: Finding positive meaning in a stressful event and coping. *Basic Applied Social Psychology, 6:* 279–295, 1985.

Ursano, R.J., Wheatley, R., Sledge, W., Rahe, A., and Carlsen, E.: Coping and recovery styles in the Vietnam era prisoner of war. *Journal of Nervous and Mental Disease, 174:* 707–714, 1986.

Veronen, L.J., and Kilpatrick, D.G.: Rape: A precursor to change. In E. Callahan, and K. McCluskey (Eds.): *Lifespan development psychology: Non-normative life events.* New York: Academic Press, 167–191, 1983.

Wagner, M.: Stress debriefing: Flight 191. *Chicago Police Star, August:* 4–7, 1979.

Wagner, M.: Airline disaster: A stress debrief program for police. *Police Stress Magazine,* 16–19, 1981a.

Wagner, M.: Trauma counselling and law enforcement. In Thomlinson, R. (Ed.): *Perspectives on industrial social work practice.* Ottawa: Family Service Canada, 1981b.

Yehuda, R.: *Psychological trauma.* Washington, DC: American Psychiatric Publishing Group, 1998.

Yehuda, R., and McFarlane, A.: *Psychobiology of posttraumatic stress disorder.* Washington, DC: American Psychiatric Press, 1997.

Yalom, I.: *The theory and practice of group psychotherapy.* (2nd ed.) New York: Basic Books, 1975.

Chapter 3

THE INTEGRATION OF TRAUMATIC EXPERIENCES: CULTURE AND RESOURCES

GISELA PERREN-KLINGLER

INTRODUCTION

THE AUTHOR'S EXPERIENCE with survivors of diverse forms of violence heightened her awareness of culture as a specific resource in the process of integrating traumatic experiences. As a clinician one can observe both universal psychophysiological reactions and culturally bound ways of appraising, dealing with, integrating and interpreting problems. It is important to take both aspects into account if one assumes that traumatic experiences must be integrated on both these levels in order to give those affected the best possible chance of survival in the future. The implications of this for professional helpers, especially in the transcultural context, is discussed.

As a psychiatrist from central Europe, my origins place me squarely in the first world. Family, professional and personal socialization have determined which culture I belong to, although some multiculturalism is inevitable after spending time in various countries in Europe during my childhood and exposure to European languages (Ponterotto, 1995). Ethically, I consider myself to be bound by the Universal Declaration of Human Rights or by the ideals proclaimed by the French Revolution. As a physician, I share the diagnostic and pathogenetically-oriented view. I define myself as a participatory observer and promoter of change in the field of mental health. The salutogenetic (i.e., resources-oriented, Antonovsky, 1988) approach, the insights of radical constructivism and the cybernetic understanding of communication (von Glaserfeld, 1987) are essential personal perceptual filters. My work is informed by the following basic assumptions. Neurobiological reactions as such, including those to stress, are similar or identical in all cultures. Physicians, with similar professional training and correspondingly similar perceptual filters, will observe these reactions everywhere. Secondly, people construct their reality (Beck, 1976), making the adoption of a salutogenetic view (Antonovsky, 1979) imperative. Thirdly, people are goal-oriented. Fourthly, people are social beings, embedded in groups according to their languages, and are formed by these languages just as they in turn form the languages. Finally, people react on both conscious and unconscious levels (Perrig, 1993).

HUMAN REACTIONS TO VIOLENCE

In all human beings, the experience of violence leads to similar observable reactions. These can be perceived on the biological (physical), psychological and social levels. Just as physical traumas heal through forming scars, so the experience of violence leaves behind scars on the psychosocial level which, in the most favorable cases, are no longer sensitive. Despite this similarity, the interpretation of traumatic reactions, and the perception of events considered threatening, vary depending on the culture of those affected. The appraisal (Lazarus, 1991) and interpretation of events and reactions are central to the integration of traumatic experiences (Frankl, 1984). In many cultures, religion offers models or rituals for working through distress after threatening experiences, and facilitates the integration of what has happened. In the so-called first world, where religion plays a less salient role in this respect, psychology and psychiatry have assumed the task of supporting the survivors when difficulties arise in dealing with the aftermath of violence. The consequences are not, however, necessarily positive.

The formulation of the diagnostic concept of Posttraumatic Stress Disorder (American Psychiatric Association, 1994) was a positive step for those victimized. At the same time, however, this medicalized concept must be seen as culturally bound. The traumatic experience, whether from war, rape or sexual abuse, is placed in the context of a disorder i.e., of an illness to be treated. However, the realization that violence in any form leads to a recurrence of the same disorders has emerged only slowly. Despite these findings, however, a kind of collective blindness is still common. A wall of silence (Asgeirsson, 1998) is built-up around the psychological consequences of violence, although they extend even to the second generation (Klien, 1974). Repeatedly, societies fall into the trap of turning the survivors of violence into heroes, victims or perpetrators. As a result, all three groups are denied the chance to psychologically integrate their experience.

CULTURALLY-INDEPENDENT REACTIONS TO VIOLENCE

People with western training recognize specific reactions to violence in members of all cultures. These reactions can be directly linked to the physical-humoral reactions of human beings in maximal negative stress situations (Kleber, 1992) and include Acute Stress Disorder (ASD) and Posttraumatic Stress Disorder (PTSD). In addition to these specific reactions, there are always non-specific reactions to violence (Mollica, 1990) which may also occur among people who have not been traumatized. They can be explained by the sense of helplessness during the exposure, and consist mainly of feelings such as shame, anger/irritation, guilt, loss of basic trust (Erikson, 1950), loss of self-coherence (Antonovsky, 1988), grief, depression and confusion (particularly with respect to values). These reactions are aptly referred to as *Shattered Assumptions* (Janoff-Bulmann, 1992). It is more difficult to observe them directly as they are expressed differently depending on the cultural context and may be beset with various taboos. Consequently, they are often not allowed to be expressed directly. They therefore assert themselves in different ways: physically, as emotional dysthymia or as dissociative disorders (van der Kolk et al., 1996) with virtually total amnesia. These culture-bound patterns of reactions are not so readily linked to the extreme event, lessening the likelihood of their being perceived as problems. Also, those affected are less likely to receive appropriate assistance.

Coping with Violence

Coping has an important role to play in dealing with ASD and PTSD. Coping abilities are part culturally-bound and part culturally independent. The conceptualization of these abilities in relation to trauma is still not clear. Of the various theoretical perspectives, the following are the easiest to observe and tend to be the most likely to be useful for structuring in the transcultural context:

- Coping functions on a cognitive (Meichenbaum, 1993), emotional, and behavioral level.
- Confrontation or avoidance to what has happened is an important way of dealing.
- Locus of control can be placed inside or outside (Horowitz, 1976).

An integral part of the traumatic experience is the virtually inseparable mixture of cognition and emotion. It manifests itself in behavior on inner (thought, emotion) and outer levels (behavior). People differ in their ability to separate cognition and emotion after a traumatic event, yet this is necessary to facilitate integration. The following are necessary for this to take place.

Cognitive confrontation with what has happened (Perren-Klingler, 1998). The person affected needs, on the one hand, to be able to face up to the experience with all its horror and unpleasant emotions and to examine what has happened. On the other hand, it is also possible to do all in one's power to avoid thinking about the experience, by suppressing all emotions and avoiding situations which could trigger one's memory. This avoidance behavior increasingly limits one's life internally (emotionally) and externally (socially). The person becomes trapped in his or her own disappointment, anger, helplessness and traumatization. Thus chances of experiencing something new or better (again), of opening the future anew, are blocked substantially. This dissociative (Janet, 1989; Spiegel, 1988) behavior is more common in some cultures than in others: "It was so terrible that I've forgotten everything" is then a typical response. It appears to be common in cultures in which the people believe it is possible to be possessed, or where the jinn (ghost) can influence people's lives.

Locus of control (LoC) also plays a role when interpreting external events. An important issue here is the extent to which the person thinks that he or she has actively participated and taken control (internal locus of control), and to what extent elements are considered to be beyond his or her influence (external locus of control). In cultures in which elements which we consider to be magical play a role, locus of control tends to be external. In cultures which emphasize personal autonomy and responsibility, locus of control is experienced internally. The locus of control is closely linked to the way in which a traumatic experience is given meaning, and is an important precondition for working through the experience.

Helpers from the first world observed several signs of ASD/PTSD in the Cambodian refugee camps in Thailand. The Cambodians themselves, however, interpreted their symptoms as a sign from their ancestors. They said the latter were angry with them because they had left the flock and no longer prepared the daily offerings for the dead. In such a situation, it would be absurd to prescribe medicines or psychotherapy (belief in the locus of control from within). In this case, only rituals which appease the ancestors and build a new relationship with them under changed circumstances can help (Eisenbruch, 1991), as the locus of control was considered as external.

Being prepared for, or the expectation that something terrible will/may happen is a protective factor (Perren-Klingler, 1990, 1996; Basolgu & Parker, 1995) and helps internalize control (I knew, I wanted, I was ready for). The capacity to hold or fantasize about positive memories, important experiences, or to belonging to a meaningful group is also important and enhances the perceived sense of internal control. The essential element is that memories are mobilized and actualized through sensory experiences.

A Palestinian who had been held incommunicado for a long time by the Israelis described to me how he coped:

> I made my eyes sharp, so that they pierced the walls of my cell and of the prison. I went to my home town. There I passed through the streets and went to visit my family: I met them and we sat together, drank coffee, chatted; I can smell the smell of the house, see and hear them. At the end of the afternoon I bid them good bye and went back to my cell.

So-called "blunting" during traumatic exposure (Miller, 1980) describes a way of withdrawing to achieve internal control (in hypnosis the term is dissociation), and indifference to the outside world while remaining secure within oneself is also a manifestation of an internal locus of control. A South American prisoner explained to me how during torture he left his body behind and was able to feel deeply peaceful within himself, triumphant in the knowledge that his tormentors could only reach his body.

Social support, help and solidarity through family, friends and political communities contribute to coping in all cultures. It often gives back the feeling of control, though it is not internal, it is inside the proper group (Teter, 1996).

In "La Libertad," a high security prison for political prisoners in Uruguay, the knowledge that the population was against their being detained was an important support. The joy and triumph was evident when they described to me that, again, this night, they had seen from their windows, the light signals of a row of cars on the bypassing main road. Such signals were important in not losing hope.

The sense of coherence (Antonovsky, 1979) where, for example, following political persecution or rape, the person's identity is not questioned during the event. Instead, it is strengthened. This has been observed with political activists who have been tortured, (Perre, 1990; Basoglu, 1995). The sense of coherence is closely linked to the concept of the locus of control.

The physical ability to resist maximum stress (in traumatic experiences such as accidents, criminal acts of violence, natural disasters, in the first world; persecution, war, torture and flight elsewhere) is partly genetic (Selye, 1980; Cannon, 1932). Security plays an important supplementary role in various circumstances. It begins with early childhood development and continues in the socialization process. Other external conditions such as the satisfaction of minimal basic needs (food, housing, medical care) are all directly related to the sense of security.

Working Through Acute Stress Reactions (ASR)

By talking about the experience in the family, with friends, or in the religious community, a narrative is constructed (Meichenbaum, 1993). The event is reviewed and a central idea is found and developed to make it easier for the listeners to understand what has happened. This leads to cognitive confrontation with the facts of the event once more. The concerned reaction of the listeners makes it easier to release one's emotions under protection of the group. The spontaneous solidarity provides a supportive climate (Fliess; Richman, both in Perren-Klingler, 1996).

The group enhances also the capacity to find a meaning for what has been experienced. This way of working has a prophylactic function and protects those marked by the experience from fixating on the stress reaction, thus preventing it from degenerating into PTSD. Political prisoners who had been tortured made spontaneous use of this technique in Chile (Becerra in Perren-Klingler, 1996). From the above it is clear that the setting of the psychological debriefing in the frame of CISM (Critical Incident Stress Management) (Mitchell, 1993; Turnbull, 1995; Dyregrov, 1997; Perren-Klingler, 1999, in press) is nothing new, but rather a ritually structured psychological group process which has reintroduced a well-tried practice into the western world.

DEALING WITH PTSD: APPROPRIATE INTERVENTIONS

Victims of torture from the military dictatorships in Latin America who had fled to Europe during the late seventies and early eighties were also treated with analytical methods in many places without much success. The treatment was lengthy and often ended with the disability of the patients. In this form of treatment, focused on pathology, the individual was "captured" in an exclusive relationship to the therapist (Baro, 1984) and the participation of the society was virtually ignored. As a reaction to these unsatisfactory and prolonged experiences, fresh attempts were made to work with the traumatized with the explicit goal of alleviating their suffering. Increasingly, different, non-psychodynamic approaches developed, some of which will be described below. Over time, there has been a steady move away from the hermeneutic-interpretative psychoanalytic approach towards totally heuristic methods. In many of these approaches words are used mainly to give instructions. The therapist no longer functions as an interpreter but instead assists the patient in overcoming what disturbs him. The therapist/patient relationship still has a role in which holding (Winnicott, 1960) is essential and must be retained for these situations.

Testimonial therapy with the politically persecuted (Agger, 1990) can be seen as an attempt at working cognitively on the past. The most detailed possible history of the events is reconstructed with the help of the therapist. The psychological consequences are also recorded, and the entire report is used as a document for political ends.

Children and youth who survived the Jupiter and Herald of Free Enterprise boat disasters in England described the support they got from the group. These group discussions worked mostly on the cognitive and emotional level separately (Yule, 1990).

Since the early eighties, Cloe Madanes (1997) has worked on a systemic approach in families in which there has been sexual or other violence. In 17 steps, she introduces not only cognition, emotion, confession, asking for forgiveness, punishment and atonement but also resocialization and relapse prevention.

Several workers (see Meichenbaum, 1994) report on cognitive and behaviorist interventions which have led to an improvement in the symptoms of PTSD over a short period. Combining these techniques with hypnosis and a salutogenetic orientation to resources available can accelerate and intensify the process (Perren-Klingler, 1990, 1999). Pharmacological relaxation has been used as a starting point for cognitive restructuring and in dealing with physical symptoms in some places for a few years now (Baettig & Verladi, personal communication).

Interventions for Understanding Trauma in Other Cultures

All societies have recognized the damaging influence of traumatic experiences on the mental heath of their members. Closer questioning has shown that most cultures have come up with appropriate interventions for working through and integrating what has happened. Rituals are a visible way of ascribing meaning to violence and its aftermath, enabling those affected to return to society. From time to time one has the fortune as a therapist from the first world to meet healers from other cultures and learn from their knowledge. A few experiences will be recorded here.

While working with Bosnian asylum seekers and refugees in the canton of Argovie in Switzerland, we learned about a Bosnian healing ritual to drive away terror. It is practiced by Muslim women in the countryside, and the knowledge is passed down from generation to generation by the women, usually from mother to daughter (cf. Loncarevic in Perren-Klingler, 1995). In central Mexico, there is a Toltec fright ritual. In Mozambique, there is a ritual for people who have killed (*Chirove,* Richman in Perren-Klingler, 1995) which enables them to return to their communities. Intervention towards reconciliation with the ancestors of Cambodian refugees in the Thai camps has been mentioned above. In all these rituals what has happened is reflected on cognitively. The emotions involved are acknowledged in a socially pro-tected framework, and through religious customs. What appears to us to be magic brings relief to those affected.

PERSONAL EXPERIENCES AND INTERVENTIONS

The author's approach will be described in some detail from very different settings. In each case, the aim was to help survivors of trau-matic experiences who were suffering from ASR or from PTSD to inte-grate what had happened and help them to take control of their lives again. In as few interventions as possible, the author or colleague want-ed to find the resources available to the clients and mobilize them for self-help and self-empowerment through homework exercises. By giv-ing clear information they hoped to guide the clients to informed con-sent and, finally, to bring the whole procedure to a satisfactory close.

Most survivors can find meaning by themselves and integrate what has happened once they are freed from the specific traumatic symp-toms. This is not an unrealistic goal as the survivors of trauma are a sample of the average population and functioned like the rest of the population prior to the traumatization. The coping abilities which have been temporarily paralyzed by the trauma must be (re)mobilized.

Intervention with an American-Swiss Patient with Acute PTSD

A 58-year-old American woman, married and living in Switzerland, survived a crash landing in which there were fatalities and injuries. As she was on Beta Blockers for high blood pressure, she had completely been dissociated in the accident. During the evacuation of the airplane she had jumped over the wing without even spraining an ankle. Three months after the accident she came for a consultation. She could not carry on because of emotional numbing and had the feeling that she needed professional help. She had found out what her problem was and what she needed to do through the Internet. She herself had made the diagnosis of PTSD. At the first consultation she was severely dissociated and could feel nothing in her body, although her neck was visibly at an angle. She denied feeling any emotions in relation to the accident. She suffered from severe lack of concentration, had difficulty in finding her words and refused to listen to music as she feared that her beloved music would be contaminated by the reemergence of the horror and that she would then never be able to listen to it again. The therapeutic procedure was explained, and why the use of hypnosis and cognitive behaviorist techniques were appropriate for her. She then gave informed consent to go through with the procedure.

Once the patient had placed her trust in me and a breathing exercise had calmed her down somewhat (i.e., once a good holding had been established), we went through the whole accident again in the first session, not leaving out any details. We worked cognitively, using hypnotic techniques. For the first time the patient became aware of the risk of being hurt, the horror, and felt these emotions intensely. We went on to talk about her "control of pain," i.e., her dissociation from the pain in her neck, and she was encouraged to have her neck vertebra examined by a doctor. After the first session she was able to listen to her music again. Whiplash, which was then diagnosed by an internist, was treated by physiotherapy, and the severe muscular tension gradually disappeared.

In further sessions we worked on her nightmares which had appeared after the first session and her hyperarousal was gradually reduced. After each session the patient received homework tasks to learn to manage her hyperarousal and to mobilize her resources. They consisted of sport activities, music and social contacts. As the dissociation gave way to normal emotion, the relationship to her husband and colleagues at work improved. The death of her mother, which happened during therapy, could be placed within its own framework and separated from the accident. She was able to fly to the United States again. Her lack of concentration was the most difficult obstacle, but it, too, gradually receded.

In seven sessions (spread over ten months), the therapy had advanced so that we were able to talk about bringing it to a close in the eighth session. I asked her to think of a ritual through which she could express her gratitude for having survived unscathed. She told me spontaneously that she would be in the United States on the anniversary of the accident and was thinking of making a donation to an art gallery in the town where she would be staying.

Soon after the Luxor act of terrorism in Egypt, which mobilized symptoms amongst many traumatized people in Switzerland, I found out in a phone call that the patient's husband had now begun to panic whenever she flew to the United States. She, however, was not at all worried.

It was easy for me as a psychiatrist and psychotherapist from a similar, enlightened culture to work with the patient. When her symptoms became intrusive after the accident, she had taken steps to inform herself and made the causal connection between the accident and the hitherto unknown disorder. I could motivate her to cooperate using common arguments. The decreasing symptoms after performing our homework exercises strengthened her conviction that she was on the right path and improved the working relationship. A typical psychiatric, psychotherapeutic setting could be built-up and the patient given the necessary support to take control of her life on her own again. We did not work on or even talk about neurotic symptoms which appeared, intensified by the traumatization, and subsided again after our work.

This patient found meaning in her survival (Frankl, 1984) and gratitude at being alive, which she expressed through the donation to the gallery. The psychotherapeutic model for trauma integration was effective. Today, almost two years after the accident, she is free of symptoms.

Intervention With Bosnian Refugees: Autumn/Winter 1994/1995

A trained eye watching television could see that the first official Bosnian refugees who were brought to Switzerland by the ICRC directly from the concentration camps in the Summer of 1992 were severely traumatized. It was not long until cries for help were heard from the centers which cared for them, as their suffering could not be over-looked. Yet, it was extremely difficult to make it clear to the refugees that the suffering expressed in their bodies was not of somatic origin, and that they needed psychological help. A frequently heard comment was ". . . I'm suffering, but I'm not mad. . . ." Under these conditions it was almost impossible to have any influence on the symptoms of PTSD directly through psychotherapy. So-called culturally adapted projects began to mushroom all over, but few managed to provide their clients with relief from their specific and non-specific symptoms of trauma.

In response to the helplessness of the helpers, a bicultural, Bosnian-Swiss project was set up to train multiplicators in mental health. A knowledge of German and the readiness to work with Bosnians towards their mental health between the training course sessions were the minimum requirements for participation. The course was planned for twelve days, six two-day sessions spread over eight months. The participants agreed to attend all units and to work as multiplicators for six months after the end of the course.

There were two levels to the goals of the project. On the one hand, the participants would have a chance, within a protected space, to come to terms with their own (hypothetical) traumatization. On the other hand—more or less as a support to their healing—they were to acquire sufficient knowledge and skills to pass on the experience, to relieve the Swiss helpers of some of the pressure on them and to support the Bosnians in a culturally appropriate way. The above goals were to be realized in the three parallel sections of the program:

1. Knowledge about normal reactions to traumatic or life-threatening experiences, PTSD and resource-orientated methods were to be taught.
2. Working through and doing exercises in small groups—always with the explicit aim of acquiring more knowledge and skills—the participants' own traumatization was to be reflected on, worked through and overcome.
3. Bicultural pairs would be set up systematically to work together as multiplicators between the courses. This would foster mutual understanding, respect and appreciation and develop greater tolerance.

The first day of the course could best be captured on film. Two groups turned up. The group of Bosnians, heads bowed, in a state somewhere between nervousness and hyperarousal. A group of concerned Swiss, some very anxious, but nevertheless calm, all involved with refugees in some way. Compulsively, the tense participants drank endless cups of coffee and smoked increasingly during the sessions, and not only in the official breaks. The atmosphere was heavy, oppressive, and hopelessly sad. Originally, I had planned to run the course based on a concept of child development. But on recognizing the obvious mood of the participants, I decided to start providing information about trauma and how to work with it immediately. The immediate work on psychological reactions to persecution, violence and uprooting, was aiming at introducing resources which they could learn to use straight away. In one of the first exercises in which we worked on resources available in our own cultures on the second day, the participants were instructed to talk about festivities in small groups. The Bosnians protested that they were unable to do this, and some said that they didn't have any festivities at home. To resolve the deadlock I added an instruction that the Swiss, who said they did have festivities, should start with the sense-specific narrative (primarily cognitive, letting the emotions flow along). Less than half an hour later each group was trying to outdo the other as to who had the better festivities. They had to explain who did what, how, and describe the special dishes that were prepared, etc. For the first time there was laughter, faces cheered up, and the atmosphere relaxed.

Tensions came up continually, also between the two national groups, when discussing security for instance. How much security does one need in order to deal with the psychological consequences of traumatization? Some of the Bosnians maintained there could only be security if they were allowed to stay in Switzerland for the next ten years (typical traumatic distortion of perceptions (Perren-Klingler, 1996). They attacked the Swiss, blaming them for the situation. Thus clarity was required on issues such as *who* is responsible for refugee politics in Switzerland, *what* comprises minimal security, *how* are adaptation difficulties expressed on both sides, and so forth. They learned to recognize that aggression can also be a sign of hyperarousal. Relating what had been said to the present situation helped everyone in a big step towards mutual understanding and understanding the effects of traumatic reactions.

Debriefing techniques in the frame of CISM, as a form of prevention were practiced in various ways to bring some order into the chaos of traumatic experiences and to clarify emotions. At the end of the twelve days of the course, the dejected and frightened participants had been transformed into a group which was ready to go into the future with hope and courage, and to support those less fortunate than themselves in several different places. In short, the solidarity (Kropotkin, 1908) had worked for them. For the course leaders it is astounding that many of the multiplicators continue to use what they have learned after the "end of the contract." Those who have returned home have taken what they have learned with them to Bosnia.

A new and different approach had been sought and found as a response to a desperate situation. The topics included information about how to act in and for a group. The strengthening of resources, by embedding them in the present context, and the mobilization of self-help and taking responsibility for oneself were the main theme, and not individualized, personalized treatment from a therapist.

The Bosnians in our group did not experience their symptoms as problems "in their heads," as individual emotions, but saw them against the background of scenes of horror and persecution. They experienced the locus of control as outside, so it would have been meaningless, and a sign of a lack of respect and understanding of the horror they had been through, to act intrapsychically/psychotherapeutically.

Initially, meaning could only be seen in relation to the malevolence of our fellow human beings, a "fate" that is against you and incomprehensible. Religion, which seeks meaning behind the incomprehensible, can sustain the belief in providence despite the helplessness experienced (Job). It is able to sharpen the perception of a new solidarity of other groups and give a new, as yet unknown, meaning in anticipation. But for most of the participants, who described themselves as atheists and Marxists, this path was not open.

My basic assumption as a course leader is that survivors have enough resources available to lead a further good life free of symptoms. My aim was to bring about changes in those traumatized to help them towards better coping. So it was clear from the beginning that the course should be future-oriented, mobilize resources and be a process of finding some peace. The idea of learning something new to pass on to people in need, i.e., the appeal to solidarity (Friere, 1980), proved to be fundamental and effective in the unexpected, much longer-lasting multiplication process. It is important to note that this process, besides the learning, consciously included not only cognition, dealing with traumatization and migration, but also confrontation with one's own resources and coping abilities. It was planned and carried out as a process of change in the integrative, healing sense. Thus it could only be implemented by someone well-versed in (psycho) therapeutic practices and working with groups.

Early Interventions with Asylum Seekers from Kosovo

Since the confrontation with the Bosnians, many Swiss professionals dealing with asylum seekers and refugees are sensitized to signs and behaviors which could stem from traumatic experiences. The massive arrival of refugees from Kosovo which nearly overwhelmed the asylum structures has, for the first time, tested the learning from the Bosnian arrivals. The professionals are aware of the need of the newly arrived persons to speak. However, they do not have the time to listen, because of the emergency in providing housing and food first.

In this specific context, the resource-oriented approach has been to organize a group of 50 persons from Kosovo and train them in debriefing techniques. This way the cultural approach is guaranteed, there is no need for interpreters and the arriving persons can construct and share their history.

The summary of a debriefing of a trigenerational family which was addressed by the carers of a center to a child psychiatric unit follows. The six year-old boy started starving himself saying that if his father was dead, he also wanted to die. However, he had not been told that his father indeed had been killed by the Serbs, but that his father was in another town in Switzerland. We decided to construct complete common history by debriefing the family who had arrived in Switzerland: Grandmother, age 55, her youngest son, age 34, with his pregnant wife, age 24, the widow mother of the boy, age 27, whose father had died. An interpreter and the director of the center, a psychologist, participated as well. In this session, the whole story of what had happened to the men (who had hidden in another place than the women) was told by the son, the only adult man left in the family. So mother, wife, sister-in-law, and the boy learned about how out of 15 eight men were killed, amongst others, the father of the boy. The man also learned what had happened to the women during hiding and that his mother had had a vision in which his dead brother told her not to go out of their hiding before night. The form of the intervention was that of a classical psychological debriefing, very tense and loaded with emotions which eased after everybody knew all of the story of the other group. It was very important to mobilize the will for survival and activity for the sake of the children, to open a future, be it in Switzerland or be it in a more peaceful Kosovo, and to talk about the ritual for the dead and what should be done more to what they already had done. It was also important to make clear that this intervention did not lead to an automatic recognition as statutory refugees, who are allowed to stay as long as they want.

STRUCTURAL SIMILARITIES IN THE INTERVENTIONS BETWEEN CULTURES

The assumption that all human brain structures are alike and therefore react in a similar way to violence is based on the observation that somatic reactions throughout the world are perceived to be similar when the same model of perception is used. Thus, intervention models which are effective in dealing with the psychological and psychosocial consequences of violent experiences can repeatedly use similar structural procedures. The contents themselves, however, vary according to society's interpretation of what has happened, the assumptions of the culture in question and, of course, the specific personality of the person affected. The following factors are important elements in this procedure.

Security is the primary precondition for a process of change. There must be a framework with a minimum of basic security, differing according to geographic and cultural understanding. The security of being accepted and supported by the community or the therapist and a minimum ability to make social contacts are essential. People who have been traumatized often have an exaggerated need for security as if, after the experience of having no control, only total control—by which they mean "total and everlasting" security—is acceptable.

The listeners must be able to keep calm and not let themselves be overwhelmed, even when the reports are terrible. They must keep on noticing and mentioning the resources of the victims, reminding them that they have survived. This salutogenetic behavior is necessary, though obviously one never loses sight of how much the victim has suffered. The optimism that as long as people live there are possibilities for changes for the better is paramount.

In the case of ASD, understanding support as to what happened and as to how life has to be organized, is structurally an important part to integrate the experience into one's life and for a personal continuity to be rediscovered, either "in spite of" or "because of" the experience. This support enables one to carry on living even after assumptions about the goodness of the world and our power to have control have been shattered, when helplessness and being overwhelmed by intense negative emotions hamper attempts to deal with the situation cognitively, and when those affected appear not to be able to get any further. Because traumatic experiences are caused by the failure of a society to provide protection (Herman, 1992) one expects from it, the function of the group is important, this time with other, "better" representatives of the society. The event can be gone through again, reinterpreted and denounced with the support of the new group. Solidarity and reparations in some form or other can be introduced. This is a form of ritual in which what has happened can be introduced, discussed, shared, and acknowledged in the society in which the affected people live.

Cognitive confrontation with what has happened occurs through talking about the event once more. Whether this happens on an informal or a formal level is immaterial, but it almost always takes place in a group, whether they be friends, comrades, family, the clan, or other people who have been affected.

Expressing the emotions and support from the community are an integral part of the above. Calming down the physical hyperarousal is achieved through explanations and actions which are prescribed, encouraged or found on one's own. Rituals can help in conquering the problems. Shattered assumptions can be rebuilt in a different way to open up the future. In short, the experience contains a new meaning different from the traumatized one. It is reconstructed.

Similar structures can also be found in dealing with PTSD. Cognitive confrontation with what has happened also takes place here. The same story is told in a changed setting, either in individual therapy or in a group, with another undertone, i.e., it is put into words, visualized or represented in an artistic form, for instance. A central theme is found to link the events and a narrative is constructed. Order is brought to the experience of chaos, and with it the precondition for the next steps to be established.

Emotions and the associated convictions or assumptions are clarified. Various techniques are used to calm down the client on a physical as well as an emotional level. Ideally, this is achieved rapidly.

Society's acknowledgement that something terrible has happened appears to be central to healing the mental wounds. Not only war, killing, destruction, persecution on the societal level, but also criminal, sexual and family (Madanes, 1997) violence are unacceptable and must be rectified. The laying of charges, condemnation, sentencing, punishment, atonement and reparations are important steps, no less so in a western world with secular values.

In order for cognitive confrontation with the traumatic events to be reached, without unleashing a flooding of feelings, various types of sensory overload are used. Watching the spoon moving horizontally over the flame and the lead being poured into the pot filled with water and hearing prayers from the Koran; the back and forth movement of the eyes following a moving finger while listening to the commentaries of the therapist in EMDR; the physical stimulation of both sides of the body accompanied by commentaries in TFT and the movement of the head from left to right accompanied by breathing in and out during a Toltec fright ritual are all ways which enable survivors protected from an overabundance of emotions to establish cognitive order. The same effect is achieved in the hypnotic techniques through so-called multiple dissociation accompanied by simultaneous instructions to mobilize resources on a physical level. Interestingly, it is not important whether everything happens on a clear conscious level or on a preconscious, "hazy" one (Perren-Klingler, in press). The culture-bound concept of time has a further role to play in the integration of what has been experienced and deserves an investigation in its own right.

CONCLUSION

The concept of trauma and of PTSD led to a boom of various, therapeutic interventions, mostly designed for individuals in the eighties. The nineties have brought us back to many traditional methods, due to the large numbers of non-European victims and their unwillingness for, or lack of understanding of, psychotherapeutic interventions. Simple interventions can help in the long term when they take place early enough and are conducted with a salutogenetic view and are as well anchored as possible in the culture in question, ideally, when they are introduced by representatives of the culture.

The salutogenetic or resources centered approach means that the persons who intervene must stick to a few presuppositions, whichever professional background they come from, medical, psychological or any other one. The persons that arrive have survived which means that they have resources, otherwise they would be dead. A respectful curiosity as to how they managed to survive is a position from which one can learn a lot about their resources, personal, community-bound and cultural/religious/ideological. The persons who have survived can cope, they dispose of enough resources to continue a meaningful life. The art of working with them consists of doing everything which lets them reopen their future. They also have the resources to find a meaning if the surroundings are able to cope with their sometimes crazy behavior. One has to accept that psychological trauma can leave scars, even if one has the salutogenetic position.

The discovery of rituals for traumatic experiences and the efficiency of these rituals in the respective cultures has taught us to develop respect and curiosity and to look for a structural common denominator with our own interventions. We have learned to be humble about our "new" techniques in the face of age-old wisdom in different traditions. That our modern culture which is often impoverished when it comes to traditions should also make use of sound, western psychological techniques goes without saying. Where other methods are available, we should have the courage and respect to examine them, so that these methods can also be used as cultural resources.

REFERENCES

Agger, I., and Jensen, B.S. (1990). Testimony as a ritual and evidence in psychotherapy for political refugees. *Journal of Traumatic Stress, 3:* 115–130, 1990.

American Psychiatric Association: *Diagnostic and statistical manual of mental disorders,* (4th ed.). Washington, DC: American Psychiatric Press, 1994.

Antonovsky, A.: *Health, stress and coping.* San Francisco: Jossey-Bass, 1979.

Antonovsky, A.: *Unravelling the mysteries of health.* San Francisco: Jossey-Bass, 1988.

Arbeitsgruppe Stolzenbachhilfe: *Nach der Katastrophe: Das Grubenunglück von Borken.* Göttingen: Vandenhoek & Rupprecht, 1992.

Asgeirsson, P.: A wall of silence. *Traumatic Stress Points, 12:* 1,2,4, 1998.

Baettig, D., and Velardi, A.: (1998). Personal communication.

Basoglu, M., and Parker, M.: Severity of trauma as predictor of long term psychological status in survivors of torture. *Journal of Anxiety Disorders, 9:* 339–353, 1995.

Baro, M.: *Guerra y Salud mental.* Estudios Centroamericanos, ECA, 1984.

Becerra, H.: Solidarity between those tortured in prison. In G. Perren-Klingler, (Ed): *Trauma.* Berne: Paul Haupt, 1996.

Bible. *Daniel, 3:* 51.

Bonhoeffer, D.: *Widerstand und Ergebung, Briefe und Aufzeichnungen aus der Haft.* München: Fischer, 1951.

Bourekat, A.: *Dix-huit Ans de Solitude.* Paris: Seuil, 1993.

Busuttill, W., Turnbull, G.J., Neal, L.A. et al.: Incorporating psychological debriefing techniques within a brief group psychotherapy programme for the treatment of PTSD. *British Journal of Psychiatry, 167:* 495–502, 1995.

Cannon, W.B.: *The wisdom of the body.* New York: Norton, 1932.

Dyregrov, A.: The process of psychological debriefings. *Journal of Traumatic Stress, 10:* 589–605, 1997.

Eisenbruch, M.: From PTSD to cultural bereavement: Diagnosis of Southeast Asian refugees. *Social Science and Medicine, 33:* 673–680, 1991.

Erickson, E.H.: *Childhood and society.* New York: Norton, 1950.

Figley, C.R. (Ed.): *Compassion fatigue.* New York: Brunner Mazel, 1995.

Fliess, C.L.: Cambodian youths in America. In Perren-Klingler (Ed.). Beane: Paul Haupt, 1996.

Frankl, V.: *Mans search for meaning.* New York: Simon & Schuster, 1984.

Freire, P.: *Education for critical consciousness.* New York: Continuum Press, 1980.

Grainger, R.D., Levin, C., Allen-Byrd, L. et al.: An empirical evaluation of EMDR with survivors of a natural disaster. *Journal of Traumatic Stress, 10:* 665–671, 1997.

Haley, J.: *Uncommon therapy: The psychiatric techniques of Milton H. Erickson.* New York: Norton, 1973.

Havel, V.: *Briefe an Olga: Identität und Existenz, Betrachtungen aus dem Gefängnis.* Hamburg: Rororo, 1984.

Hermann, J.: *Trauma and recovery: The aftermath of violence.* New York: Harper-Collins, 1992.

Horowitz, M.J.: *Stress response syndromes.* New York: Jason Aronson, 1976.

Janet, P.: *L'automatisme Psychique*. Reprint (1973), Paris, 1989.

Janoff-Bulman, R.: *Shattered assumptions: Towards a new psychology of trauma*. New York: Free Press, 1992.

Jingsheng, W.: *Lettres de prison, 1981–1993*. Paris: Bibliographie, 1998.

Kleber, R.J.: *Coping with trauma*. Amsterdam: Swets and Zeitlinger, 1992.

Klein, H.: *Delayed affects and after effects of severe traumatization*. Israel Annals of Psychiatry, *12:* 12–20, 1974.

Kropotkin, P.: *Gegenseitige Hilfe in der Tier-und Menschenwelt*, Reprint (1975), Berlin, 1908.

Lazarus, R.S.: *Emotion and adaptation*. New York: Oxford University Press, 1991.

Loncarevic. M.: MIR: A socio-cultural integration project for Bosnian refugees. In G. Perren-Klingler (Ed.): *Trauma*. Berne: Paul Haupt, 1996.

Macksoud, M.: *Helping children cope with the stresses of war*. New York: UNICEF, 1993.

Madanes, C.: *Sex, love and violence*. New York: Norton, 1990.

Meichenbaum, D., and Fitzpatrick, D.: A constructionist narrative perspective on stress and coping. In Goldberg and Breznitz (Eds.): *Handbook of Stress*. New York: Free Press, 1993.

Miller, S.M.: When is a little information a dangerous thing? Coping with stressful events by monitoring vs blunting. In Levine and H. Ursin (Eds.): *Coping and health*. New York: Plenum, 1980.

Mitchell, J.T., and Everly, G.S.: *Critical incident stress debriefing: An operations manual for the prevention of traumatic stress among emergency services and disaster workers*. Ellicott City, MD: Chevron Publishing, 1993.

Mollica, R.F.: Assessing symptom change in Southeast Asian refugee survivors of mass violence and torture. *American Journal of Psychiatry, 147:* 83–88, 1990.

Niederland, W.: Survivor syndrome. *Journal of the American Psychiatric Association, 29:* 413–425, 1981.

Pennebaker, J.W., Mayne, T.J., and Francis, M.E. (1997). Linguistic predictors of adaptive bereavement. *Journal of Personality and Social Psychology, 72:* 863–871, 1997.

Perren-Klingler, G.: Le Stress post traumatique, développement d'un concepte. *Rev. Méd. Suisse Rom., 110:* 77, 1990.

Perren-Klingler, G.: Human reactions to traumatic experience: In G. Perren-Klingler, (Ed.). *Trauma*. Berne: Paul Haupt, 1996.

Perren-Klingler, G.: Psychotrauma: A change in perspective: From pathology to coping, from individual to community, from victim to survivor. In G. Perren-Klingler (Ed.): *Stiftung für Kinder: Children and War*. Hamburg: UNICEF, 1996.

Perren-Klingler, G.: Hypnotische Behandlung von post traumatischen Belastungsstörungen. In B. Peter, and D. Revenstorf, D. (Hg): *Handbuch der Hypnose*. im Druck, 1998.

Perren-Klingler, G. (Ed.): *Debriefing und Andere Frühe Interventionen nach Trauma*. Bern: im Druck, 1999.

Perrig, W.J., Wippich, W., and Perreig-Chielleo, P.: *Unbewusste Informationsverarbeitung*. Bern/Toronto: Hans Huber, 1993.

Ponteretto, J.G., Casas, J.M., Suzuki, L.A., and Alexander, C.M.: *Handbook of multi-cultural counseling, Appendix I: Guidelines for providers of psychological services to ethnic, linguistic and culturally diverse populations.* London: Sage, 1995.

Richman, N., Mucache E., and Draimba, F.: A school-based community mental health programme for helping war affected children. In G. Perren-Klingler (Ed.): *Stiftung für Kinder: Children and War.* Hamburg: UNICEF, 1996.

Rosencof, M., and Huidobro, E.F.: *Memorias del Calabozo. Novarra, dt. Wie Efeu an der Mauer.* Hamburg: 1993.

Selye, H. (Ed.): *Guide to stress research.* New York: McGraw-Hill, 1980.

Shazer, S. de: *Clues, investigating solutions in brief therapy.* London: Norton, 1988.

Spiegel, D.: Dissociation and hypnosis in PTSD. *Journal of Traumatic Stress, 1:* 11–33, 1988.

Terr, L.: Forbidden games. Posttraumatic child's play. *Journal of the American Academy of Child Psychiatry, 20:* 547–621, 1981.

Teter, H.: Mass violence and community treatment. In G. Perren-Klingler (Ed.). *Trauma.* Berne: Paul Haupt, 1996.

van der Kolk, B.A., Pelcovitz, D., Roth, S., et al.: Dissociation, somatization and affect dysregulation: The complexity of adaptation to trauma. *American Journal of Psychiatry, 153 (Suppl):* 83–93, 1996.

Von Glasersfeld, E.: *Siegener Gespräche über Radikalen Konstruktivismus in Der Diskurs des Radikalen Konstruktivismus.* Frankfurt: Schmidt, 1987.

Yule, W., and Williams, R.: Posttraumatic stress reactions in children. *Journal of Traumatic Stress, 3:* 279–295, 1990.

Chapter 4

BRIEF PREVENTION PROGRAMS
AFTER TRAUMA

I.V.E. Carlier and B.P.R. Gersons

INTRODUCTION

CRISIS THEORY HAS TAUGHT US that people who have been involved in traumatic events are inclined by nature to share their experiences and emotions with one another (Wollman, 1993; Carlier & Gersons, 1997). There is evidence, however, that the process of trauma resolution often fails to operate. That may, for example, be due to a macho culture that prevails in trauma-sensitive occupations such as police, fire fighting and military work.

The frequent failure of spontaneous trauma resolution has prompted efforts to develop professionalized intervention methods aimed at fending off posttraumatic stress disorder, or PTSD (Carlier & Gersons, 1995). This psychiatric disorder, formerly known as traumatic neurosis, has also achieved some notoriety as a consequence of the many damage claims filed by trauma victims. Public enterprises, the military, police and fire departments, and other organizations where employees are at risk have therefore seized on the idea that professional care might help to avert later damage. Beyond the concrete support that employees receive, the structured trauma response programs are a meaningful acknowledgment of the problems they face in terms of traumatic experiences at work. Such traumatic work experiences can be regarded as occupational risks, and PTSD as an occupational illness (Carlier & Gersons, 1992, 1994; Carlier et al., 1996, 1997).

Professionalized trauma intervention is often referred to as debriefing. Although stress debriefing was originally developed as an initial psychosocial intervention for groups that had been affected by trauma, the technique is now also used for individuals, couples and families. Debriefing is by no means new, although its popularity has been increasing since the 1980s. The word itself is originally a military term for a postcombat interview (Salmon, 1919; see also Marshall, 1944). In the early 1980s, the method was adapted by Mitchell (1983) for the care of rescue personnel such as police, fire fighters, ambulance workers and Red Cross relief workers. He named it Critical Incident Stress Debriefing, or CISD.

We first examine the core elements of debriefing and the various stages in its application, and we discuss several theories about its preventive effects. We then review the research on the outcomes of debriefing and examine some alternative preventive programs for PTSD. We close with some tentative conclusions and suggestions about crisis intervention in the wake of traumatic events.

THE CORE ELEMENTS OF PROFESSIONALIZED TRAUMA INTERVENTION

Mitchell's (1983) debriefing model is now applied worldwide, and not just for rescue workers. Others have developed modified versions (e.g., Raphael, 1986; Armstrong et al., 1991; Talbot et al., 1992). According to the general model, debriefing is preferably performed within 24 to 72 hours of the traumatic event. A debriefing session lasts an average of two hours, but this can be slightly shorter for individual debriefings and longer for group sessions. A debriefing session normally comprises seven phases, which may also be applied in combination with each other (Mitchell, 1983; Dyregrov, 1997):

1. Introduction—explanation of the main "rules of play" (confidentiality, constructive attitude etc.)
2. Facts—reconstruction of the factual elements of the event (what exactly happened?)

3. Thoughts–thoughts that occurred during the event (what did you think when you first saw the chaos?)
4. Experiencing–emotions that occurred (emotional ventilation or catharsis)
5. Symptoms–physical and psychological stress reactions
6. Education–explanation of the stress reactions (normalization) and of useful coping strategies
7. Closing–answers to any remaining questions and information on opportunities for further care.

In practice there are only minor differences between debriefing models. These lie not in the intervention method or its format, but in details such as the timing (time span between traumatic event and intervention), intensity and duration (one or several sessions), practitioners (lay people versus professionals) or number of participants (individual versus group intervention). The professionalized intervention consistently includes the same core aspects: giving the participants the opportunity, within a confidential, supportive environment, to rid themselves of all the internal tensions they have built up as a result of the incident, and to let off emotional steam. Debriefing is also thought to help participants maintain or regain control over themselves (Dyregrov, 1997). By reconstructing the traumatic event they can create a more realistic perception of it. They are then asked about their stress reactions and, by way of reassurance, informed about possible posttraumatic stress reactions in the future which would be part of the normal resolution of the trauma. Information is also provided about useful coping strategies, and about opportunities for follow-up care if the stress symptoms persist.

In the event that the intervention does not occur until a later point in time (a month or more after the traumatic event), and if stagnation has occurred in the process of resolving the trauma, participants can be referred on to some kind of further counseling, since debriefing is not the same as treatment. At this later point in time, more attention can also be focused on any changes in the participants' lives that have occurred as a result of the traumatic experience. These could be practical changes, such as time off work, but especially changes in values, norms and view of life (for example, "I can't trust anybody any more"). Changes can also be positive ("Since that happened, I've had more confidence in myself"). The debriefing can also address how to deal with reactions from the environment, at home or at work.

THEORIES ABOUT THE PREVENTIVE
EFFECTS OF DEBRIEFING

Theories that explain the preventive effect of intervention may emphasize a range of different factors (Wollman, 1993; Shalev, 1994; Everly, 1995; Mitchell & Everly, 1995). A psychodynamic approach assumes that the emotional ventilation (catharsis) induced by debriefing will set free the internal tension that has been bottled up since the traumatic experience. Ultimately this should counter the development of posttraumatic stress symptomatology (see also Krystal, 1978; Benyakar et al., 1989). The verbalization of the recent traumatic experience can be seen in the same light–it, too, may facilitate the normal resolution process (Greenberg & van der Kolk, 1987; Pennebaker & Susman, 1988). Horowitz (1976) has stressed the similarities between PTSD and bereavement, focusing on the potential therapeutic role of bereavement processes in debriefing.

The cognitive perspective places more emphasis on the role of effective coping strategies and the importance of cognitive restructuring (Lazarus & Folkman, 1984). The latter is achieved during debriefing by reconstructing the traumatic event (creating a more realistic and complete perception) and by repairing any cognitive schemata that have been damaged (moderating generalizations like "The world is rotten to the core"). The role of coping strategies in debriefing is rather complex. In some people, reactions such as denial or avoidance can expedite the resolution process, while in others it can hinder it (Lazarus, 1982; Shalev, 1994; see also Jones, 1995).

An additional factor sometimes seen as a possible determinant of the effect of debriefing is the *promptness* of the intervention within a few hours or days posttrauma (Friedman et al., 1988; Everly, 1995). Finally, in group interventions, the *group process* itself is believed to aid in the resolution of the trauma. This is specifically due to therapeutic group factors such as mutual identification, support, exchange of information, and self-help through helping others (Jones, 1985; Everly, 1995).

Systematic Research on the Effects of Debriefing

Two types of systematic assessments of debriefing have been made: satisfaction assessments and outcome evaluations. These are reviewed in the sections to follow.

Satisfaction Assessments

Satisfaction studies give an indication of how satisfied people feel with an intervention they have undergone, in this case debriefing. The conclusion of most such studies has been that a large majority of the participants valued the debriefing, rating it from "reasonably satisfied" to "very satisfied" (Robinson & Mitchell, 1993; Turner et al., 1993; Jenkins, 1996; Carlier et al., 1998). This finding is consistent with the observation that recently traumatized people have a natural need for emotional support, compassion, mutual identification, understanding and endorsement. But research has further shown that satisfaction with debriefing is not associated with a positive outcome of the intervention. That is, high levels of satisfaction are not statistically correlated with lower levels of symptomatology, less sick leave or earlier work resumption (Doctor et al., 1994; Lee et al., 1996; Bisson et al., 1997; Carlier et al., 1998).

Much of the satisfaction research consists of exploratory, descriptive studies of posttraumatic stress symptomatology in subjects who have all undergone debriefing, without comparison to a control group. Most studies have reported a reduction in symptomatology following the debriefing (Sloan, 1988; Alexander & Wells, 1991; Flannery et al., 1991; Johnson et al., 1992; Alexander, 1993; Stallard & Law, 1993; Robinson & Mitchell, 1993; Turner et al., 1993; Busuttil et al., 1995; Chemtob et al., 1997; Jenkins, 1996; Saari et al., 1996). Given the absence of control groups of non-debriefed subjects, however, this apparent improvement cannot be taken as an unquestionable positive effect of the intervention. This brings us to the second type of assessments, the controlled outcome studies.

Outcome Evaluations

Outcome evaluations compare the levels of posttraumatic stress symptomatology in a group of debriefed traumatized subjects with those in a group who received no debriefing. The presence of a control group of non-debriefed respondents, preferably allocated at random, is essential for reaching any firm conclusions about the effects of the intervention (Sibbald & Roland, 1998). Three randomized, controlled trials of debriefing have been published so far (Hobbs et al., 1996; Lee et al., 1996; Bisson et al., 1997), mostly involving one-session interventions. In the Lee study, individual debriefing was performed two weeks posttrauma. At a 4-month follow-up, no significant differences in symptomatology were detected between debriefed and non-debriefed participants. The Hobbs study of individual debriefing 24–48 hours posttrauma recorded *more* symptomatology in the debriefed group than in the non-debriefed control group. In the Bisson study, debriefing was carried out, individually or in couples, from 2 to 19 days (an average of 6 days) posttrauma. At a 3-month follow-up, no significant differences were evident between debriefed and non-debriefed respondents. However, at a 13-month follow-up, the debriefed group reported significantly more symptomatology (more PTSD, more anxiety and more depression) than the group that had undergone no debriefing. These researchers further showed that the outcomes of the intervention were not influenced by other potentially relevant variables such as the level of training of the debriefers (lay people, paraprofessionals, professionals), satisfaction with debriefing, number of participants in debriefing sessions (individual versus couple debriefing) or the gender of the debriefed subjects. The Bisson group noted moreover that the adverse effects of the debriefing were stronger (more symptomatology was induced) the longer the debriefing sessions themselves had lasted.

We can conclude that the three randomized trials have produced no evidence for any positive effect of debriefing, that is, that debriefing has no preventive effect on the development of posttraumatic stress symptomatology. The negative effects found in two of the three trials suggest that debriefing may induce symptomatology. Some studies (e.g., Matthews, 1998) have proposed that the unexpected negative outcomes of debriefing were caused by applying it too early (48–72 hours posttrauma).

The findings of these randomized, controlled studies of debriefing are consistent with the results of several non-randomized controlled studies (McFarlane, 1988; Hytten & Hasle, 1989; Deahl et al., 1994; Doctor et al., 1994; Griffith & Watts, 1994; Kenardy et al., 1996; Carlier et al., 1998; Matthews, 1998). Most of the latter studies involved group debriefing. Hence, there is little or no support for the idea (e.g., Busuttil & Busuttil, 1995) that the lack of positive effects in the randomized studies in individualized contexts may be attributable to the absence of therapeutic group factors like support and mutual identification. Raphael et al. (1995) had argued earlier that the group process is not the deciding factor for a positive outcome of debriefing. It is even conceivable that participants in group debriefing sessions become retraumatized by hearing the traumatic stories of their fellow group members.

Other authors (Watts, 1994; Turnbull et al., 1997) have blamed the lack of positive outcomes in controlled studies on the fact that in most cases only a single debriefing session was provided. The assumption here is that multiple sessions would have a more powerful impact in averting posttraumatic stress symptomatology. Recent findings by Carlier et al. (submitted) and by Brom et al. (1993), however, have cast doubt on that possibility. The Carlier study investigated the efficacy of a departmental debriefing program in the police force. It provided for structured intervention in the form of three sequential individual debriefing sessions (informally known as the three-stage debriefing model). A more or less similar model is also applied outside police contexts (Brom & Kleber, 1989; van der Velden et al., 1997). The core elements of the debriefing sessions were in agreement with those described above. The three sessions normally took place over a period of three months, calculated from the traumatic event: within 24 hours, one month, and three months posttrauma. The first debriefing session was devoted mainly to reconstructing the event (the victim's trauma narrative) in a calm, structured context. Emphasis in the second and third interviews was more on depth, integration and education. These last two interviews also highlighted an important additional function of structured intervention, the detection of any stagnation in the resolution of the trauma. This would enable the debriefers to extend the intervention, if necessary, by referring the victim to occupational social workers or medical officers. In many cases, two debriefing sessions were deemed sufficient (see van der Velden et al., 1997). That occurred especially when the victim did not perceive, or no longer perceived, the event as terrifying, or when the stress reactions had strongly, or even fully, remitted.

The Carlier study compared traumatized, debriefed police officers with an internal and an external control group, neither of which had received any debriefing. At the assessment point 24 hours posttrauma, no significant differences appeared between the comparison groups in symptomatology or work resumption. At one week posttrauma, significantly more posttraumatic stress reactions had emerged in the debriefed group than in the two non-debriefed groups, although no such differences were evident in work resumption or sick leave. Six months posttrauma, there were no longer any significant differences between the groups in symptomatology, work resumption or sick leave. These results replicate those in the controlled study by Brom et al. (1993), which evaluated a trauma response program that strongly resembled the three-stage police debriefing model. The Brom assessments were carried out at one and at six months posttrauma. In spite of the satisfaction expressed with the intervention, the debriefed and non-debriefed groups did not significantly diverge in their levels of symptomatology.

ALTERNATIVE PROGRAMS FOR PTSD PREVENTION

In some cases, debriefing is applied not within 72 hours of the trauma, but several weeks or months afterwards (Dyregrov, 1997). One benefit of this is that victims can be screened for PTSD, since they would then satisfy DSM-IV Criterion E that the PTSD symptoms be present for more than one month. This section describes some alternative preventive programs, which are normally applied in cases of acute PTSD (duration of symptoms less than three months). These are not so much debriefing programs as treatment interventions. Their purpose is not the prevention of acute PTSD, but of *chronic* PTSD (duration of symptoms three months or longer). In all cases they are very brief trauma treatment programs, averaging from three to six treatment sessions. They are sometimes referred to in the literature as crisis intervention counseling (Bordow & Porritt, 1979; Cryer & Beutler, 1980; Kilpatrick

& Veronen, 1983; Viney et al., 1985). We highlight here three alternatives for which favorable results have recently been published. Given the focus of this book, we have left aside preventive programs for coping with bereavement.

The first example is Ford et al.'s (1997) Time-Limited Psychotherapy. This eclectically-oriented program, averaging three treatment sessions, devotes systematic attention to the following aspects: reconstruction of the trauma, psychoeducation, affect focusing (Gendlin, 1979), cognitive restructuring (McCann & Pearlman, 1990; Meichenbaum, 1994) and interpersonal problem-solving (D'Zurilla & Goldfried, 1971; Stanton & Figley, 1978; Frank & Spanier, 1995). The brief treatment was administered to combat veterans two to nine months after the Gulf War. The treatment group finished with more favorable symptom scores than the control group, although the differences were not statistically significant. The authors attributed that to the absence of a specific trauma exposure component.

An approach called the Brief Prevention Program (Foa et al., 1995) did contain trauma exposure, and it delivered significant improvement. It was applied in the prevention of chronic PTSD in female victims of sexual or other types of violence. It was administered approximately one month posttrauma, as soon as PTSD could be diagnosed, and it encompassed four treatment sessions. The following cognitive-behavioral techniques were applied (see also Foa et al., 1991): (a) psychoeducation, (b) relaxation training, (c) imaginal exposure, (d) in vivo exposure and (e) cognitive restructuring. At two months posttrauma, the treatment group exhibited significantly less PTSD symptomatology than the control group, and at five-and-a-half months posttrauma the treatment group reported significantly fewer depressive and reexperiencing symptoms. Despite the small number of respondents (N=10), these results seem promising at the least.

Busuttil et al. (1995) reported an evaluation of their program known as Brief Group Psychotherapy (see also Ford et al., 1993). It involved an inpatient treatment which also went by the name of Royal Air Force Wroughton PTSD Rehabilitation Programme. The treatment was comprised of 12 days of group psychotherapy, supplemented if necessary with several follow-up sessions extending over a year's time. Five phases were distinguished: (1) introduction and group integration, (2) detailed reconstruction of the traumatic event, (3) psychoeducation, relaxation training and homework assignments, (4) problem-solving and behavioral exposure (the compulsory viewing of an entire movie on people with PTSD), coupled to homework assignments, and (5) family reintegration and psychoeducation. This program can best be characterized as an information-processing model supplemented by cognitive-behavioral techniques. The evaluation included 43 patients and no control group. Half the patients were war victims and the other half had suffered other types of traumas, such as traffic accidents. Participants had either acute or chronic PTSD—for some, many years had elapsed between the traumatic event and the treatment program. The study noted significantly lower symptom scores at posttest than at pretest.

DISCUSSION

A considerable number of controlled studies of debriefing, some of them randomized, are now available. None of the controlled studies found any confirmation of the purported prophylactic effect of debriefing on stress symptomatology. In view of the consistency of the results, it would be unscientific to ignore them (see also Raphael et al., 1996; Bisson & Jenkins, 1997). These disappointing findings have been obtained for both individual and group debriefing, regardless of the number of debriefing sessions or the debriefers' level of professional training. Nor does a high degree of satisfaction with a debriefing intervention correspond statistically to lower levels of stress symptoms, a swifter resumption of work, or a shorter spell of sick leave in the aftermath of the traumatic experience. For organizations it is therefore important to realize that if employees give high satisfaction ratings to trauma response programs at work, that is mainly an indication that they appreciate this type of employee welfare facility. In itself that is no small achievement. Low-threshold trauma response facilities can also detect any difficulties employees might be having in resolving traumas, to ensure their prompt referral for additional counseling. Hopefully that will keep employees with PTSD from procrastinating for years before seeking professional help.

Adverse effects of debriefing are most likely brought on by the emotional catharsis and/or by the instruction given about stress reactions. It has been argued on a number of occasions (Hobbs et al., 1996; Bisson et al., 1997; Kraus, 1997; Turnbull et al., 1997; Carlier et al., 1998) that acute interventions like debriefing carry an emotional and cognitive overload that interferes with the natural trauma resolution process. In the light of the research findings, two solutions now remain: (1) to adapt the present model of debriefing (for instance by omitting the educational or emotional components) and (2) to apply one of the alternative preventive models for PTSD. In the present state of the art, the Foa model would seem the best alternative choice (Foa et al., 1995). This preventive PTSD program is more tightly structured than the debriefing method currently in use, and it is applied later and exclusively to traumatized subjects who have already developed acute PTSD. These two possible solutions need to be systematically assessed in future research, possibly in some combined form. This could be in the form of a stepped care model. An initial trauma response intervention could be delivered on the basis of a new model (Solution 1), and then, if PTSD develops, that could be followed up by acute treatment with Foa's preventive program (Solution 2) consisting of four weekly sessions (Guscott & Grof, 1991; Cooper et al., 1996; Treasure et al., 1996; Wilfley & Cohen, 1997). The first author of this chapter has recently begun a study in the Netherlands based on such a stepped care model.

REFERENCES

Alexander, D.A.: Stress among police body handlers. A long-term follow-up. *British Journal of Psychiatry, 163:* 806–808, 1993.

Alexander, D.A., and Wells, A.: Reactions of police officers to body-handling after a major disaster. A before and after comparison. *British Journal of Psychiatry, 159:* 547–555, 1991.

Armstrong, K., O'Callahan, W., and Marmar, C.R.: Debriefing Red Cross disaster personnel: The multiple stressor debriefing model. *Journal of Traumatic Stress, 4:* 581–593, 1991.

Benyakar, M., Krutz, I., Dasberg, H., and Stern, M.J.: The collapse of structure: A structural approach to trauma. *Journal of Traumatic Stress, 2:* 431–450, 1989.

Bisson, J.I., and Jenkins, P.L.: Psychological debriefing for victims of acute burn trauma. *British Journal of Psychiatry, 171:* 583, 1997.

Bisson, J.I., Jenkins, P.L., Alexander, J., and Bannister, C.: Randomised controlled trial of psychological debriefing for victims of acute burn trauma. *British Journal of Psychiatry, 171:* 78–81, 1997.

Bordow, S., and Porritt, D.: An experimental evaluation of crisis intervention. *Social Science and Medicine, 13a:* 251–256, 1979.

Brom, D., and Kleber, R.J.: Prevention of posttraumatic stress disorder. *Journal of Traumatic Stress, 2:* 335–351, 1989.

Brom, D., Kleber, R.J., and Hofman, M.C.: Victims of traffic accidents: Incidence and prevention of posttraumatic stress disorder. *Journal of Clinical Psychology, 49:* 191–195, 1993.

Busuttil, A., and Busuttil, W.: Psychological debriefing. *British Journal of Psychiatry, 166:* 676–681, 1995.

Busuttil, W., Turnbull, G.J., Neal, L.A., Rollins, J., West, A.G., Blanch, N., and Herepath, R.: Incorporating psychological debriefing techniques within a brief group psychotherapy program for the treatment of posttraumatic stress disorder. *British Journal of Psychiatry, 167:* 495–502, 1995.

Carlier, I.V.E., and Gersons, B.P.R.: Development of a scale for traumatic stress incidents in police work. *Psychiatrica Fennica (supplementum), 23:* 59–70, 1992.

Carlier, I.V.E., and Gersons, B.P.R.: Trauma at work: Posttraumatic stress disorder: An occupational health hazard. *The Journal of Occupational Health and Safety, Australia and New Zealand, 19:* 254–266, 1994.

Carlier, I.V.E., and Gersons, B.P.R.: Partial PTSD; the issue of psychological scars and the occurrence of PTSD symptoms. *The Journal of Nervous and Mental Disease, 183:* 107–109, 1995.

Carlier, I.V.E., and Gersons, B.P.R.: Stress reactions in disaster victims following the Bijlmermeer plane crash. *Journal of Traumatic Stress, 10:* 329–335, 1997.

Carlier, I.V.E., Fouwels, A.J., Lamberts, R.D., and Gersons, B.P.R.: Posttraumatic stress disorder and dissociation in traumatized police officers. *The American Journal of Psychiatry, 153:* 1325–1328, 1996.

Carlier, I.V.E., Lamberts, R.D., and Gersons, B.P.R.: Risk factors for posttraumatic stress symptomatology in police officers. *The Journal of Nervous and Mental Disease, 185:* 498–506, 1997.

Carlier, I.V.E., Uchelen, J.J. van, Lamberts, R.D., and Gersons, B.P.R.: Disaster-related posttraumatic stress in police officers; a field study of the impact of debriefing. *Stress Medicine, 14:* 143–148, 1998.

Chemtob, C.M., Thomas, S., Law, W., and Cremniter, D.: Postdisaster psychosocial intervention: A field study of the impact of debriefing on psychological distress. *American Journal of Psychiatry, 154:* 415–417, 1997.

Cooper, P.J., Coker, S., and Fleming, C.: An evaluation of the efficacy of supervised cognitive behavioral self-help for bulimia nervosa. *Journal of Psychosomatic Research, 40:* 281–287, 1996.

Cryer, L., and Beutler, L.: Group therapy: An alternative treatment approach for rape victims. *Journal of Sex and Marital Therapy, 6:* 40–46, 1980.

Deahl, M.P., Gilham, A.B., Thomas, J., Searle, M.M., and Srinivasan, M.: Psychological sequelae following the Gulf War. Factors associated with subsequent morbidity and the effectiveness of psychological debriefing. *British Journal of Psychiatry, 165:* 60–65, 1994.

Doctor, R.S., Curtis, D., and Isaacs, G.: Psychiatric morbidity in policemen and the effect of brief psychotherapeutic intervention: A pilot study. *Stress Medicine, 10:* 151–157, 1994.

Dyregrov, A.: The process in psychological debriefings. *Journal of Traumatic Stress, 10:* 589–605, 1997.

D'Zurilla, T., and Goldfried, M.: Problem solving and behavior modification. *Journal of Abnormal Psychology, 78:* 107–126, 1971.

Everly, G.S.: The role of the critical incident stress debriefing (CISD) process in disaster counseling. *Journal of Mental Health Nursing, 17:* 278–290, 1995.

Flannery, R.B., Fulton, P., Tausch, J., and Deloffi, A.Y.: A program to help staff cope with psychological sequelae of assaults by patients. *Hospital and Community Psychiatry, 42:* 935–938, 1991.

Foa, E.B., Rothbaum, E.O., Riggs, D., and Murdock, T.: Treatment of PTSD in rape victims: A comparison between cognitive-behavioral procedures and counseling. *Journal of Consulting and Clinical Psychology, 59:* 715–723, 1991.

Foa, E.B., Hearst-Ikeda, D., and Perry, K.J.: Evaluation of a brief cognitive-behavioral program for the prevention of chronic PTSD in recent assault victims. *Journal of Consulting and Clinical Psychology, 63:* 948–955, 1995.

Ford, J.D., Shaw, D., Sennhauser, S., Greaves, D., Thacker, B., Chandler, B., Schwartz, L., and McClain, V.: Psychosocial debriefing after Operation Desert Storm: Marital and family assessment and intervention. *Journal of Social Issues, 49:* 73–102, 1993.

Ford, J.D., Greaves, D., Chandler, P., Thacker, B., Shaw, D., Sennhauser, S., and Schwartz, L.: Time-limited psychotherapy with Operation Desert Storm veterans. *Journal of Traumatic Stress, 10:* 655–664, 1997.

Frank, E., and Spanier, C.: Interpersonal psychotherapy for depression. *Clinical Psychology, 2:* 349–369, 1995.

Friedman, R., Framer, M., and Shearer, D.: Early response to posttraumatic stress. *EAP Digest,* 45–49, 1988.

Gendlin, E.: Experiential psychotherapy. In R. Corsini (Ed.): *Current Psychotherapies.* Itasca, IL, 1979.

Greenberg, M.S., and Kolk, B.A. van der: Retrieval and integration of traumatic memories with the "painting cure." In B.A. van der Kolk (Ed.), *Psychological Trauma* (pp. 191–216). Washington, DC: American Psychiatric Press, 1987.

Griffith, J., and Watts, R.: *The Kensey and Grafton bus crashes: The aftermath.* East Lismore: Instructional Design Solutions, 1994.

Guscott, R., and Grof, P.: The clinical meaning of refractory depression: A review for the clinician. *American Journal of Psychiatry, 148:* 695–704, 1991.

Hobbs, M., Mayou, R., and Harrison, B.: A randomized controlled trial of psychological debriefing for victims of road traffic accidents. *British Medical Journal, 313:* 1438–1439, 1996.

Horowitz, M.J.: *Stress response syndromes.* New York: Jason Aronson, 1976.

Hytten K., and Hasle, A.: Fire fighters: A study of stress and coping. *Acta Psychiatrica Scandinavica (supplementum), 80:* 50–55, 1989.

Jenkins, S.R.: Social support and debriefing efficiency among emergency medical workers after a mass shooting incident. *Journal of Social Behavior and Personality, 11:* 7–492, 1996.

Johnson, L.B., Cline, D.W., Marcum, J.M., and Intress, J.L.: Effectiveness of a stress recovery unit during the Persian Gulf War. *Hospital and Community Psychiatry, 43:* 829–830, 1992.

Jones, D.R.: Secondary disaster victims. *American Journal of Psychiatry, 142:* 303–307, 1985.

Jones, L.: Response to stress is not necessarily pathological. *British Medical Journal, 311:* 509–510, 1995.

Kenardy, J.A., Webster, R.A., Lewin, T.J., Carr, V.J., Hazell, P.L., and Carter, G.L.: Stress debriefing and patterns of recovery following a natural disaster. *Journal of Traumatic Stress, 9:* 37–50, 1996.

Kilpatrick, D.G., and Veronen, L.J.: Treatment for rape-related problems: Crisis intervention is not enough. In L. Cohen, W. Claiborn and G.A. Specter (Eds.): *Crisis Intervention* (pp. 165–185). New York: Human Sciences Press, 1983.

Kraus, R.P.: Psychological debriefing for victims of acute burn trauma. *British Journal of Psychiatry, 171:* 583, 1997.

Krystal, H.: Trauma and affect. *Psychoanalytical Study of the Child, 33:* 81–116, 1978.

Lazarus, R.S.: The costs and benefits of denial. In S. Bereznits (Ed.), *The denial of stress* (pp. 1–30). Madison, CT: International Universities Press, 1982.

Lazarus, R.S., and Folkman, S.: Cognitive appraisal processes. In R.S. Lazarus and S. Folkman (Eds.): *Stress appraisal and coping* (pp. 22-52). New York: Springer Publishing Company, 1984.

Lee, C., Slade, P., and Lygo, V.: The influence of psychological debriefing on emotional adaptation in women following early miscarriage: A preliminary study. *British Journal of Medical Psychology, 69:* 47–58, 1996.

Marshall, S.L.A.: *Island victory.* New York: Penguin Books, 1944.

Matthews, L.R.: Effect of staff debriefing on posttraumatic stress symptoms after assaults by community housing residents. *Psychiatric Services, 49:* 207–212, 1998.

McCann, L., and Pearlman, L.: *Psychological trauma and the adult survivor.* New York: Brunner/Mazel, 1990.

McFarlane, A.C.: The aetiology of posttraumatic stress disorders following a natural disaster. *British Journal of Psychiatry, 151:* 116–121, 1988.

Meichenbaum, D.: *A clinical handbook/practical therapist manual.* Waterloo, Canada: Institute Press, 1994.

Mitchell, J.T.: When disaster strikes. *Journal of Emergency Medical Services, 8:* 36–39, 1983.

Mitchell, J.T., and Everly, G.S.: *Critical incident stress debriefing: An operations manual for the prevention of trauma among emergency service and disaster workers.* Baltimore, MD: Chevron, 1995.

Pennebaker, J.W., and Susman, J.R.: Disclosure of trauma and psychosomatic processes. *Social Science and Medicine, 26:* 327–332, 1988.

Raphael, B.: *When disaster strikes: A handbook for the caring professions.* London: Unwin Hyman, 1986.

Raphael, B., Meldrum, L., and McFarlane, A.C.: Does debriefing after psychological trauma work? *British Medical Journal, 310:* 1479–1480, 1995.

Raphael, B., Wilson, J., Meldrum, L., and McFarlane, A.C.: Acute preventive interventions. In B.A. van der Kolk, A.C. McFarlane, and L. Weisaeth (Eds.): *Traumatic stress: The effects of overwhelming experience on mind, body and society* (pp. 463–479). New York: Guilford Press, 1996.

Robinson, R.C., and Mitchell, J.T.: Evaluation of psychological debriefings. *Journal of Traumatic Stress, 6:* 367–382, 1993.

Saari, S., Lindeman, M., Verkasalo, M., and Prytz, H.: The Estonia disaster: A description of the crisis intervention in Finland. *European Psychologist, 1:* 135–139, 1996.

Salmon, T.W.: The war neuroses and their lesson. *New York State Journal of Medicine, 51:* 993–994, 1919.

Shalev, A.Y.: Debriefing following traumatic exposure. In R.J. Ursano, B.G. McCaughey, and C.S. Fullerton (Eds.): *Individual and community responses to trauma and disaster: The structure of human chaos* (pp. 201–219). Cambridge: Cambridge University Press, 1994.

Sibbald, B., and Roland, M.: Why are randomized controlled trials important? *British Medical Journal, 316:* 201, 1998.

Sloan, P.: Posttraumatic stress in survivors of an airplane crash-landing: A clinical and exploratory research intervention. *Journal of Traumatic Stress, 1:* 211–229, 1988.

Stallard, P., and Law, F.: Screening and psychological debriefing of adolescent survivors of life-threatening events. *British Journal of Psychiatry, 163:* 660–665, 1993.

Stanton, M., and Figley, C.R.: Treating the Vietnam veteran within the family. In C.R. Figley (Ed.): *Stress disorders among Vietnam veterans* (pp. 281–291). New York: Brunner/Mazel, 1978.

Talbot, A., Menton, M., and Dunn, P.J.: Debriefing the debriefers: An intervention strategy to assist psychologists after a crisis. *Journal of Traumatic Stress, 5:* 45–62, 1992.

Treasure, J., Schmidt, U., Troop, N., Tiller, J., Todd, G., and Turnbull, S.: Sequential treatment for bulimia nervosa incorporating a self-care manual. *British Journal of Psychiatry, 168:* 94–98, 1996.

Turnbull, G., Busuttil, W., and Pitman, S.: Psychological debriefing for victims of acute burn trauma. *British Journal of Psychiatry, 171:* 582, 1997.

Turner, S.W., Thompson, J., and Rosser, R.M.: The King's Cross fire: Early psychological reactions and implications for organizing a "phase-two" response. In J.P. Wilson and B. Raphael (Eds.): *International handbook of traumatic stress syndromes* (pp. 451–459). New York: Plenum Press, 1993.

Velden, P.G. van der Eland, J., and Kleber, R.J.: *Handbook for care after disasters and calamities* (Dutch version only). Utrecht: Instituut voor Psychotrauma, 1997.

Viney, L.L., Clark, A.M., Bunn, T.A., and Benjamin, Y.N.: Crisis intervention counseling: An evaluation of long- and short-term effects. *Journal of Counseling Psychology, 32:* 29–39, 1985.

Watts, R.: The efficacy of critical incident stress debriefing for personnel. *Bulletin of the Australian Psychological Society, 16:* 6–7, 1994.

Wilfley, D.E., and Cohen, L.R.: Psychological treatment of bulimia nervosa and binge eating disorder. *Psychopharmacology Bulletin, 33:* 437–454, 1997.

Wollman, D.A.: Critical incidents stress debriefing and crisis groups: A review of the literature. *Group, 17:* 70–83, 1993.

Chapter 5

THERE ARE NO SIMPLE SOLUTIONS TO COMPLEX PROBLEMS

RICHARD GIST AND S. JOSEPH WOODALL

INTRODUCTION

THE PAST DECADE HAS WITNESSED increasing concern within academic and professional communities alike regarding the trend toward reflexive application of rigid, routinized, quasi-therapeutic protocols employed in any stressful event—often at the expense of exploring the natural support and adaptation processes that facilitate resilience and growth (Gist & Woodall, 1999). The significance of these concerns has risen not only because reliable empirical evidence indicating demonstrable preventive effect is lacking (cf. Bisson & Deahl, 1994; Foa & Meadows, 1997; Gist, 1996a, 1996b; Gist et al., 1997; Gist & Woodall, 1995, 1998; Kenardy & Carr, 1996; Raphael et al., 1995, Stephens, 1997), but also because any observed palliative effect is no greater than that afforded by more traditional venues of discussion and social support (cf. Alexander & Wells, 1991; Hytten & Hasle, 1989; Gist et al., 1998; Stephens, 1997; Thompson & Solomon, 1991). Systematic research suggesting the superiority of the most dominant of these protocols, Critical Incident Stress Debriefing (CISD) Mitchell (1983), has not been forthcoming. Of greater concern are the paradoxical effects, possibly of iatrogenic origin, noted in several independent studies (Bisson et al., 1997; Gist et al., 1998; Hobbs et al., 1996; McFarlane, 1988). Overall, the more rigorous the study, the more objective its measurements, the more independent the researchers, and the more discerning the publication, the more likely has been a neutral to negative assessment (Gist et al., 1997; Gist & Woodall, 1998).

The thrust of contemporary scientific debate now transcends CISD itself, challenging fundamental assumptions long accepted as postulates in the arena of immediate crisis response. Bisson et al. (1997) questioned the principal assumption of immediate intervention, suggesting that it may effectively inhibit the distancing needed in the immediate aftermath of traumatic disruption. Gist, Lubin, and Redburn (1998) have similarly questioned this fundamental tenet, noting that models which provide effective social comparison, facilitate salutogenic social constructions of the problem, and selection of productive solution schemata may prove directly helpful while attempts at emotional catharsis prior to such constructions may, in fact, disrupt these essential elements of adaptive resolution.

Charlton and Thompson (1996) reported that persons exposed to the novelty and intensity of traumatic experiences initially adopt diverse coping strategies, but found that only cognitive reframing and psychological distancing proved beneficial. Both of these coping mechanisms stand specifically contrary to the presumption inherent in debriefing models that early emotional venting and other forms of emotion-based coping are essential to resolution. Gump and Kulik's (1997) demonstration of social contagion in settings characterized by shared traumatic exposure further illustrates how group interventions might just as readily promote paradoxically maladaptive responses as encourage constructive coping.

Taken together, these findings emphasize the need to explore alternative mechanisms for enhancing resiliency in individuals, communities, and organizations. Programs that harbor, whether implicitly or explicitly, goals of promoting interventionist causes that stimulate "overhelping" (Gilbert & Silvera, 1996) may ultimately disempower those they purport most to aid by depriving them, to greater or lesser degrees, of the very essence of resilient resolution—the sense of personal mastery that flows from coping with adversity.

CONTEMPORARY PERSPECTIVES ON FIRE FIGHTER STRESS

Recognition of stress as a significant determinant of fire fighter health and safety no longer meets resistance within the industry. Professional acknowledgement, as well as references to stress and stress management in fire service literature and instruction, testify to this growing acceptance. However, complimentary growth in systematic research and intervention has been lacking (Gist & Woodall, 1999). With respect to intervention, attention remains focused on Mitchell's (1983 et seq.) construction of occupational stress (i.e., "critical incident stress") and a specific model of peer intervention: CISD (Gist & Woodall, 1999).

The foundation of CISD and similar pathogenic models are their assumption that exposure to any traumatic event disrupts the capacity of those involved to function normally (cf. Mitchell, 1983; Mitchell, 1988a; Mitchell & Bray, 1990; Mitchell & Everly, 1993). The premise that these exposures, if not contravened through direct and focused rapid interventions, will lead to posttraumatic stress disorder and related psychiatric maladies (cf. Mitchell, 1992) has become so ubiquitous that this assumption, rather than any critical scientific evaluation of response and intervention effectiveness, has been the platform for advocating its adoption. The ease with which this popular model has been assimilated stands in contrast to attempts to specify and test its component constructs. For example, it fails to accommodate how organizational context (Alexander & Wells, 1991; Gist et al., 1998) and individual circumstances, history and predispositions (Cook & Bickman, 1990; McFarlane, 1988, 1989) have proven more predictive of impact than such features as proximity and exposure alone.

The growing criticism and increasing calls for caution from research and academic arenas have not impeded the use of popular trauma intervention models. Arguments from proponents have shifted from attempts to assert unique and phenomenal efficacy (cf. Mitchell, 1992) to contentions that no component can be tested outside complete adherence to a collection of activities and interventions termed "CISM" (critical incident stress management) (Mitchell and Everly, 1997). Scientific evidence for CISM (Mitchell & Everly, 1997) appears to consist primarily of unpublished presentations, theses, articles from trade magazines, and trade books (Gist & Woodall, 1998).

DEVELOPING CONSTRUCTIONS OF
OCCUPATIONAL STRESS RESILIENCE

Taylor (1983) argued that cognitive adaptation to stressful events might be more effectively characterized from a salutogenic, developmental perspective. Subsequent empirical research (e.g., Taylor & Brown, 1988; Taylor & Lobel, 1989) affirmed and refined these propositions to develop testable constructions of individual and collective adjustment to negative events (Taylor, 1991). These constructions both acknowledged the unique salience and impact of extraordinary threats as stressors, while emphasizing also that adversity can constitute a stimulus for growth and the development of resilience. Such constructions represent more appropriate frameworks for conceptualizing traumatic stress phenomena in fire and rescue services.

Exposure to critical incidents is not only unavoidable in fire and rescue work, it is the essence of the enterprise. For most providers in most situations, these encounters are not sources of threat or loss, but are rather episodes of challenge in which skills and effort central to one's personal and professional role identity are focused on the legitimate demands of the occupation (McCrae, 1984). While the organization remains responsible for ensuring that personnel are adequately prepared, equipped, deployed, and configured for effective response, and for ensuring that the impact of equivocal events is effectively addressed in organizational and operational review (Gist & Taylor, 1996), individual decisions, actions, coping patterns, and responses are also highly salient determinants of adjustment. These interact with organizational determinants in complex and sometimes unpredictable ways that render uniform approaches to remediation suspect, if not overtly dangerous (Moran, 1998). Accordingly, strategies for intervention and assistance must address the unique and interactive contributions of organizational, situational, and individual factors in facilitating individual and group resilience.

In contrast to constructs built on pathogenic assumptions regarding trauma, those built on resiliency facilitate the interpretation of subjective discomfort as signs of disequilibrium attendant to, and essential for, salutogenic processes of adaptation and accommodation (rather than as "symptoms" of disorder and dysfunction) (Gist & Woodall, 1999; Solomon & Canino, 1990). These disparities have contributed to sometimes remarkable differences in estimation of pathology following traumatic exposure (Rubonis & Bickman, 1991), and have fueled substantial differences in the nature, scope, visibility, and intrusiveness of intervention modalities. However, the integration of posited determinants of resiliency into intervention and prevention strategies has been far less extensive or systematic (Gist & Woodall, 1999).

The essential characteristics associated with resilience have included dispositional features, especially certain protective factors demonstrated to offset the negative impacts of life experiences; emotional ties to family and primary social relationships; and both the extent and the quality of external support systems that can serve to buffer the impact of negative life events and reinforce the election and successful execution of positive coping strategies (Basic Behavioral Sciences Advisory Board, 1996; Garmezy, 1991; Matsen, Best, & Garmezy, 1990; Werner, 1994a, 1994b). Effective intervention and assistance must accommodate strategies to enhance resilience, and must integrate these strategies with approaches that supplement and reinforce resilient responses of individuals and organizations; that is, they must occur without supplanting the natural contacts and supports that promote autonomy and resilience with artificial structures that may instead reinforce vulnerability or encourage reliance on inappropriate, ineffective, or ill-timed coping strategies.

A Systematic View of Occupational Stress

Motowidlo et al. (1986) offered an interactive schematic suggesting how several factors might interact to result in perceptions of occupational stress and influence attitudinal and behavioral concomitants to those perceptions. This schematic illustrated how job conditions and certain personal characteristics (e.g., job experience, fear of negative evaluation) influence the experience and interpretation of events in one's working life (Gist & Woodall, 1999). These factors interact with both the frequency and the intensity of stressful events to influence subjective reactions and the affective experience of events and their contexts. It is not some specific and conceptually isolated set of "critical incidents" that can be posited to determine the most salient links in the processes of reaction and resolution; it is the backdrop of "daily hassles" (personal and organizational strain) that ultimately define the relative impact of a given stressor.

This was highlighted in Beaton and Murphy's (1993) study of fire fighter/paramedics and fire fighter EMTs wherein past critical incidents ranked well below job conditions (e.g., sleep disruption, wages and benefits, labor/management issues, personal safety, job skill concerns, and family/financial strains) as elements of perceived job stress. Indeed, past critical incidents failed to significantly enter regression equations predicting job satisfaction and morale for paramedic fire fighters and barely achieved significance for fire fighter/EMTs. Moreover, Wright (1993) reported that, for career paramedics, the principal factors influencing perceptions of stress in a series of hypothetical calls hinged not on the manifest content of the encounter or even on patient outcome, but rather on perceptions of personal and organizational success in the address of component evolutions.

Managing occupational stress interventions in these professions must start with enhancing those organizational and support factors that promote effective response and personal resilience. Similarly, incident-specific interventions should maintain the operation and, if necessary, the regeneration of these same factors through the least intrusive means consistent with individual and organizational circumstances and needs. Moreover, conflicts between individual and organizational interests are inevitable. Separate routes of intervention with clearly specified client relationships will generally be required for the system to operate ethically and effectively.

Client Relationships and the CISD Model

The cornerstone of the critical incident model, the CISD Team (see Mitchell, 1988b; Mitchell & Bray, 1990; or Mitchell & Everly, 1993), typically comprises self-selected personnel who have attended at least two consecutive days of training. Although certification is offered, there are no requirements for examination or other verification of skill or competence. Ethical issues regarding competence thus need to be addressed.

Client relationships, definitions of roles and expectations, and attendant legal and ethical responsibilities are critical components of professional practice. Specific identification of client relationships for

CISD teams and their interventions has proven elusive, particularly in relation to issues of informed consent in contexts where programs are often mandatory (Gist & Woodall, 1999). The urgent need to attend to these ethical concerns is heightened by the potential for paradoxical outcomes and the growing implication of iatrogenesis for certain participants (Gist & Woodall, 1999). The application of any intervention should require appropriate licensure, informed consent, clear definition of client relationships, and full documentation on an individual basis of services rendered and results derived.

Pursuing a More Reasoned Course

Gist & Taylor (1996) outlined a series of organizationally based strategies designed to promote maximum resiliency in individuals exposed to stressful occupational events. That strategy focused on the incorporation of enhanced information and more effective practices into existing organizational relationships affecting management, command, supervision, and human resource support, and on the addition of skills and resources to supplement existing patterns wherever deficits might exist or develop. Moreover, they specifically advocated empowerment in daily activities and responses over remedial interventions.

Woodall (1994) reported on a pilot program designed to incorporate this strategy into an organizationally integrated, theoretically grounded approach to issues identified as affecting both organizational and individual resilience in the workplace (Gist, Taylor, Woodall, & Magenheimer, 1994). This approach concentrated first on identification, development, and consistent reinforcement of workplace dynamics, systems and structures that held demonstrated capacity to develop, enhance and maintain individual resilience factors. The subsequent combination of these with posttrauma exposure strategies designed to minimize intrusion and visibility of the intervention while mobilizing and enhancing the capacity of existing roles and relationships to bolster buffering characteristics during times of uncommon duress constituted the basis of the program.

The pilot presentations were modularized to preserve the possibility of tailoring the program to the social and organizational profile of each individual organization. The relative implications of alternative strategies of presentation and configuration were also explored as components of the evaluation. Component modules, their rationales, and the routes of address adopted are briefly summarized below.

Overview of Occupational Stress, Organizational Strain, and Personal Reactivity

This module utilized case studies, literature review, and operational analyses to introduce the premises and arguments that provided the foundations for psychosocial, ecological, and community treatments of occupational stress and its management.

Building Healthy Baseline Behaviors

This component, which had been routinely presented in fire recruit training and as a recertification class for emergency medical technicians, reviewed implication of the model suggested by Motowidlo et al. (1986) and discussed individually-based elements associated with resiliency at each point in the schematic.

Contributing to and Working Within an Effective Organizational Climate

It is "organizational strain," the daily interactions and issues of the workplace (cf. Beaton & Murphy, 1993), that largely determine the stressor impact of any given event. This presentation discussed elements of leadership from working and operating levels of professional service delivery organizations, with particular emphasis on team building and effective supervision.

Controlling CIS (Critical Incident Stress) through ICS (Incident Command System)

This module, adapted from material routinely used in recruit training and officer development, prepares personnel to work effectively within an Incident Management System built to ensure safe, focused, and effective partitioning of incident components and responsibilities, and to develop a broader understanding of its implications in daily operations of as well as in the delineation of capacity, capability, and accountability factors in effective incident response.

Family, Peer, and Professional Support Systems

This component emphasized the importance of social support to resilience and concentrated on such issues as boundaries and relationships in the often compartmentalized lives of the professional fire service responder. Given a role for these "daily hassles" that defines the stressor impact of major events (Wagner et al., 1988), the management of life strain outside the job was postulated as essential for maintaining the buffering capacity of these support systems. Also addressed were the roles of such human resource support services as employee assistance programs and agency chaplains, and their effective use to assist with the various problems in living that can complicate progress in any professional career—as well as those problems made especially prominent by the unique nature of fire and rescue service.

The second day centered on specific applications and techniques. It comprised four modules defined by level of work team involvement and the formality of the response set contemplated. Routine, consistent consideration and discussion of personal impacts of daily human services delivery were defined as role responsibilities of immediate supervisors (company officers), while broader, more formal, strategies were contemplated at the management level (e.g., battalion chiefs) for events that produced impacts and required participation beyond the basic unit of the system. The more formal responses were reserved for events that transcend the ordinary organizational unit, while other paths for involvement of the informal system to facilitate the instrumental and emotional support of individuals and their families were also presented.

The group process model utilized for the most formal version of postincident intervention was functionally similar to a CISD format, reflecting a relatively direct application of a common group counseling format (Corey, 1995). The placement and conduct of such formal exercises, their centrality to the overall program, and the parameters surrounding utilization and deployment, however, are almost orthogonally distinct.

CISD paradigms portray the group process as a focal intervention (cf. Mitchell, 1993; Mitchell & Everly, 1993). The alternative tested by Woodall afforded a much less critical role to any specific intervention set or technique, being organized instead along a continuum from least formal, structured, and intrusive approaches (given declarative precedence) to the most visible and the most structured. Where the CISD is protocol-bound and driven, with highly mechanized strategies proposed for description and application, the alternative system was designed to promote fluid adaptation of a range of process and provider options to meet the specific needs of the organizational circumstance, favoring always the least formal, least intrusive, and more conservative of available options.

Comparative Tests of the Models

Woodall (1994) compared this organizationally-based model (Gist, Taylor, Woodall, & Magenheimer, 1994) against the CISD (Mitchell, 1983) model of critical incident stress management amongst law enforcement, fire service, EAP, and education professionals directly acquainted with the latter approach. Participants critically reviewed the suitability and impact of each component, and of the components combined as a package. Participants reported the program's objectives as highly salient to workplace goals and showed strong preference for its construction, strategies, and grounding. Moreover, the emergent diversity of organizations, disciplines, and jurisdictions clearly rendered the CISD program unworkable and inappropriate in practice.

The approach finally recommended included selecting modules to fit an overall design specifically tailored to each individual organization and circumstance; it also clearly delineated the need to construe organizational intervention as a specific set of procedures developed for uniquely designated organizational clients, and to distinguish these from individual-level interventions where the client relationship must be unique to the employee and based on thorough individual assessments (Moran, 1998).

Back to Basics

These findings stimulated a fundamental reconsideration of the most basic assumptions and foundations regarding adjustment of these professionals to the experiences of their careers, particularly those that had stood as axiomatic assumptions in the social evolution of pathogenic movements:

- What emotions are commonly experienced by fire fighters in emergency situations, both critical and routine?
- What emergency situations or circumstances commonly elicit the strongest emotional reactions?
- How are those emotions managed, both in the immediate situation and in the processes of personal and occupational resolution?
- How might their personal and colloquial descriptions of coping strategies be digested to provide a preliminary set of constructs and hypotheses from which to develop a more grounded picture of occupational adjustment in the contemporary enterprise?

Although common challenges and shared loss united fire and rescue personnel at a professional level, a striking finding was the diversity of personality and views in the contemporary profession. This critically important factor had been seriously misinterpreted and hence misrepresented in the foundational arguments of pathogenic approaches. Mitchell has stated (see interview by Hopper, 1988, p. 7, as an example) that emergency services personnel could be distinguished by characteristic personality traits that rendered them uniquely similar, and that these had been demonstrated through definitive empirical research, to wit: "Our recent study using the Milan (sic) Personality Inventory clearly shows that the police officer/fire fighter/paramedic personality is significantly, statistically different from the average population" (quoted by Hopper, 1988, p. 7).

Despite lack of empirical support, this contention has been made repeatedly (Gist & Woodall, 1998) and remains central to CISD training (International Critical Incident Stress Foundation, 1998); it has been argued that uniform and routinized strategies for intervention are not only apt for this population, but are mandated by their homogeneity of personality and coping. The findings of Woodall (1996, 1997), especially when combined with the reports of Gist, Lubin, and Redburn (1998) and Fullerton et al. (1993) regarding the dominant role of support systems outside the occupational context, suggest that effective organizational support strategies must reflect this diversity of values, affiliations, and coping styles. Diversity must be accommodated to ensure that coping strategies provide both the distance needed to gain or maintain some level of objectivity in the performance of one's social roles, and the perspective needed to assimilate difficult and disconcerting life events with some level of meaning and equanimity are encouraged. Distancing, boundaries, and reframing are critical to the processes of integration and resolution; these essential components are too often directly (and probably paradoxically) countered by the most basic premises of the debriefing rubric (Gist & Woodall, 1999).

The matters that emerge as most significant to fire fighter resilience are, essentially, functions of characteristics that can't be taught, can't be trained, and cannot be created after the fact by a highly prescribed, standardized ritual or routine. These features of resilience include such intangibles as optimism and determination, commonwealth and commitment. We'll always do better, we suspect, to point quietly and persistently toward their realization than to wave and shout about obstacles, real or imagined, that may sometimes block the path.

REFERENCES

Alexander, D.A., and Wells, A.: Reactions of police officers to body handling after a major disaster: A before and after comparison. *British Journal of Psychiatry, 159:* 547–555, 1991.

Basic Behavioral Science Task Force: Basic behavioral science research for mental health: Vulnerability and resistance. *American Psychologist, 51:* 22–28, 1996.

Beaton, R.D., and Murphy, S.A.: Sources of occupational stress among fire fighter/EMTs and fire fighter/paramedics and correlations with job-related outcomes. *Prehospital and Disaster Medicine, 8:* 140–150, 1993.

Bisson, J.I., and Deahl, M.P.: Psychological debriefing and prevention of posttraumatic stress: More research is needed. *British Journal of Psychiatry, 165:* 717–720, 1994.

Bisson, I.J., Jenkins, P.L., Alexander, J., and Bannister, C.: A randomized controlled trial of psychological debriefing for victims of acute harm. *British Journal of Psychiatry, 171:* 78–81, 1997.

Charlton, P.F.C., and Thompson, J.A.: Ways of coping with psychological distress after trauma. *British Journal of Clinical Psychology, 35:* 517–530, 1996.

Cook, J.D., and Bickman, L.: Social support and psychological symptomatology following a natural disaster. *Journal of Traumatic Stress, 3:* 541–556, 1990.

Corey, G.: *Theory and Practice of Group Counseling* (4th ed.). Pacific Grove, CA: Brooks/Cole, 1995.

Foa, E.B., and Meadows, E.A.: Psychosocial treatments for posttraumatic stress disorder: A critical review. *Annual Review of Psychology, 48:* 935–938, 1997.

Fullerton, C.S., Wright, K.M., Ursano, R.J., and McCarroll, J.E.: Social support for disaster workers after a mass-casualty disaster: Effects on the support provider. *Nordic Journal of Psychiatry, 47:* 315–324, 1993.

Garmezy, N.: Resilience and vulnerability to adverse developmental outcomes associated with poverty. *American Behavioral Scientist, 34:* 416–430, 1991.

Gilbert, D.T., and Silvera, D.H.: Overhelping. *Journal of Personality and Social Psychology, 70:* 678–690, 1996.

Gist, R.: Is CISD built on a foundation of sand? *Fire Chief, 40:* 38–42, 1996a.

Gist, R.: Dr. Gist responds (Letter to the editor). *Fire Chief, 40:* 19–24, 1996b.

Gist, R., Lohr, J.M., Kenardy, J.A., Bergmann, L., Meldrum, L., Redburn, B.G., Paton, D., Bisson, J.I., Woodall, S.J., and Rosen, G.M.: Researchers speak on CISM. *Journal of Emergency Medical Services, 22:* 27–28, 1997.

Gist, R., Lubin, B., and Redburn, B.G.: Psychosocial, ecological, and community perspectives on disaster response. *Journal of Personal and Interpersonal Loss, 3:* 25–51, 1998.

Gist, R., and Taylor, V.H.: Line of duty deaths and their effects on co-workers and their families. *Police Chief, 63:* 34–37, 1996.

Gist, R., Taylor, V.H., Woodall, S.J., and Magenheimer, L.K.: *Personal, organizational, and agency development: The psychological perspective.* Phoenix, AZ: St. Luke's Behavioral Health System/Phoenix Fire Department, 1994.

Gist, R., and Woodall, S.J.: Occupational stress in contemporary fire service. *Occupational Medicine: State of the Art Reviews, 10:* 763–787, 1995.

Gist, R., and Woodall, S.J.: Social science versus social movements: The origins and natural history of debriefing. *Australasian Journal of Disaster and Trauma Studies, 1998–1.* Online serial at www.massey.ac.nz/~trauma, 1998.

Gist, R., and Woodall, S.J.: There are no simple solutions to complex problems: The rise and fall of critical incident stress debriefing as a response to occupational stress in the fire service. In R. Gist and B. Lubin (Eds.): *Response to Disaster: Psychosocial, community and ecological approaches.* Philadelphia: Taylor & Francis, 1999.

Gump, B.B., and Kulik, J.A.: Stress, affiliation, and emotional contagion. *Journal of Personality and Social Psychology, 72:* 305–319, 1997.

Hobbs, M., Mayou, R., Harrison, B., and Worlock, P.: A randomised controlled trial of psychological debriefing for victims of road traffic accidents. *British Medical Journal, 313:* 1438–1439, 1996.

Hopper, L.: Stress recovery: An interview with Jeffrey Mitchell, Ph.D. *PM (Public Management),* 5–8, 1988.

Hytten, K., and Hasle, A.: Firefighters: A study of stress and coping. *Acta Psychiatrica Scandinavia, 355(supp.):* 50–55, 1989.

International Critical Incident Stress Foundation: *Course brochure and outline.* (Mass mailing), 1998.

Kenardy, J.A., and Carr, V.: Imbalance in the debriefing debate: What we don't know far outweighs what we do. *Bulletin of the Australian Psychological Society, 18:* 4–6, 1996.

Matsen, A.S., Best, K.M., and Garmezy, N.: Resilience and development: Contributions from the study of children who overcome adversity. *Development and Psychopathology, 2:* 425–444, 1991.

McCrae, R.R.: Situational determinants of coping responses: Loss, threat, and challenge, *Journal of Personality and Social Psychology, 46:* 919–928, 1984.

McFarlane, A.C.: The longitudinal course of posttraumatic morbidity: The range of outcomes and their predictors. *Journal of Nervous and Mental Disease, 176:* 30–39, 1988.

McFarlane, A.C.: The aetiology of posttraumatic morbidity: Predisposing, precipitating, and perpetuating factors. *British Journal of Psychiatry, 154:* 221–228, 1989.

Mitchell, J.T.: When disaster strikes: The critical incident stress debriefing process. *Journal of Emergency Medical Services, 8:* 36–39, 1983.

Mitchell, J.T.: The history, status, and future of critical incident stress debriefing. *Journal of Emergency Medical Services, 13:* 49–52, 1988a.

Mitchell, J.T.: Development and functions of a critical incident stress debriefing team. *Journal of Emergency Medical Services, 13:* 42–46, 1988b.

Mitchell, J.T.: Protecting your people from critical incident stress. *Fire Chief, 36:* 61–67, 1992.

Mitchell, J.T.: Personal correspondence, 1993.

Mitchell, J.T., and Bray, G.: *Emergency Services Stress.* Englewood Cliffs, NJ: Brady, 1990.

Mitchell, J.T., and Everly, G.S.: *Critical incident stress debriefing: An operations manual for the prevention of traumatic stress among emergency services and disaster workers.* Ellicott City, MD: Chevron Publishing, 1993.

Mitchell, J.T., and Everly, G.S., Jr.: The scientific evidence for critical incident stress management. *Journal of Emergency Medical Services, 22:* 86–93, 1997.

Moran, C.C.: Individual differences and debriefing effectiveness. *Australasian Journal of Disaster and Trauma Studies, 1998–1:* Online serial: www.massey.ac.nz/~trauma., 1998.

Motowidlo, S.J., Packard, J.S., and Manning, M.R.: Occupational stress: Its causes and consequences for job performance. *Journal of Applied Psychology, 71:* 618–629, 1986.

Raphael, B., Meldrum, L., and McFarlane, A.C.: Does debriefing after psychological trauma work? Time for randomised controlled trials. *British Journal of Psychiatry, 310:* 1479–1480, 1995.

Rubonis, A.V., and Bickman, L.: Psychological impairment in the wake of disaster: The disaster-psychopathology relationship. *Psychological Bulletin, 109:* 384–399, 1991.

Solomon, S.D., and Canino, G.J.: Appropriateness of the DSM-III-R criteria for post-traumatic stress disorder. *Comprehensive Psychiatry, 31:* 227–237, 1990.

Stephens, C.: Debriefing, social support, and PTSD in the New Zealand police: Testing a multidimensional model of organizational traumatic stress. *Australasian Journal of Disaster and Trauma Studies, 1.* Online serial: http://massey.ac.nz/~trauma/issues/1997-1/cvs.htm., 1997.

Taylor, S.E.: Adjusting to threatening events: A theory of cognitive adaptation. *American Psychologist, 38:* 1161–1173, 1983.

Taylor, S.E.: Asymmetrical effects of positive and negative events: The mobilization-minimization hypothesis. *Psychological Bulletin, 110:* 67–85, 1991.

Taylor, S.E., and Brown, J.D.: Illusion and well-being: A social psychological perspective on mental health. *Psychological Bulletin, 103:* 193–211, 1998.

Taylor, S.E., and Lobel, M.: Social comparison activity under threat: Downward evaluation and upward contacts. *Psychological Review, 96:* 569–575, 1989.

Thompson, J., and Solomon, M.: Body recovery teams at disasters: Trauma or challenge. *Anxiety Research, 4:* 235–244, 1991.

Wagner, B.M., Compas, B.E., and Howell, D.C.: Daily and major life events: A test of an integrative model of psychosocial stress. *American Journal of Community Psychology, 16:* 189–205, 1988.

Werner, E.E.: Overcoming the odds. *Journal of Developmental and Behavioral Pediatrics, 15:* 131–136, 1994a.

Werner, E.E.: Risk, resilience, and recovery: Perspectives from the Kauai Longitudinal Study. *Development and Psychopathology, 5:* 503–515, 1994b.

Woodall, S.J.: *Personal, organizational, and agency development: The psychological dimension. A closer examination of critical incident stress management.* National Fire Academy Executive Fire Officer program, available through Learning Resource Center, National Emergency Training Center, Emmitsburg, MD [(800) 638-1821], 1994.

Woodall, S.J.: *Hearts on fire: Ethnographic exploration of the emotional world of firefighters.* National Fire Academy Executive Fire Officer program, available through Learning Resource Center, National Emergency Training Center, Emmitsburg, MD [(800) 638-1821], 1996.

Woodall, S.J.: Hearts on fire: An exploration of the emotional world of fire fighters. *Clinical Sociology Review, 15:* 153–162, 1997.

Wright, R.M.: *Any fool can face a crisis: A look at the daily issues that make an incident critical.* In R. Gist (Moderator), New information, new approaches, new ideas. Center for Continuing Professional Education, Johnson County Community College, Overland Park, KS, 1993.

Chapter 6

THE EFFECTS OF TRAUMATIC DISCLOSURE ON PHYSICAL AND MENTAL HEALTH: THE VALUES OF WRITING AND TALKING ABOUT UPSETTING EVENTS

JAMES W. PENNEBAKER

INTRODUCTION

DIRECTLY AND INDIRECTLY, sudden life transitions can profoundly influence people's social, family, physical, and psychological lives. One traditional goal within psychology has been to understand and develop ways by which to reduce the adverse impact of individual and collective traumas. Four major issues surrounding coping with emotional upheavals are discussed in the current paper. The first concerns the natural sequence of coping that occurs in most disasters. The second focuses on the advantages of talking about upsetting experiences and, conversely, the dangers of not talking about emotional upheavals. The third section, which has been central to our lab's approach, deals with evidence that writing about upsetting experiences is beneficial to health and well-being. The final part of the paper discusses these findings within the context of Critical Incident Stress Management (CISM) debriefing strategies.

THE NATURAL SEQUENCE OF COPING WITH
SHARED TRAUMAS

Although a traumatic event may unfold quickly—as in the case of an earthquake or the sudden death of a friend—its impact may persist for days, months, or years. Similarly, coping strategies that may be quite effective in the hours or days after the event, such as denial or distancing, may be maladaptive in the long run.

Surprisingly, few researchers have focused on the ways that people change in their coping with an event over time. Kubler-Ross (1966) was one of the first clinicians to suggest that people progressed through distinct coping stages on learning of their impending death. Her model included five stages, sequenced as denial, anger, bargaining, depression, and acceptance. Closer scrutiny by researchers, however, revealed that Kubler-Ross' five-stage model was not a valid formulation since most individuals did not experience all of the stages, did not necessarily progress through the stages in the same order, and often would bounce back and forth between stages (cf., Pennebaker & Harber, 1993 for review).

Since the introduction of Kubler-Ross' model, more sophisticated quasi-stage approaches have been put forward. Drawing on his psychoanalytic training, Horowitz (e.g., 1976) has provided evidence to suggest that people typically progress through three phases in dealing with a personal trauma: intrusive thoughts and denial, working through, and assimilation. The goal of therapy, in Horowitz's view, is to facilitate the working through of the trauma. The process of working through can include talking about or acting out parts of the trauma so that the experience can be cognitively assimilated.

Despite the intuitive appeal of stage models, the empirical evidence to support them is scanty. In summarizing the results of several large-scale studies, Wortman and Silver (1989) concluded that only about 50 percent of people who have faced a massive trauma evidence high levels of psychological distress in the weeks following the trauma. Of these, over half return to normal functioning within a year. At best, according to Wortman and Silver, only 30 percent of people evidence possible signs of progressing through clear-cut stages in coping.

Virtually all theories and research dealing with the stages of traumatic experience have been intrapsychic; they have focused more on what people said about what they were thinking and feeling than what was happening in their social lives. Further, most traditional approaches have relied more on self-reports than objective indicators of distress. In recent years, our strategy has been to explore the *social* stages of traumas rather than just the intrapsychic stages. Further, we have been interested in tracking people's modal responses to upheavals over time.

When a large-scale event affects an entire region or society, a common response is for people to openly talk about it. In two related studies on a natural disaster (the San Francisco Bay Area, or Loma Prieta, earthquake of 1989) and responses to the Persian Gulf War, the degree of self-reported talking and thinking about these events was startling (Pennebaker & Harber, 1993). In both of these studies, weekly or semi-weekly samples of residents of San Francisco (for the earthquake project) and of Dallas, Texas (for the war project) were interviewed using random-digit dialing sampling methods immediately after the war or quake through at least 3 months later. Among the questions that both groups of samples were asked was "How many times in the last 24 hours have you talked with someone about the quake (or war)." Similar questions asked the number on times subjects thought and heard about the quake or war.

Across the 789 people surveyed in the earthquake and 361 in the Persian Gulf War study, we discovered three distinct social stages following the respective upheavals. During the *emergency phase,* the degree of social sharing and ruminating about these events was remarkably high during the first 2–3 weeks following the quake and the onset of the war. Not only were people discussing these events to a high degree, but they were bombarded with features of the events via the media. People would spontaneously note how the upheaval had "brought us together"–both their neighborhoods and the country in general. The number of times people talked per day about the upheavals (8–12 times, depending on the event) and the number of people with whom they talked was striking. Interestingly, in both of these studies, various indicators of distress hint that people are actually coping quite well during this period. Illness rates, crime rates, reports of anger or aggressive behavior, and even dreams about the disasters are quite low. People appear to cope remarkably well in the face of a trauma.

About two to three weeks after the event, however, a striking social shift occurs. Almost overnight, people report that they are continuing to think about the upheaval at high rates but that they drastically reduce the rates they talk to others. This *inhibition phase,* which lasts 4–8 weeks, is characterized by an active avoidance of the topic. Indeed, this is precisely when the mental health workers and news media leave. Although people no longer talk about the event, there are increasing signs that the communities are stressed. Rates of illness, nightmares, fights, and aggravated assaults all peak during this phase.

Why don't people talk during the inhibition phase? There appears to be a number of forces driving this social phenomenon. One is that there is an emerging value among residents to "get on with life." In our surveys among people in the Loma Prieta earthquake, we discovered that whereas people reported that they wanted to talk about and hear about other people's experiences in the first 3 weeks after the quake, they changed at the three-week point by saying that they would still like to tell others about their experiences but were not interested in hearing others' stories. It was during this time that t-shirts began appearing in the San Francisco Bay area that pronounced, "Thank you for not sharing your earthquake experience."

The inhibition phase in the two studies we have conducted passed about 8–12 weeks after the onset of the quake and war and gave way to the *adaptation phase*–a period where people were neither talking or thinking about the events. It is during this time that people begin to return to normal. When the adaptation phase begins probably varies with the nature of the trauma and on who is being interviewed.

In recent years, we have examined this idea on the internet. Here there are opportunities for people to talk about a variety of topics. After local, national, or international upheavals, web sites immediately appear allowing people to talk about the events. Soon after the Oklahoma bombing, we monitored how frequently people wrote entries on the web and AOL and also collected samples of how they talked. In line with social stage models, during the first 2–3 weeks after the bombing, the rates of postings were very high. At 3-weeks, there was a dramatic drop in postings. By 2 months after the bombing, the rates of postings dropped to very low levels.

The ways people talked changed as well. Using a text analytic strategy (see Pennebaker & Francis, 1996), we discovered that the ways people used language shifted from generally positive tones to much darker, angrier tones at the 3-week point. Particularly striking was the use of first person plural (e.g., we, us, our) and first person singular (I, me, my). Overall, rates of first person plural were remarkably high during the first three weeks and then dropped off. First person singular, although always higher than plural, increased significantly at week 3. It was as though there was a change in the collective identity of people.

Clearly, the social dynamics of a trauma change drastically over time. Many of the natural healing ingredients—social support, open disclosure, a sense of community—are apparent soon after the disaster. Mental health intervention may be particularly valuable during the inhibition period—perhaps even more so than during the emergency phase.

HEALTH RISKS OF NOT TALKING ABOUT UPHEAVALS

As suggested by the inhibition phase of collective traumatic experiences, not talking about upsetting experiences appears to be a health risk. Indeed, our research program on disclosure began by noting that people who had faced early traumatic experiences and who had not talked about them were much more likely to have a variety of health problems compared to people who had had comparable traumas but who had shared them with others (e.g., Pennebaker & Susman, 1988). Similarly, individuals whose spouses had died suddenly were far more likely to have health problems a year after the death if they didn't talk to others (or even pray) about the death (Pennebaker & O'Heeron, 1984).

Holding back or inhibiting oneself about an important emotional topic is a stressor. The work of inhibition can be seen biologically in both the short run, as measured by increases in autonomic activity, as well as over time, as measured by health changes (see Pennebaker, 1989, 1997b). Findings to support this inhibition model of psychosomatics are growing. Individuals who conceal their gay status (Cole et al., 1996), traumatic experiences in their past (Pennebaker, 1993), or who are considered inhibited or shy by others (e.g., Kagan, Reznick, & Snidman, 1988) exhibit more health problems than those less inhibited. Inhibition, then, appears to contribute to long-term health problems. The task of researchers is to now demonstrate that if we can get people to talk about upsetting experiences, the adverse effects of inhibition can be counteracted.

Parameters of Writing and Talking Associated with Health Improvements

Over the last decade, several laboratories have been exploring the value of writing or talking about emotional experiences. Confronting deeply personal issues has been found to promote physical health, subjective well-being, and selected adaptive behaviors. In this section, the general findings and limitations of the disclosure paradigm are discussed. Whereas a few studies have asked individuals to disclose personal experiences through talking, most involve writing.

The Basic Writing Paradigm

The standard laboratory writing technique has involved randomly assigning participants to one of two or more groups. All writing groups are asked to write about assigned topics for 3–5 consecutive days, 15–30 minutes each day. Writing is generally done in the laboratory with no feedback given. Those assigned to the control conditions are typically asked to write about superficial topics, such as how they use their time. The standard instructions for those assigned to the experimental group are a variation on the following:

> For the next (three) days, I would like for you to write about your very deepest thoughts and feeling about an extremely important emotional issue that has affected you and your life. In your writing, I'd like you to really let go and explore your very deepest emotions and thoughts. You might tie your topic to your relationships with others, including parents, lovers, friends, or relatives, to your past, your present, or your future, or to who you have been, who you would like to be, or who you are now. You may write about the same general issues or experiences on all days of writing or on different topics each day. All of your writing will be completely confidential. Don't worry about spelling,

sentence structure, or grammar. The only rule is that once you begin writing, continue to do so until your time is up.

The writing paradigm is exceptionally powerful. Participants—from children to the elderly, from honor students to maximum security prisoners—disclose a remarkable range and depth of traumatic experiences. Lost loves, deaths, sexual and physical abuse incidents, and tragic failures are common themes in all of our studies. If nothing else, the paradigm demonstrates that when individuals are given the opportunity to disclose deeply personal aspects of their lives, they readily do so. Even though a large number of participants report crying or being deeply upset by the experience, the overwhelming majority report that the writing experience was valuable and meaningful in their lives.

Effects of Disclosure on Outcome Measures

Researchers have relied on a variety of physical and mental health measures to evaluate the effect of writing. As depicted in Table 6.1, writing or talking about emotional experiences relative to writing about superficial control topics has been found to be associated with significant drops in physician visits from before to after writing among relatively healthy samples. Writing and/or talking about emotional topics has also been found to influence immune function in beneficial ways, including t-helper cell growth (using a blastogenesis procedure with the mitogen PHA), antibody response to Epstein-Barr virus, and antibody response to hepatitis B vaccinations.

Self reports also suggest that writing about upsetting experiences, although painful in the days of writing, produce long-term improvements in mood and indicators of well-being compared to controls. Although a number of studies have failed to find consistent mood or self-reported distress effects, a recent meta-analysis by Smyth (1998) on written disclosure studies indicates that, in general, writing about emotional topics is associated with significant reductions in distress.

Behavioral changes have also been found. Students who write about emotional topics evidence improvements in grades in the months following the study. Senior professionals who have been laid off from their jobs get new jobs more quickly after writing. Consistent with the direct health measures, university staff members who write

Table 6.1
EFFECTS OF DISCLOSURE ON VARIOUS OUTCOME PARAMETERS

Physician Visits in the Months Surrounding Writing

± 2 months:	Cameron & Nicholls (1996)
	Greenberg & Stone (1992)
	Greenberg, Stone, &
	Wortman (1996)
	Krantz & Pennebaker (1996)
	Pennebaker & Francis (1996)
	Pennebaker, Kiecolt-Glaser, &
	Glaser (1988)
	Richards, Pennebaker, &
	Beal (1996)
± 6 months:	Francis & Pennebaker (1992)
	Pennebaker & Beall (1986)
	Pennebaker, Colder, &
	Sharp (1990)
± 1.4 years:	Pennebaker, Barger, &
	Tiebout (1989)

Physiological Markers

LONG-TERM IMMUNE AND OTHER SERUM MEASURES

Blastogenesis (t-helper cell response to PHA):	Pennebaker et al. (1988)
Epstein-Barr virus antibody titers:	Esterling et al. (1994)
	Lutgendorf et al. (1994)
Hepatitis B antibody levels:	Petrie et al. (1995)
NK cell activity:	Christensen et al. (1996)
CD-4 (t-lymphocyte) levels:	Booth, Petrie, & Pennebaker (1996)
Liver enzyme levels (SGOT):	Francis et al. (1992)

IMMEDIATE CHANGES IN AUTONOMIC AND MUSCULAR ACTIVITY

Skin conductance and/or heart rate:	Dominguez et al. (1995); Hughes,
	Uhlmann, & Pennebaker (1994)
	Pennebaker, Hughes, &
	O'Heeron (1987)
	Petrie et al. (1995)
Corrugator activity:	Pennebaker et al. (1987)
	Yogo et al. (1996)

Behavioral Markers

Grade point average:	Cameron et al. (1996)
	Krantz et al. (1996)
	Pennebaker et al. (1990);
	Pennebaker & Francis (1996)
Reemployment following job loss:	Spera, Buhrfeind, &
	Pennebàker (1994)
Absenteeism from work:	Francis et al. (1992)

Self-Reports

Physical symptoms:	Greenberg & Stone (1992)
	Pennebaker & Beall (1986);
	Richards et al. (1996)
Failure to find effects:	Pennebaker et al. (1990)
	Pennebaker et al. (1988)
	Petrie et al. (1995)
Distress, Negative Effect, or Depression:	Greenberg et al. (1992)
	Greenberg et al. (1996)
	Murray & Segal (1994)
	Rimé (1995)
	Spera et al. (1994)
	Schoutrop et al. (1996).
Failure to find effects:	Pennebaker & Beall (1986)
	Pennebaker et al. (1988)
	Pennebaker & Francis (1996)
	Petrie et al. (1995)

Note: Only studies published or submitted for publication are included. Several studies find effects that are qualified by a second variable (e.g., stressfulness of topic). See also Smyth (1996) for detailed account.

about emotional topics are subsequently absent from their work at lower rates than controls. Interestingly, relatively few reliable changes emerge using self-reports of health-related behaviors. That is, after writing, experimental participants do not exercise more or smoke less. The one exception is that the study with laid-off professionals found that writing reduced self-reported alcohol intake.

Procedural Differences That Affect the Disclosure Effects

Writing about emotional experiences clearly influences measures of physical and mental health. In recent years, several investigators have attempted to define the boundary conditions of the disclosure effect. Some of the most important findings are as follows:

1. Writing versus talking about traumas. Most studies comparing writing alone versus talking either into a tape recorder (Esterling et al., 1994) or to a therapist (Murray, Lamnin & Carver, 1989; Donnelly & Murray, 1991) find comparable biological, mood, and cognitive effects. Talking and writing about emotional experiences are both superior to writing about superficial topics.

2. *Topic of disclosure.* Whereas two studies have found that health effects only occur among individuals who write about particularly traumatic experiences (Greenberg & Stone, 1992; Lutgendorf et al., 1994), most studies have found that disclosure is more broadly beneficial. Choice of topic, however, may selectively influence the outcome. For beginning college students, for example, writing about emotional issues about coming to college influences grades more than writing about traumatic experiences (Pennebaker & Beall, 1986; Pennebaker, Colder, & Sharp, 1990). It is also of interest that a recent large-scale study by Stroebe and Stroebe (1996) on recently bereaved older adults failed to find benefits of writing—suggesting that some types of upheavals may benefit from writing more than others.

3. *Length or days of writing.* Different experiments have variously asked participants to write for 1 to 5 days, ranging from consecutive days to sessions separated by a week, ranging from 15 to 30 minutes for each writing session. In Smyth's meta-analysis, he found a promising trend suggesting that the more days over which the experiment lapses, the stronger the effects. Although this was a weak effect, it suggests that writing once each week over a month may be more effective than writing four times within a single week. Self-reports of the value of writing do not distinguish shorter writing from longer writing sessions.

4. *Actual or implied social factors.* Unlike psychotherapy, the writing paradigm does not employ feedback to the participant. Rather, after individuals write about their own experiences, they are asked to place their essays into an anonymous-looking box with the promise that their writing will not be linked to their name. In one study comparing the effects of having students either write on paper that would be handed in to the experimenter versus write on a "magic pad" (wherein the writing disappears when the person lifts the plastic writing cover), no autonomic or self-report differences were found (Czajka, 1987).

5. *Individual differences.* No consistent personality or individual difference measures have distinguished who does versus does not benefit from writing. Most commonly-examined variables unrelated to outcomes include age, anxiety (or Negative Affectivity), and inhibition or constraint. Interestingly, Smyth's meta-analysis suggests that males may benefit more from writing than females—presumably because females tend to naturally disclose problems more than the more inhibited males. The one study that preselected participants on hostility found that those high in hostility benefited more from writing than those low in hostility (Christensen & Smith, 1993).

6. *Educational, linguistic, or cultural effects.* Within the United States, the disclosure paradigm has benefited senior professionals with advanced degrees at rates comparable to maximum security prisoners with 6th grade education (Spera et al., 1994; Richards et al., 1996). Among college students, we have not found differences as a function of the students' ethnicity or native language. The disclosure paradigm has produced consistently positive results among French-speaking Belgians (Rimé, 1995), Spanish-speaking residents of Mexico City (Dominguez et al., 1995), multiple samples of adults and students in The Nether-lands (Schoutrop, Lange, Brosschot, & Everaerd, 1996), and even Eng-lish-speaking New Zealand medical students (Petrie et al., 1995).

When individuals write or talk about personally upsetting experi-ences in the laboratory, consistent and significant health improvements are found. The effects include both subjective and objective markers of health and well-being. The disclosure phenomenon appears to gener-alize across settings, most individual differences, many western cul-tures, and is independent of social feedback.

WHY DOES WRITING WORK?

Most of the research on disclosure has been devoted to demon-strating its effectiveness rather than on identifying the underlying mechanisms. Two very broad models that have attempted to explain the value of disclosure are those that invoke inhibitory processes and cognitive processes.

1. *Inhibition and disclosure.* The original theory that motivated the first studies on writing was based on the assumption that not talking about important psychological phenomena was a form of inhibition. Drawing on the animal and psychophysiological literatures, it was posited that active inhibition was a form of physiological work. This inhibitory work, which is reflected in autonomic and central nervous system activity, could be viewed as a long-term low-level stressor (cf., Selye, 1976). Such stress, then, could cause or exacerbate psychoso-matic processes thereby increasing the risk of illness and other stress-related disturbances. Just as constraining thoughts, feelings, or behaviors linked to an emotional upheaval was stressful, letting go and talking about these experiences should, in theory, reduce the stress of inhibition (for a full discussion of this theory, see Pennebaker, 1989).

2. Cognitive changes associated with writing. In the last decade, several studies have persuasively demonstrated that writing about a trauma does more than allow for the reduction of inhibitory processes. For example, a recent study randomly assigned students to either express a traumatic experience using bodily movement, to express an experience using movement and then write about it, or to exercise in a prescribed manner for 3 days, 10 minutes per day (Krantz & Pennebaker, 1996). Whereas the two movement expression groups reported that they felt happier and mentally healthier in the months after the study, only the movement plus write group evidenced significant improvements in physical health and grade point average. The mere expression of a trauma is not sufficient. Health gains appear to require translating experiences into language.

In recent years, we have begun analyzing the language that individuals use in writing about emotional topics. Our first strategy was to have independent raters evaluate the essays' overall contents to see if it was possible to predict who would benefit most from writing. Interestingly, judges noted that essays of people who benefit from writing appeared to be "smarter," "more thoughtful," and "more emotional" (Pennebaker, 1997a). However, the relatively poor interjudge reliability led us to develop a computerized text analysis system.

In 1991, we created a computer program called LIWC (Linguistic Inquiry and Word Count) that analyzed essays in text format. LIWC had been developed by having groups of judges evaluate the degree to which about 2,000 words or word stems were related to each of several dozen categories (for a full description, see Pennebaker & Francis, 1996; Pennebaker, Mayne, & Francis, 1997). The categories included negative emotion words (sad, angry), positive emotion words (happy, laugh), causal words (because, reason), and insight words (understand, realize). For each essay that a person wrote, we were able to quickly compute the percentage of total words that these and other linguistic categories represented.

Analyzing the experimental subjects' data from 6 writing studies, three linguistic factors reliably predict improved physical health. First, the more that individuals use positive emotion words, the better their subsequent health. Second, a moderate number of negative emotion words predicts health. Both very high and very low levels of negative emotion word use correlate with poorer health. Third, and most important, an increase in both causal and insight words over the course of writing is strongly associated with improved health (Pennebaker, Mayne, & Francis, 1997). Indeed, this increase in cognitive words covary with judges' evaluations of the construction of a story or narrative. That is, people who benefit from writing begin with a poorly organized description and progress to a coherent story by the last day of writing.

The language analyses are particularly promising in that they suggest that certain features of essays predict long-term physical health. Further, these features are congruent with current views on narratives in psychology. The next issue that is currently being addressed is the degree to which cohesive stories or narratives predict changes in real world cognitive processes. That is, does a coherent story about a trauma produce improvements in health by reducing ruminations or flashbacks? Does a story ultimately result in the assimilation of an unexplained experience that allows the person to get on with life?

IMPLICATIONS FOR CRITICAL INCIDENT STRESS DEBRIEFING (CISD)

The creators of critical incident stress debriefing, including Jeffrey Mitchell and George Everly (e.g., Mitchell & Everly, 1996), have done an invaluable job in designing a program that helps both victims and emergency workers in dealing with massive traumas. In settings where no one had ever done any systematic research, they developed a program based on their own experiences in understanding emergency situations. It is now time to stand back and evaluate which aspects of CISD work and which parts may need to be changed. The critical incident stress management world shares many of the same assumptions as those in the writing research. Using our writing approach as a base, I propose a number of points of discussion.

The Importance of Exploring Why Talking Works

The CISD strategy has been focused more on what seems to work than exploring why it might work. Simple catharsis or abreaction models are clearly inadequate to explain why talking about problems is generally beneficial. Rather, the active ingredients in the expression of emotions that appear to promote health are cognitive in nature. When individuals are able to talk about and acknowledge emotional causes and responses to significant experiences, they are far better off than if they do not do so. Emotion expression through language, then, is only one part of the broader phenomenon of the telling of the story about the emotional event.

The Clear Need for Objective Assessment

Despite the wide popular appeal of CISD, there are very few strong studies proving its effectiveness (e.g., Friedman, 1996). Indeed, there are as many published articles questioning the effectiveness of CISD (e.g., Matthews, 1998; Kenardy et al., 1996) as there as studies supporting it (e.g., Jenkins, 1996; Chemtob et al., 1996). Strong studies require random assignment to a CISD group and a comparably-timed control group. Admittedly, this is extremely difficult to accomplish in highly volatile traumatic situations where an overriding desire to help the victims can take precedence over scientific concerns. A central value of assessment studies would be to discover which aspects of CISD work and which may not.

When is the best time to intervene? CISD is based on the assumption that the most important time of debriefing is within the first 48 hours of the incident (Mitchell & Dyregrov, 1993) and, if possible, a follow-up. Ironically, the strongest published supportive study on the benefits of CISD were based on a treatment that was introduced 6 months after a devastating disaster (Chemtob et al., 1996). Based on our own research, some form of debriefing may be maximally beneficial at a minimum of 3 weeks posttrauma. During the first two weeks, many of the natural debriefing processes occur within people's social networks. More consideration, then, should be given to more detailed and systematic follow-up sessions.

The Issue of Distancing

The formal CISD procedure differs from the writing technique in an important respect. Whereas CISD demands returning to the images and feelings of the event in a powerful way, writing encourages people to approach it at their own speed without any social pressure. There are no explicit or implicit ways of thinking about the event. For some, the trauma may be upsetting because of the recurring images; for others, the implications for their own financial or social lives. With writing, people work on their own issues at their own pace.

Individual Differences

Statistically, those people most likely to have long-term problems are the very ones who have had previous problems. The trauma is more than what has just happened. It evokes thoughts, images, and fears of previous upheavals. CISD (and writing, for that matter) may work better on some people than others. Indeed, it may be harmful for a subgroup of people. Any way of systematically identifying these individual differences is important.

Identifying the Appropriate Outcome Variables

The writing research clearly affects physical health and, possibly, indicators of mental health. What outcome measures should CISD affect the most: physical health, ruminations, somatic symptoms, other PTSD symptoms? It cannot do everything for everyone. A more systematic approach in measurement of outcomes is clearly needed.

REFERENCES

Bisson, J.I.: Is post-traumatic stress disorder preventable? *Journal of Mental Health, 6:* 109–111, 1997.
Booth, R.J., Petrie, K.J., & Pennebaker, J.W.: Changes in circulating lymphocyte numbers following emotional disclosure: Evidence of buffering? *Stress Medicine, 13:* 23–29, 1997.

Cameron, L.D., and Nicholls, G.: Expression of stressful experiences through writing: Effects of a self-regulation manipulation for pessimists and optimists. *Health Psychology, 17:* 84–92, 1998.

Chemtob, C.M., Tomas, S., Law, W., and Cremniter, D.: Postdisaster psychosocial intervention: A field study of the impact of debriefing on psychological distress. *American Journal of Psychiatry, 154:* 415–417, 1997.

Christensen, A.J., and Smith, T.W.: Cynical hostility and cardiovascular reactivity during self-disclosure. *Psychosomatic Medicine, 55:* 193–202, 1993.

Cole, S.W., Kemeny, M.E., Taylor, S.E., and Visscher, B.R.: Elevated physical health risk among gay men who conceal their homosexual identity. *Health Psychology, 15:* 243–251, 1996.

Czajka, J.A.: Behavioral Inhibition and Short Term Physiological Responses. Unpublished master's thesis. Southern Methodist University, 1987.

Dominguez, B., Valderrama, P., Meza, M.A., Perez, S.L., Silva, A., Martinez, G., Mendez, V.M., and Olvera, Y.: The roles of emotional reversal and disclosure in clinical practice. In J.W. Pennebaker (Ed.): *Emotion, disclosure, and health.* Washington, DC: American Psychological Association, 1995.

Donnelly, D.A., and Murray, E.J.: Cognitive and emotional changes in written essays and therapy interviews. *Journal of Social and Clinical Psychology, 10:* 334–350, 1991.

Eppley, K.R., Abrams, A.I., and Shear, J.: Differential effects of relaxation techniques on trait anxiety. *Journal of Clinical Psychology, 45:* 957–974, 1989.

Esterling, B.A., Antoni, M.H., Fletcher, M.A., Margulies, S., and Schneiderman, N.: Emotional disclosure through writing or speaking modulates latent Epstein-Barr virus reactivation. *Journal of Consulting and Clinical Psychology, 62:* 130–140, 1994.

Francis, M.E., and Pennebaker, J.W.: Putting stress into words: Writing about personal upheavals and health. *American Journal of Health Promotion, 6:* 280–287, 1992.

Friedman, M.J.: PTSD diagnosis and treatment for mental health clinicians. *Community Mental Health Journal, 32:* 173–189, 1996.

Greenberg, M.A., and Stone, A.A.: Writing about disclosed versus undisclosed traumas: Immediate and long-term effects on mood and health. *Journal of Personality and Social Psychology, 63:* 75–84, 1992.

Greenberg, M.A., Wortman, C.B., and Stone, A.A.: Emotional expression and physical health: Revising traumatic memories or fostering self-regulation. *Journal of Personality and Social Psychology, 71:* 588–602, 1996.

Horowitz, M.J.: *Stress Response Syndromes.* New York: Jacob Aronson, 1976.

Hughes, C.F., Uhlmann, C., and Pennebaker, J.W.: The body's response to psychological defense. *Journal of Personality, 62:* 565–585, 1994.

Jenkins, S.R.: Social support and debriefing efficacy among emergency medical workers after a mass shooting incident. *Journal of Social Behavior and Personality, 11:* 477–492, 1996.

Kagan, J., Reznick, J.S., and Snidman, N.: Biological bases of childhood shyness. *Science, 240:* 167–171, 1988.

Kenardy, J.A., Webster, R.A., Lewin, T.J., Carr, V.J., Hazell, P.L., and Carter, G.L.: Stress debriefing and patterns of recovery following a natural disaster. *Journal of Traumatic Stress, 9:* 37–50, 1996.

Krantz, A., and Pennebaker, J.W.: Bodily versus written expression of traumatic experience. Manuscript submitted for publication, 1996.

Kubler-Ross, E.: *On death and dying.* Toronto: Macmillan, 1966.

Lutgendorf, S.K., Antoni, M.H., Kumar, M., and Schneiderman, N.: Changes in cognitive coping strategies predict EBV-antibody titre change following a stressor disclosure induction. *Journal of Psychosomatic Research, 38:* 63–78, 1994.

Matthews, L.R.: Effect of staff debriefing on posttraumatic stress symptoms after assaults by community housing residents. *Psychiatric Services, 49:* 207–212, 1998.

Mitchell, J.T., and Dyregrov, A.: Traumatic stress in disaster workers and emergency personnel. In J.P. Wilson and B. Raphael (Eds.): *International handbook of traumatic stress syndromes* (pp. 905–914). New York: Plenum Press, 1993.

Mitchell, J.T., and Everly, G.S.: *Critical incident stress debriefing (CISD): An operations manual.* Ellicott City: Chevron, 1996.

Murray, E.J., Lamnin, A.D., and Carver, C.S.: Emotional expression in written essays and psychotherapy. *Journal of Social and Clinical Psychology, 8:* 414–429, 1989.

Pennebaker, J.W.: Mechanisms of social constraint. In D.M. Wegner and J.W. Pennebaker (Eds.): *Handbook of mental control* (pp. 200–219). Englewood Cliffs, NJ: Prentice Hall, 1993.

Pennebaker, J.W.: Confession, inhibition, and disease. In L. Berkowitz (Ed.): *Advances in experimental social psychology* (Vol. 22, pp. 211–244). New York: Academic Press, 1989.

Pennebaker, J.W.: *Opening up: The healing power of expressing emotion* (revised edition). New York: Guilford Press, 1997a.

Pennebaker, J.W.: Writing about emotional experiences as a therapeutic process. *Psychological Science, 8:* 162–166, 1997b.

Pennebaker, J.W., Barger, S.D., and Tiebout, J.: Disclosure of traumas and health among Holocaust survivors. *Psychosomatic Medicine, 51:* 577–589, 1989.

Pennebaker, J.W., and Beall, S.K.: Confronting a traumatic event: Toward an understanding of inhibition and disease. *Journal of Abnormal Psychology, 95:* 274–281, 1986.

Pennebaker, J.W., Colder, M., and Sharp, L.K.: Accelerating the coping process. *Journal of Personality and Social Psychology, 58:* 528–537, 1990.

Pennebaker, J.W., and Francis, M.E.: Cognitive, emotional, and language processes in disclosure. *Cognition and Emotion, 10:* 601–626, 1996.

Pennebaker, J., and Harber, K.: A social stage model of collective coping: The Persian Gulf War and other natural disasters. *Journal of Social Issues, 49:* 15–145, 1993.

Pennebaker, J.W., Hughes, C.F., and O'Heeron, R.C.: The psychophysiology of confession: Linking inhibitory and psychosomatic processes. *Journal of Personality and Social Psychology, 52:* 781–793, 1987.

Pennebaker, J.W., Kiecolt-Glaser, J., and Glaser, R.: Disclosure of traumas and immune function: Health implications for psychotherapy. *Journal of Consulting and Clinical Psychology, 56:* 239–245, 1988.

Pennebaker, J.W., Mayne, T.J., and Francis, M.E.: Linguistic predictors of adaptive bereavement. *Journal of Personality and Social Psychology, 72:* 863–871, 1997.

Pennebaker, J.W., and O'Heeron, R.C.: Confiding in others and illness rates among spouses of suicide and accidental deaths. *Journal of Abnormal Psychology, 93:* 473–476, 1984.

Pennebaker, J.W., and Susman, J.R.: Disclosure of traumas and psychosomatic processes. *Social Science and Medicine, 26:* 327–332, 1988.

Petrie, K.J., Booth, R., Pennebaker, J.W., Davison, K.P., and Thomas, M.: Disclosure of trauma and immune response to Hepatitis B vaccination program. *Journal of Consulting and Clinical Psychology, 63:* 787–792, 1995.

Richards, J.M., Pennebaker, J.W., and Beal, W.E.: *The effects of criminal offense and disclosure of trauma on anxiety and illness in prison inmates.* Paper presented at the Midwest Psychological Association, Chicago and currently submitted for publication, 1995.

Rimé, B.: Mental rumination, social sharing, and the recover from emotional exposure. In J.W. Pennebaker (Ed.): *Emotion, disclosure, and health.* Washington, DC: American Psychological Association, 1995.

Schoutrop, M.J.A., Lange, A., Brosschot, J., and Everaerd, W.: *The effects of writing assignments on reprocessing traumatic events: Three experimental studies.* Paper presented at The (Non) Expression of Emotions and Health and Disease Conference, Tilburg, The Netherlands, 1996.

Selye, H.: *The stress of life.* New York: McGraw-Hill, 1976.

Smyth, J.M.: Written emotional expression: Effect sizes, outcome types, and moderating variables. *Journal of Consulting and Clinical Psychology, 66:* 174–184, 1998.

Spera, S.P., Buhrfeind, E.D., and Pennebaker, J.W.: Expressive writing and coping with job loss. *Academy of Management Journal, 37:* 722–733, 1994.

Stroebe, M. and Stroebe, W.: *Writing assignments and grief.* Paper presented at The (Non) Expression of Emotions and Health and Disease Conference, Tilburg, The Netherlands, 1996.

Van Rood, Y.R., Bogaards, M., Goulmy, E., and Van Houwelingen, H.C.: The effects of stress and relaxation on the in vitro immune response in man: A meta-analysis. *Journal of Behavioral Medicine, 16:* 163–181, 1993.

Wortman, C.B., and Silver, R.C.: The myths of coping with loss. *Journal of Consulting and Clinical Psychology, 57:* 349–357, 1989.

Chapter 7

HARDINESS AS A RESILIENCY FACTOR FOR UNITED STATES FORCES IN THE GULF WAR

PAUL T. BARTONE

INTRODUCTION

SOME OF THE MOST EXTREME of human stressors are those encountered by soldiers in combat. Wartime exposure can have both short and long-term damaging effects on the mental health of military personnel (Grinker & Spiegel, 1945; Solomon & Flum, 1988; Kulka et al., 1990). Although the 1991 Persian Gulf War with Iraq was over relatively quickly and with relatively few United States casualties, research indicates this war was no exception. A growing number of studies document the negative health consequences of exposure to war zone stress in the Gulf War (e.g., Lehman, 1993; Elder, Shanahan & Clipp, 1997). Many of these studies examine reservist units, which are relied upon more heavily in the smaller, post-Cold War military force structure (Griffith, 1995). By one count (Lakhani & Fugita, 1993), reserves comprised 18% of all American troops deployed to the Gulf (102,000 out of 569,000). Studies with Gulf War veterans generally report higher levels of psychological symptoms related to stress exposure (Sutker, Uddo, Brailey & Allain, 1993; Wolfe, Keane & Young, 1996; Ford et al., 1993; Stuart & Bliese, 1998; Holmes, Tariot & Cox, 1998).

But while these studies agree regarding increased risk for ill-effects associated with exposure to war-related stress, little attention is paid to understanding differential responses to stress, and why so many exposed individuals remain healthy. For example, Holmes, Tariot & Cox (1998) report that in an Air National Guard unit mobilized during the Gulf War, 6.8% of those who deployed to the Gulf showed elevated PTSD (Posttraumatic Stress Disorder) scores afterwards, compared to only 1.7% of those who were not deployed. Apart from the effects of deployment itself, these authors make no attempt to explain differences in reported PTSD symptoms, or why the vast majority of those deployed apparently do not develop symptoms. This is typical of such studies, where the focus is on ill health and psychiatric breakdown rather than good health and resilience.

Several personality or dispositional constructs have been posited to confer stress resistance or resiliency upon those possessing them. Notable among these are Antonovsky's (1979) "sense of coherence," "hardiness" as presented by Kobasa (1979) and Maddi and Kobasa (1984), and characteristic optimism as described by Scheier and Carver (1985) and elaborated by Seligman (1991). In this chapter, I will focus on the dimension of hardiness as a resiliency factor for U.S. soldiers operating in the Persian Gulf War. Research studies with a variety of occupational groups have found that hardiness appears to function as a significant moderator or buffer of stress (e.g., Bartone, 1989; Contrada, 1989; Kobasa, Maddi & Kahn, 1982; Roth et al., 1989; Wiebe, 1991). In exploring the role of hardiness as a resiliency factor for soldiers, I will draw from the results of two research efforts. Both examine hardiness and posttraumatic stress (PTS) symptomatology in soldiers following the Gulf War, with the first utilizing a large sample of active duty Army forces (Bartone et al., 1992; Bartone, 1993), and the second using a sample of Army Reserve medical units (Bartone, 1999). Results from both studies demonstrate that personality hardiness is a significant protective or resiliency factor for active duty and reservist forces exposed to war-related stress. These results are discussed in terms of possible mechanisms of action for hardiness-based stress resiliency, and implications for training and future research.

HARDINESS

Before presenting these research findings in some detail, it is useful to review some conceptual and measurement issues related to the hardiness construct. Conceptually, hardiness is a personality variable that develops early in life and is reasonably stable over time, though amenable to change under certain conditions (Maddi & Kobasa, 1984). Hardy persons have a high sense of life and work commitment, a stronger belief of control, and are more open to change and challenges in life. They tend to interpret stressful and painful experiences as a normal aspect of existence, part of life that is overall interesting and worthwhile. Originally developed by Salvatore Maddi and Suzanne Kobasa Ouellette (Maddi, 1967, 1970; Kobasa, 1979; Maddi & Kobasa, 1984), the concept of personality hardiness is rooted in existential psychology and personality theory (Kobasa & Maddi, 1977; Kierkagaard, 1954; Keen, 1970). Theoretically, as a function of their own psychosocial developmental history, hardy (authentic) persons are more open to experience on a variety of levels, and are more solidly grounded and confident in their sense of self and place in the social world.

The critical implication of hardiness theory for stress resiliency is that hardy personality types are not as easily threatened or psychologically disrupted by ordinarily painful aspects of the human condition. This theoretical underpinning sets hardiness apart from constructs such as "optimism" (Scheier & Carver, 1985) or "hope" (Snyder et al., 1991), which imply a quite simple process whereby stressful or painful experiences are disregarded or ignored. In contrast, the hardy person accepts disruptive and even painful experiences as a normal part of life in all its richness. Maddi (1967) even argues that due to this existential and open approach to life, the hardy person is more accepting, and less fearful of death. If true, this would have particular relevance to the domain of combat-related stress, and how soldiers cope with the prospect of their own and their comrades' imminent death.

At least in part as a function of this theoretical depth and complexity, the hardiness has proved difficult to measure. Much of the published work on hardiness uses measures that have been criticized as flawed in several important ways, including poor reliability, and negative wording of all items (Funk & Houston, 1987). Both studies reported here utilize a hardiness measure that improves substantially over earlier versions. The first study used a 30-item hardiness scale (Dispositional Resilience Scale) that corrects many problems associated with earlier self-report hardiness measures (Bartone et al., 1989; Bartone, 1991). In his review of hardiness measures, Funk (1992) recommended this Dispositional Resilience Scale as the best of several available hardiness measures. It includes ten items each to measure the three general characteristics or hardiness facets of commitment, control, and challenge. The Dispositional Resilience Scale is balanced for positive and negative items, with an equal number (15) of each. The correlation between the 30-item form and 27 non-overlapping items (6 alienation from self, 2 alienation from work, 7 powerlessness, 10 security, 2 cognitive structure) from the original hardiness scale used in the Chicago studies (Maddi and Kobasa, 1984) is .74 (bus driver sample, N=753; Bartone, 1991). Scores on the 30-item hardiness or DRS scale have demonstrated appropriate correlations with theoretically related (convergent) and unrelated (discriminant) variables, and are generally predictive of continued mental and physical health under a variety of environmental stressors (e.g., Bartone et al., 1990; Bartone, 1989b). For example, scores on this measure were found to discriminate Army disaster assistance workers who remain healthy from those reporting stress-related symptoms over time (Bartone et al., 1989). The reliability of the DRS is also good. A six-month stability coefficient of .57 was found in a sample (N=80) of Army officers, and a three-month stability coefficient of .58 was obtained in a small (N=21) group of Army personnel workers. Cronbach's alpha for the total scale ranges from .70 to .85 depending on the sample. Reliability and factor analyses with various samples generally confirm the presence of the 3 facets of commitment, control and challenge, though internal consistency for the challenge scale is only moderate (.62).

In examining the hardiness facets of commitment, control and challenge, it is important to keep in mind that these subscales were never intended to fully describe "hardiness" from a theoretical point of view. Rather, these were suggested by Kobasa as "three general characteristics" that "hardy persons are considered to possess" (1979, p. 3). As such, when taken together these characteristics can provide a useful operational (if theoretically incomplete) indicator of the personality style described by Maddi (1967) as "hardy." Put another way, the "whole" of personality hardiness is greater than the sum of its commitment, control and challenge parts (Maddi, Bartone & Puccetti, 1987).

Following the development of the 30-item "Dispositional Resiliency" hardiness scale, additional psychometric testing with multiple samples led to a shortened form that keeps the best 15-items of the set (Bartone, 1995). Study Two, reported below, uses this 15-item short hardiness scale. This 15-item scale includes positively and negatively keyed items, and covers the facets of commitment, control and challenge with 5 items each. Cronbach's alpha for the total measure is .82 and for the facets, .77 (commitment), .68 (control), and .69 (challenge) (Bartone, 1999). In a sample of 105 (West Point) college students, the three-week test-retest reliability coefficient for this scale is .78.

STUDY 1: GULF WAR ACTIVE DUTY FORCES

As part of a larger study by investigators at the Walter Reed Army Institute of Research (Gifford et al., 1996), questionnaires were administered to a total of 8,632 U.S. Army soldiers who had deployed to Saudi Arabia during the war. These questionnaires were administered over the 3–12 months following the end of the Gulf War. Surveys were also obtained on a control group of 465 soldiers who did not participate in the wartime deployment (Bartone et al., 1992). Surveys were collected at Army home-station locations in Germany and the United States. In addition to demographics, measures included a 31-item combat exposure inventory; soldier cohesion scales (both "horizontal" or peer-to-peer, and "vertical" or subordinate-to-leader); personality hardiness (the 30-item "DRS" form, as described above); several measures of psychiatric/psychological outcome including the Brief Symptoms Inventory (BSI; Derogatis, 1975) and the Impact of Events Scale (IES; Horowitz, Wilner & Alvarez, 1979); and a specially constructed indicator of risk for Posttraumatic Stress Disorder (PTSD) based on DSM-III(R) diagnostic criteria. To form this PTSD scale, items were selected from the BSI and the IES that corresponded to the 17 symptoms listed under DSM III-R for PTSD, including 4 intrusion items, 7 avoidance items, and 6 arousal items (Bartone, Adler & Vaitkus, 1994). A short survey was administered to a smaller sample of soldiers (N=833) just prior to the ground war offensive, permitting some prospective analyses to be done (see Martin et al., 1992, and Gifford et al., 1996 for additional details on the Walter Reed Army Institute of Research Gulf War studies).

STUDY 2: GULF WAR RESERVE FORCES

In Study 2, the resiliency factor of hardiness was explored in a group of Army reserve medical units that were mobilized for the Gulf War. A voluntary questionnaire was distributed to six Army National Guard and Reserve medical units from three states 4–6 months after the end of the Gulf War. All 6 units represented Army field hospitals that had been mobilized for the war effort. The survey was endorsed by senior commanders, and distributed through local command channels. Participation ranged from 25% to 75% across the six units involved in the study. Units with the lowest response rates also experienced more distribution problems. The overall response rate was approximately 50%, quite good for surveys of this type. Of the 6 Reserve units surveyed, three deployed to Saudi Arabia, one deployed to Germany as backup for Germany-based units that deployed to the Persian Gulf, and two units, though mobilized, remained in the United States. Thus, there is a range of exposure to war-related stress across these units. The sample was 45% women, which although high for Army units in general, is not unusual for medical units. Other characteristics of the sample: Age, X=34, sd=10.6; military rank, 68% enlisted and non-commissioned officers, 32% officers; 55% married; and 32% with college or graduate degrees.

The questionnaire included items on demographic and background variables, such as military rank, age, education, gender, ethnic background, and marital status. To measure war-related stress, a 15-item scale asked about stressors specific to the Gulf War experience (e.g., "Threat of enemy missile attack," "Exposure to dead or dying," "Caring for traumatically injured patients"). As with Study 1, this survey also included the Brief Symptom Inventory (Derogatis & Melisaratos, 1983), and the Impact of Events scale (Horowitz et al., 1979) which assesses symptoms related to posttraumatic stress disorder (PTSD). In what follows, results are presented from both studies showing that hardiness interacts with combat stress to predict PTSD-related outcomes. The focus is on outcome indicators most relevant to PTSD symptomatology, the "Impact of Events Scale" (IES), and (for Study 1) the constructed measure of PTSD risk, as described above. The IES is thought to be an especially sensitive indicator of reactions to extreme or traumatic stressors (Horowitz, Wilner & Alvarez, 1979). In Study 1, unit cohesion was also examined as a possible resiliency factor at the group level.

Table 7.1

STEPWISE MULTIPLE REGRESSION PREDICTING IMPACT OF
EVENTS (IES) SCORES GULF WAR, ACTIVE DUTY
(CROSS-SECTIONAL) SAMPLE (N=7,924)

Predictor Variable	R^2	Beta	T	p<
Anxiety	.231	.44	43.5	.0001
Combat Exposure	.253	.20	11.4	.0001
Combat Expos. X Cohesion (H)	.254	−.06	−3.4	.001
Hardiness	.255	−.03	−2.9	.003

Multiple R = .50
R^2 = .25
F (4,7920) = 678.7
p<.0001

RESULTS: STUDY 1

Table 7.1 summarizes results from a stepwise multiple regression analysis, predicting IES Total scores for the postcombat (N=7,924) active duty sample. Scores on a generalized anxiety measure were entered as a covariate to control for the possible confounding effects of neuroticism. Costa & McCrae (1985) have argued that characteristic anxiety or neuroticism can lead people to overreport stressors as well as symptoms, generating artificially high correlations between stress and symptoms measures. Funk (1992) pointed out that hardiness scores can be similarly contaminated by neuroticism. By controlling for anxiety scores, we take a conservative approach in that anxiety scores in soldiers who are about to go to war very likely indicate realistic responses to actual stressful circumstances, to some degree. That is, by partialling out the effects of anxiety on IES scores, we may be removing some of the variance we wish to identify and explain. Nevertheless, this was done in order to ensure that results are not a simple function of trait anxiety or neuroticism.

Not surprisingly, anxiety emerged as a strong independent predictor of IES total scores. The model also showed significant independent effects for Combat Exposure and Hardiness, as well as a Combat Exposure X Horizontal Cohesion interaction effect. Figure 7.1 plots the regression lines for high vs. low cohesion soldiers (median split). This shows that cohesion exerts its strongest effect on symptoms under high stress (combat exposure) conditions.

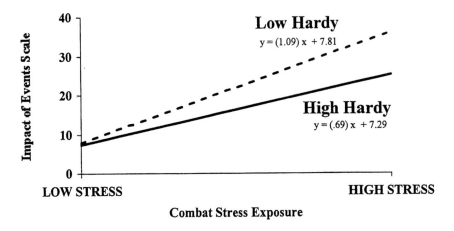

* Displays Hardy x CSE interaction (p < .0001) from Table 2,
  N=824 active duty, unstandardized betas used to map regression lines

Figure 7.1. Gulf War Combat Stress Exposure (CSE) predicting IES scores for Low and High Hardy groups, *active duty* sample*

Also as part of Study 1, prospective data were examined for a smaller sample (N=824) of soldiers who had completed both pre- and post-combat surveys. For this group, the precombat survey was administered 1–4 weeks before the launch of offensive ground operations. With these data, it was possible to control for actual precombat generalized anxiety levels, rather than postcombat levels. This provides a better control for generalized anxiety or neuroticism, since scores could not be influenced by actual combat events that came later in time. Still, it is a conservative approach in that precombat anxiety scores may reflect a realistic appraisal of events likely to follow, rather than generalized worry or neuroticism.

As Table 7.2 shows, precombat anxiety is a significant predictor of postcombat IES scores. With the effects of precombat anxiety removed, the remaining significant effects in the model are for Combat Exposure and a Combat Exposure X Hardiness interaction term. Thus, the independent main effect of hardiness on soldier adjustment in the cross-sectional data is replaced by an interaction effect (with Combat Exposure) when actual precombat levels of anxiety are controlled.

Figure 7.2 plots the regression lines for high and low hardy soldiers (median split). Similar to cohesion in the cross-sectional data, hardiness appears to have its greatest influence on symptoms under high

Table 7.2
STEPWISE MULTIPLE REGRESSION PREDICTING IMPACT OF
EVENTS (IES) SCORES GULF WAR, ACTIVE DUTY
(PROSPECTIVE) SAMPLE (N=824)

Predictor Variable	R^2	Beta	T	p<
Combat Exposure	.089	.82	8.3	.0001
Anxiety (precombat)	.153	.22	7.0	.0001
Hardiness X Combat Expos.	.183	−.54	−5.5	.0001

Multiple R = .43
R^2 = .18
F (3,821) = 61.3
p<.0001

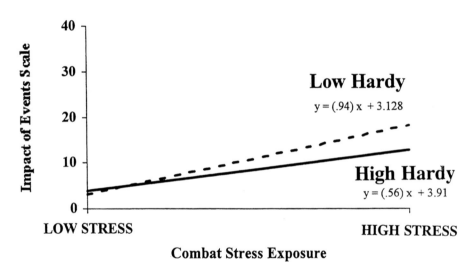

* Displays Hardy x CSE interaction (p < .002) from Table 5,
N=700 reservists, unstandardized betas used to map regression lines

Figure 7.2. Gulf War Combat Stress Exposure (CSE) predicting IES scores for Low and High Hardy groups, *reservist* sample*

stress (combat exposure) conditions. These findings are supportive of a "stress-buffering" hypothesis, wherein persons who possess the personality style of hardiness are less vulnerable to the disruptive effects of severe stress.

Table 7.3
STEPWISE MULTIPLE REGRESSION PREDICTING PTSD (DSM III-R)
GULF WAR, ACTIVE DUTY (CROSS-SECTIONAL) SAMPLE (N=7,924)

Predictor Variable	R^2	Beta	T	p<
Anxiety	.163	.37	34.7	.0001
Combat Exposure	.167	.48	8.2	.0001
Combat Expos. X Cohesion (V)	.172	−.06	−2.2	.0001
Combat Expos. X Hardiness	.175	−.33	−5.4	.0001
Hardiness	.176	.05	3.0	.002
Combat Expos. X Cohesion (H)	.177	−.06	−2.5	.01

Multiple R =.42
R^2 = .177
F (6,7918) = 283.3
p<.0001

As another check on hardiness as a resiliency factor, a similar stepwise multiple regression was examined, but with the above described PTSD variable as the dependent variable. Scores on this variable reflected whether or not respondents met DSM III-R criteria for PTSD, based on their answers to 17 symptom items. Even with the possible confounding effects of anxiety removed, results showed a main effect for hardiness, and an interaction between hardiness and combat exposure (Table 7.3). Additional independent predictors of PTSD were vertical and horizontal cohesion in interaction with combat exposure.

RESULTS: STUDY 2

A majority of the reservist sample (N=389) reported having deployed to the Persian Gulf (Saudi Arabia or Kuwait), while N=145 deployed to U.S. Army stations in Germany. Another 236, though mobilized and assigned full-time to reserve unit duties, remained in the United States. The first set of analyses examines levels of reported stress and symptoms across the deployment groups. Those soldiers closest to the combat situation (Saudi Arabia) should experience the highest levels of combat stress, as well as any related symptoms or health problems. Table 7.4 compares the three groups in terms of combat and life stress, and the total score of the Impact of Events scale (IES).

Table 7.4
MEANS AND STANDARD DEVIATIONS (SD) FOR STRESS AND
HEALTH MEASURES FOR THREE DEPLOYMENT GROUPS

Health measure		Deployment Group		
		1 Deployed, within U.S. N=236	2 Deployed to Germany N=145	3 Deployed to Persian Gulf N=389
SLE – Stressful	X	8.2(3)	8.5	9.3(1)
Life Events	sd	5.6	5.1	5.6
Combat Stress	X	.2(2,3)	8.5(1,3)	13.5(1,2)
Exposure	sd	1.1	3.9	2.4
IES – Impact	X	4.0(2,3)	9.3(1,3)	13.8(1,2)
Of Events	sd	7.2	9.7	9.7

Note: Numbers in parentheses indicate groups that are significantly different (at .05 level or better) from this group mean, based on Least-Square Difference post-hoc test. Homogeneity of variance verified across groups for all measures.

These results confirm that proximity to the battlefield is associated with significantly higher levels of combat stress exposure, as well as increased IES scores. In general, the U.S.-based group reports the lowest levels of stress and health complaints, the group deployed to Germany reports the next highest, and the group deployed to the Persian Gulf reports the highest levels.

To test for possible mediating roles, stress and hardiness scores were entered into a direct, or simultaneous entry regression model, along with relevant interaction terms, predicting IES scores. Results are summarized in Table 7.5. A main effect was found for combat stress exposure, and hardiness also interacts with combat stress to predict IES scores.

Again, in order to clarify the direction of the interaction effect, separate regressions were computed for high and low hardiness groups, and results plotted (Figure 7.2). These results show clearly that the positive effects of hardiness increase as combat stress exposure increases. Thus, it is under high-stress conditions that hardiness seems to matter most.

Table 7.5
STANDARD MULTIPLE REGRESSION OF STRESS AND HARDINESS
VARIABLES PREDICTING IES (IMPACT OF EVENTS) GULF WAR,
RESERVIST SAMPLE (N=700)

Predictor Variable	Beta	T	p<
Hardiness	−.07	−.68	ns
Stressful Life Events	−.10	−.73	ns
Combat Stress Exposure	.72	3.95	.001
Hardiness X Stressful Life Events	.35	1.99	.05
Hardiness X Combat Stress Exposure	−.50	−2.37	.02
Hardiness X Combat Stress X Stress. Life Events	.07	.55	ns

Multiple R = .50
R^2 = .25
F (6,594) = 76.07
p<.001

DISCUSSION

Results from Study 1 demonstrate that both unit cohesion and the personality style of "hardiness" can have significant and independent effects on postcombat adjustment for U.S. soldiers. These effects pertain even when the possible confounding influence of generalized anxiety is controlled for. Perhaps more importantly, hardiness was found to interact with combat exposure, lending support to the theorized function of hardiness as a stress-resistance resource (Maddi, 1976). A similar, though less pronounced interaction effect was seen between combat exposure and horizontal cohesion. With these empirical effects demonstrated in samples of U.S. soldiers exposed to actual combat, it now remains for additional research to identify the manner and form in which the personality style of hardiness develops, how it is influenced by group processes such as leadership and cohesion, and the degree to which it can be trained or modeled. It is also the task of future research to identify the underlying mechanisms, cognitive, emotional, and physiological, wherein unit cohesion and the generalized orientation of "hardiness" serve to buffer the ill-effects of environmental stressors.

Study 2 has also demonstrated that the stress of exposure to combat is substantially related to PTSD symptoms in a large group of Army reserve personnel mobilized for the Persian Gulf War. Yet as has been observed, the relation between war-related stress and illness is far from perfect, and a majority of those exposed show no ill-effects at all (Rundell & Ursano, 1996). Many soldiers in the reservist sample experienced life and combat-related stress, with no apparent negative health consequences. The present results suggest that the personality variable hardiness can at least partly explain why some soldiers remain healthy under war-related stress. Hardiness was found to interact with combat stress to predict fewer symptoms under stress. The pattern of results further suggests that those who are experiencing, or have recently experienced, significant major stressful life events, in addition to being exposed to combat stressors, are at the greatest risk for psychological symptoms of various kinds. It also appears that while personality hardiness exerts modest salubrious effects under low-stress conditions, it generally has a stronger influence under high-stress conditions. This corresponds to similar findings in various occupational groups (Bartone, 1989; Bartone et al., 1989; Bartone, 1996; Contrada, 1989; Kobasa, Maddi & Kahn, 1982; Roth et al., 1989; Wiebe, 1991).

How might hardiness influence the relationship between combat stress and health? A recent study of Vietnam veterans suggests that hardiness operates through social support to increase resistance to Posttraumatic Stress Disorder (King et al., 1998). In an earlier study, Kobasa and Puccetti (1983) reported similar findings, with hardiness and social support interacting to predict continued good health in corporate managers. One possibility they suggest is that hardy persons are better able to develop and utilize social support resources.

Another possible mechanism for the positive hardiness effect involves the cognitive interpretation that individuals make when exposed to stressful events and life circumstances. The tendency to find positive meaning in life, especially at work, is a defining feature of personality hardiness (Kobasa, 1979; Maddi, 1967; Maddi & Kobasa, 1984). People with a hardy personality style are more inclined to attach or create positive meaning and importance to their work activities, and are also less vulnerable to the ill effects of work and life stress. (Kobasa, Maddi & Kahn, 1982). In a study of city bus drivers, Bartone (1989) found that those high in hardiness had a strong sense of meaningfulness and pride in their work, and were also more resilient and healthy when subjected to work-related stressors. In several recent studies with military units performing contingency and peacekeeping operations, hardiness was found to reduce the impact of stress (including mission stressors like boredom) on depression and psychiatric symptoms (Bartone, 1996; Bartone & Adler, 1999). Given the likelihood of boredom or loss of meaning during peacekeeping operations in particular, and the apparent potential harm to morale, health, well-being, and mission performance (Siebold, 1996), more attention is needed to this problem.

The research results summarized here show that personality hardiness is an important factor contributing to continued resiliency and mental health, for reservist as well as active duty forces confronted with a spectrum of real war-related stressors. While these results are suggestive regarding underlying mechanisms, additional work is needed. Future studies should seek to clarify how and under what conditions hardiness protects against stress, and with respect to what kinds of stressors. It is also important to explore how hardy cognitive appraisals and behaviors might be increased amongst those who must undergo severe stressors, not only in the occupation of soldier, but also fire fighters, police, and rescue workers. Some initial work along these lines has been done by Maddi and colleagues (Maddi, 1999), who find that structured training programs can increase hardiness levels to some degree, and the kinds of behaviors under stress that seem to characterize high-hardy persons. Organizations like the military should be able to develop new training programs for employees, or adjust existing stress management programs to emphasize hardy responses on a cognitive and behavioral level.

While these results are based on individual differences and responses to stressful situations, there are also implications for resiliency at the organizational level. In military as well as other large organizations, the social environment or climate is heavily influenced by how leaders behave, as well as their programs and policies. It would seem that in principle, leaders could increase the frequency of "hardy" cognitive interpretations and behaviors through enlightened policies aimed at fostering such responses. For example, providing increased recognition and praise to soldiers (employees) for their work and contributions to the mission should increase the overall level of commitment, a key facet of hardiness. Likewise, a psychologically beneficial increase in sense of control would likely result when leaders give subordinates more power and autonomy in their jobs, and resist the tendency to "micromanage." Likewise, leaders who model positive responses to change and unpredictability during operations are setting an important example for subordinates, who are more likely then to display similar positive responses to change and uncertainty. Atella (1999) reports two organizational case studies that support this notion, where specific leader efforts and organizational policies guided by hardiness theory apparently improved employee attitudes, teamwork and performance.

The possibility that resiliency levels can be increased in individuals, and even in whole organizations, is an intriguing one with potentially huge implications. Additional empirical work is needed to clarify the nature and mechanisms of stress-resiliency, whether considered in terms of hardiness or some other theoretical framework. The empirical findings to date with respect to hardiness as a resiliency factor certainly suggest that it is a good place to narrow the search.

REFERENCES

Antonovsky, A.: *Health, stress, and coping.* San Francisco: Jossey-Bass, 1979.

Atella, M.D.: Case studies in the development of organizational hardiness: From theory to practice. *Consulting Psychology Journal, 51:* 125–134, 1999.

Bartone, P.T.: Predictors of stress related illness in city bus drivers. *Journal of Occupational Medicine, 31:* 657–663, 1989a.

Bartone, P.T.: *Hardiness, optimism, and health: A construct validity study.* 60th Annual Meeting of the Eastern Psychological Association, Boston, MA., 1989b.

Bartone, P.T.: *Development and validation of a short hardiness measure.* Presented at the 3rd Annual Convention of the American Psychological Society, Washington, DC, 1991.

Bartone, P.T.: *Psychosocial predictors of soldier adjustment to combat stress.* Paper presented at the Third European Conference on Traumatic Stress, Bergen, Norway, 1993.

Bartone, P.T.: *A short hardiness scale.* Paper presented at the Annual Convention of the American Psychological Society, New York, 1995.

Bartone, P.T.: Family notification and survivor assistance: Thinking the unthinkable. In R.J. Ursano and A.E. Norwood (Eds.): Emotional *aftermath of the Persian Gulf War: Veterans, families, communities and nations* (pp. 315–350). Washington, DC: American Psychiatric Press, 1996a.

Bartone, P.T.: *Stress and hardiness in U.S. peacekeeping soldiers.* Paper presented at the Annual Convention of the American Psychological Association, Toronto, 1996b.

Bartone, P.T.: Hardiness protects against war-related stress in Army reserve forces. *Consulting Psychology Journal, 51:* 72–82, 1999.

Bartone, P.T., and Adler, A.: Cohesion over time in a medical peacekeeping task force. *Military Psychology, 11:* 85–107, 1999.

Bartone, P.T., Adler, A.B., and Vaitkus, M.A.: *Assessing posttraumatic stress disorder and PTSD symptomatology in U.S. Army personnel.* Paper presented at the 30th International Congress on Military Medicine, Augsburg, Germany, 1994.

Bartone, P.T., Gifford, R.K., Wright, K.M., Marlowe, D.H., and Martin, J.A.: *U.S. soldiers remain healthy under Gulf War stress.* Presented at the 4th Annual Convention of the American Psychological Society, San Diego, CA, 1992.

Bartone, P.T., McCarroll, J.E., Wright, K.M., Ursano, R.J., and Fullerton, C.S.: *Personality hardiness and resiliency in high-stressed military populations.* Presented at the 98th Annual Convention of the American Psychological Association, Boston, MA, 1990.

Bartone, P.T., Ursano, R.J., Wright, K.M., and Ingraham, L.H.: The impact of a military air disaster on the health of assistance workers: A prospective study. *Journal of Nervous and Mental Disease, 177:* 317–328, 1989.

Contrada, R.J.: Type A behavior, personality hardiness, and cardiovascular responses to stress. *Journal of Personality and Social Psychology, 57:* 895–903, 1989.

Costa, P.T., and McCrae, R.R.: Hypochondriasis, neuroticism, and aging: when are somatic complaints unfounded? *American Psychologist, 40:* 19–28, 1985.

Department of Defense, Washington Headquarters Services: DoD active duty military personnel strength levels, fiscal years 1950-1997. Washington, DC: DoD Directorate for Information Operations and Reporting (http://web1.whs.osd.mil/mmid/military/trends.htm), 1998.

Derogatis, L.R., and Melisaratos, N.: The Brief Symptom Inventory: An introductory report. *Psychological Medicine, 12:* 595–605, 1983.

Derogatis, L.R.: *Brief Symptom Inventory.* Baltimore: Clinical Psychometric Research, 1975.

Derogatis, L.R.: *BSI–Brief symptoms inventory: Administration, scoring and procedures manual.* Minneapolis, MN: National Computer Systems Inc., 1993.

Elder, G.H., Shanahan, M.J., and Clipp, E.C: Linking combat and physical health: The legacy of World War II in men's lives. *American Journal of Psychiatry, 154:* 330–336, 1997.

Ford, J.D., Shaw, D., Sennhauser, S., Greaves, D., Thacker, B., Chandler, P., Schwartz, L., and McClain, V.: Psychosocial debriefing after Operation Desert Storm: Marital and family assessment and intervention. *Journal of Social Issues, 49:* 73–102, 1993.

Funk, S.C.: Hardiness: A review of theory and research. *Health Psychology, 11:* 335–345, 1992.

Funk, S.C., and Houston, B.K.: A critical analysis of the hardiness scale's validity and utility. *Journal of Personality and Social Psychology, 53:* 572–578, 1987.

Gifford, R.K., Martin, J.A., Marlowe, D.H., Wright, K.M., and Bartone, P.T.: Unit cohesion during the Persian Gulf War. In Martin, J.A., Sparacino, L.R. and Belenky, G. (Eds.): *The Gulf War and mental health* (pp. 155-160). Westport, CT: Praeger, 1996.

Griffith, J.: The Army reserve soldier in operation Desert Storm: Perceptions of being prepared for mobilization, deployment and combat. *Armed Forces and Society, 21:* 195–215, 1995.

Grinker, R.R., and Spiegel, J.P.: *Men under stress.* New York: McGraw-Hill, 1945.

Holmes, D.T., Tariot, P.N., and Cox, C.: Preliminary evidence of psychological distress among reservists in the Persian Gulf War. *Journal of Nervous and Mental Disease, 186:* 166–173, 1998.

Horowitz, M., Wilner, N., and Alvarez, W.: Impact of Event Scale: A measure of subjective stress. *Psychosomatic Medicine, 41:* 209–218, 1979.

Keen, E.: *Three faces of being: Toward an existential clinical psychology.* New York: Appleton-Century-Crofts, 1970.

Kierkagaard, S.: *The sickness unto death.* New York: Doubleday, 1954.

King, L.A., King, D.W., Fairbank, J.A., Keane, T.M., and Adams, G.A.: Resilience-recovery factors in posttraumatic stress disorder among male and female Vietnam veterans: hardiness, postwar social support, and additional stressful life events. *Journal of Personality and Social Psychology, 74:* 420–434, 1998.

Kobasa, S.C.: Stressful life events, personality and health: An inquiry into hardiness. *Journal of Personality and Social Psychology, 37:* 1–11, 1979.

Kobasa, S.C., and Maddi, S.R.: Existential personality theory. In R. Corsini (Ed.): *Existential Personality Theories.* Itasca, IL: Peacock, 1977.

Kobasa, S.C., Maddi, S.R., and Kahn, S.: Hardiness and health: A prospective study. *Journal of Personality and Social Psychology, 42:* 168–177, 1982.

Kobasa, S.C., and Puccetti, M.A.: Personality and social resources in stress resistance. *Journal of Personality and Social Psychology, 45:* 839–850, 1983.

Kulka, R.A., Schlenger, W.E., Fairbank, J.A., Hough, R.L., Jordan, B.K., Marmar, C.R., and Weiss, D.S.: *Trauma and the Vietnam War generation.* New York: Brunner/Mazel, 1990.

Lakhani, H., and Fugita, S.S.: Reserve/Guard retention: Moonlighting or patriotism? *Military Psychology, 5:* 113–125, 1993.

Lehman, D.R. (1993). Continuing the tradition of research on war: The Persian Gulf War. *Journal of Social Issues, 49:* 1–14, 1993.

Maddi, S.R.: The existential neurosis. *Journal of Abnormal Psychology, 72:* 311–325, 1967.

Maddi, S.R: The search for meaning. In M. Page (Ed.): *Nebraska Symposium on Motivation.* Lincoln, NE: University of Nebraska Press, 1970.

Maddi, S.R.: *Personality theories: A comparative analysis* (3rd ed.). Homewood, IL: Dorsey Press, 1976.

Maddi, S.R.: Comments on trends in hardiness research and theorizing. *Consulting Psychology Journal, 51:* 67–71, 1999.

Maddi, S.R., Bartone, P.T., and Puccetti, M.A.: Stressful events are indeed a factor in physical illness: Reply to Schroeder and Costa (1984). *Journal of Personality and Social Psychology, 52:* 833–843, 1987.

Maddi, S.R., and Kobasa, S.C.: *The hardy executive.* Homewood, IL: Jones-Irwin, 1984.

Manning, F.R.: Morale, Cohesion and Esprit de Corps. In R. Gal and A.D. Mangelsdorff (Eds.): *Handbook of Military Psychology*. Chichester, UK: Wiley, 1991.

Martin, J.A., Vaitkus, M.A., Marlowe, D.H., Bartone, P.T., Gifford, R.K., and Wright, K.M.: Psychological well-being among U.S. soldiers deployed from Germany to the Gulf War. *Journal of the U.S. Army Medical Department (September/October)*: 29–34, 1992.

Office of the Secretary of Defense: Report of the Quadrennial Defense Review: Section V, Forces and Manpower. Washington, DC: Office of the Secretary of Defense (http://www.defenselink.mil/pubs/qdr/sec5.html), 1997.

Roth, D.L., Wiebe, D.J., Fillingim, R.B., and Shay, K.A.: Life events, fitness, hardiness, and health: A simultaneous analysis of proposed stress-resistance effects. *Journal of Personality and Social Psychology, 57:* 136–142, 1989.

Rundell, J.R., and Ursano, R.J.: Psychiatric responses to war trauma. In R.J. Ursano and A.E. Norwood (Eds.): *Emotional aftermath of the Persian Gulf War: Veterans, families, communities and nations* (pp. 43–81). Washington, DC: American Psychiatric Press, 1996.

Scheier, M.F., and Carver, C.S.: Optimism, coping, and health: Assessment and implications of generalized outcome expectancies. *Health Psychology, 4:* 219–247, 1985.

Seligman, M.E.P.: *Learned Optimism*. New York: Alfred A. Knopf, 1991.

Siebold, G.L.: Small Unit Dynamics: Leadership, cohesion, motivation and morale. In R.H. Phelps and B.J. Farr (Eds.): *Reserve component soldiers as peacekeepers* (pp. 237–236). Alexandria, VA: U.S. Army Research Institute for the Social and Behavioral Sciences, 1996.

Solomon, Z., and Flum, H.: Life events, combat stress reaction and posttraumatic stress disorder. *Social Science and Medicine, 26:* 319–325, 1988.

Snyder, C.R., Harris, C., Anderson, J.R., Holleran, S.A., Irving, L.M., Sigmon, S.T., Yoshinobu, L., Gibb, J., Langelle, C., and Harney, P.: The will and the ways: Development and validation of an individual differences measure of hope. *Journal of Personality and Social Psychology, 60:* 570–585, 1991.

Stouffer, S.A., Lumsdaine, A.A., Lumsdaine, M.H., Williams, R.M., Smith, M.B., Janis, I.L., Star, S.A,. and Cottrell, L.S.: *The American soldier. (Vol. 2): Combat and its aftermath*. Princeton, NJ: Princeton University Press, 1949.

Stuart, J.A., and Bliese, P.D.: The long-term effects of Operation Desert Storm on the psychological distress of U.S. Army Reserve and National Guard veterans. *Journal of Applied Social Psychology, 28:* 1–22, 1998.

Sutker, P.B., Uddo, M., Brailey, K., and Allain, A.N.: *Journal of Social Issues, 49:* 1–14, 1993.

Walker, W.E.: Comparing Army reserve forces: A tale of multiple ironies, conflicting realities, and more certain prospects. *Armed Forces and Society, 18:* 303–322, 1992.

Wiebe, D.J.: Hardiness and stress moderation: A test of proposed mechanisms. *Journal of Personality and Social Psychology, 60:* 89–99, 1991.

Wilson, B.J. (Ed.): *The Guard and Reserve in the total force: The first decade, 1973–1983*. Washington, DC: National Defense University Press, Fort McNair, 1985.

Wolfe, J., Keane, T.M., and Young, B.L.: From soldier to civilian: Acute readjustment patterns of returned Persian Gulf veterans. In R.J. Ursano and A.E. Norwood (Eds.): *Emotional aftermath of the Persian Gulf War: Veterans, families, communities and nations* (pp. 477–500). Washington, DC: American Psychiatric Press, 1996.

Chapter 8

EARLY POSTTRAUMATIC INTERVENTIONS: FACILITATING POSSIBILITIES FOR GROWTH

LAWRENCE G. CALHOUN AND RICHARD G. TEDESCHI

INTRODUCTION

TRAUMATIC EVENTS ARE NOT UNCOMMON for people in general and critical incidents are a routine part of the work for persons in a variety of occupations (Murphy, Hurrell, Sauter, & Keita, 1995; Norris, 1992). Police officers, fire fighters, military and emergency medical personnel, for example, routinely face extremely stressful, and sometimes life-threatening situations. Such highly demanding situations as earthquakes, fires, riots, floods, major transportation accidents and situations where children are at great risk or are seriously harmed, can place those exposed to these events at risk for significant levels of distress and posttraumatic life disruption. Intrusive thoughts and images, highly distressing emotions, negative changes in behavior, and a variety of physical symptoms and complaints can occur in the aftermath of a traumatic situation or critical incident (Tedeschi & Calhoun, 1995).

There is also considerable evidence, however, suggesting that the struggle with highly challenging circumstances can produce significant positive changes for many persons coping with trauma. We have termed these changes *posttraumatic growth*. Posttraumatic growth is positive change that the individual experiences as a result of the struggle with a traumatic event (Calhoun & Tedeschi, 1999). Persons facing such difficult and diverse events as the death of a loved one, cancer, a house fire, criminal assault, serious accident, paraplegia, the birth of a medically fragile infant, rheumatoid arthritis, serious heart attack, the sinking of a ship, and military combat have reported significant positive changes in their struggle with the aftermath of the trauma (Tedeschi & Calhoun, 1995).

Posttraumatic growth, although it may have some similarities with hardiness, resilience, and related concepts is distinctly different from them. The words hardy, resilient, and their synonyms have been used to describe persons who, in spite of exposure to highly stressful and demanding life circumstances, nevertheless withstand or bounce back psychologically without developing deficiencies or psychological problems. Posttraumatic growth refers to something different. The experience of posttraumatic growth is one in which the individual describes significant positive changes arising from the struggle. Individuals do not simply survive without negative effects, they experience themselves as *better* than they were before the traumatic event.

The kinds of posttraumatic growth reported tend to fall into three general categories, as follows: changes in one's sense of self, changes in relationships with others, and changes in one's spirituality or religion. In this chapter, we will describe these three general domains of growth, and then discuss how a posttraumatic growth perspective might be applied in the context of posttraumatic interventions.

POSTTRAUMATIC GROWTH

It is important to underscore, at the beginning of this discussion, two general trends in the findings on posttraumatic growth. First, although these changes are commonly reported, they do not inevitably occur in all persons struggling with trauma. Second, the experience of growth does not necessarily indicate that the individual will be free of the potentially negative consequences of traumatic events. Growth is not guaranteed and it will not necessarily eliminate the pain. With those caveats in place, we turn to a summary of the general domains of posttraumatic growth.

Changes in Self

A common response of persons who have faced highly challenging situations is the sense that if they have managed somehow to cope with the traumatic event, then they must be capable of facing just about anything. A man who had become paraplegic as the result of an accident, for example, reported that once he went through the arduous rehabilitation process that was required of him, he knew that he could face just about anything in life. This general sense of increased self-reliance is a frequently noted element of the experience of persons grieving the death of a spouse. Eighty-eight percent of the sample of widows and widowers we interviewed reported that they felt better able to face other life crises (Calhoun & Tedeschi, 1989–90).

Although this kind of growth has been reported by persons coping with a variety of crises (Tedeschi & Calhoun, 1995), persons whose life roles have restricted their past options may find unique opportunities for change in the struggle with circumstances forced on them by traumatic loss. This was the case with the older women in the sample of widows described above. Having been married and lived in a cultural climate that severely limited the roles available to women, widows were required to begin to deal with and learn to manage challenges that they had not had to before. "I feel I can take better care of business affairs. . . ," "I am now more assured," "I now do things . . . I am no longer just an extension of a marriage" (Calhoun & Tedeschi, 1989–90, p. 268).

This view of oneself as stronger and having higher levels of self-efficacy that many persons experience in the struggle with trauma may, paradoxically, coexist with an increased experience of being vulnerable to life's tragedies. We have referred to this kind of growth experience as seeing oneself as vulnerable, yet stronger. A typical posttraumatic change in self-perception is that although there is an increased recognition that one's life may not be as safe and predictable as one previously assumed (Janoff-Bulman, 1992), there is also an increased sense that the individual now has greater strength to meet any other challenges that life may offer (Tedeschi & Calhoun, 1995).

Changes in Relationships with Others

As people struggle with traumatic events, it is not uncommon for them to report a significant change in their relationships and their orientation to other people. One common theme is "now I know who my real friends are and we are so much closer than before I had to go through this." For example, some families report becoming closer as a result of the struggle with grief, and some couples report becoming significantly closer as a result of coping with a heart attack in one of the spouses (Tedeschi, Park, & Calhoun, 1998). The struggle with a serious life-threatening illness, such as cancer, may serve as a catalyst for individuals to strip away false social masks. And, the increased self-disclosure can serve as a catalyst for the further deepening of interpersonal relationships.

For some people, having to face critical life events leads them to experience a greater sense of compassion for other people who also are suffering. "I know what they are going through and my heart goes out to them" is how this general change might be summarized. Although the data is still quite limited, there is some suggestion that in addition to an increased sense of compassion for others who, there is an increase in altruistic behavior (Wuthnow, 1991). For example, a highly successful attorney who herself had experienced the serious and life-threatening illness of her husband, actively began to do pro bono work, representing the rights of individuals with AIDS. The struggle with traumatic events can have the effect of strengthening and deepening some of the individual's connections to other people, and in some ways can lead to an increase in a sense of greater connectedness to other human beings in general.

In the words of poet John Donne, many individuals who have faced critical life problems themselves have no need to ask "for whom the bell tolls"—they very much experience the tolling of the bell as calling for something from them. For example, emergency personnel who have experienced significant distress during critical incidents in the past, may very well be more attuned to the possible need for personal support by others facing critical incidents.

It is important to remember that positive change in interpersonal relationships arising from the struggle with trauma is neither inevitable nor universal. Traumatic circumstances can also put a strain on intimate social connections, producing both short-term and long-term impairment in the quality of relationships. For example, while some families who have experienced the death of a loved one draw closer in the tragic aftermath, others are pushed apart (Lehman et al., 1993).

Changes in Spirituality and Life Orientation

Life's critical incidents tend to shake the cognitive foundations upon which world views are built (Calhoun & Tedeschi, 1998). Much like an earthquake that can shake the foundations of buildings, perhaps to the point of leading them to crumble and cause the building to collapse, traumatic events can shatter the assumptions on which people build their everyday lives (Calhoun & Tedeschi, 1998; Janoff-Bulman, 1992). In the cognitive processing that usually follows life trauma, individuals may experience significant positive changes in their world view. Traumatic events call into question the previous way of understanding one's life and one's place in the world. Most people try to make sense out of what has happened, and in this process of posttraumatic cognitive review and rumination, significant growth can occur. Individuals may experience a significant change in life priorities, an increased appreciation for life, and for some individuals, an increased importance and positive growth in their spiritual or religious lives.

Critical life events can serve as a reminder of what should be more and what should be less important in life. Persons who have been diagnosed with cancer, for example, often report a radical change in their sense of what is important in life (Taylor, Lichtman, & Wood, 1984). Elements that in the past had received less time and attention may be given new importance, and other elements may be relegated to much lower priority. The goal of rapid promotion in a career may give way to the importance of taking life easier, enjoying it more, and spending more time with one's family and friends. Or, perhaps a much simpler and more specific shift is illustrated by the emergency medical technician who, as a result of treating children severely injured in an automobile accident, simply goes home and hugs the children, and makes a personal commitment to "just love them even more than I have, and show it too."

"I just appreciate each day so much more now." This is also a change often reported by persons who have had to struggle with life trauma. What might have, before the crisis, not been noticed at all now may be imbued with much greater significance. The small and simple things can become much more appreciated: a sunset, a walk on the beach, a child's smile, or even the bad jokes told by a fellow police officer in attempts to break the monotony or the tension. As Richard Belzer remarked about his own illness, life trauma can be "a cosmic slap in the face." For many persons struggling with trauma, the "cosmic slap" not only leads them to change priorities, but for some persons it can lead to significant positive change in their spirituality or religion.

In one of our studies (Calhoun, Tedeschi, & Lincourt, 1992, August), we talked to people who had experienced highly traumatic events (e.g., victim of violent crime, sudden death of a loved one in an accident) and asked them how their spiritual beliefs had been affected. Although there were a variety of different trajectories described, a significant portion of the respondents reported that in the struggle with trauma their spiritual and religious beliefs had become stronger and had assumed a more important role in their lives. The traumatic event can, for some persons, be a reckoning time. The trauma can lead to a significant degree of ruminating, "chewing the cud," about one's life path, and in the process of facing the reckoning time, some persons develop a deeper and more meaningful spiritual or religious life. As with other domains of posttraumatic growth, this process of existential or spiritual development does not happen to all persons struggling with crises and there may be significant positive changes in some spiritual domains but not in others. But, it is important to remember that for some persons trauma may produce a loss of faith and meaning (Herman, 1992).

These three general clusters of posttraumatic growth encountered in the struggle with the aftermath of trauma, suggest that an expansion of the way posttraumatic interventions are understood. In agreement with general paradigm shifts that are already underway (Antonovsky, 1987; Dunning, 1999; O'Leary, Alday, & Ickovis, 1998), we are suggesting an expansion of the perspectives used in posttraumatic interventions. The way the usual interventions are undertaken and the ways in which they are conceptualized, could profitably be expanded to include considerations about posttraumatic growth–a posttraumatic growth perspective on posttraumatic interventions.

INTERVENTIONS: A POSTTRAUMATIC GROWTH PERSPECTIVE

As illustrated in other chapters in this volume, there are a variety of specific approaches, having a variety of different names, that have been developed to address exposure to job-related traumatic events. Critical incident stress debriefing, emotional first aid, psychological debriefing, defusing, multiple stressor debriefing, and crisis intervention are among the labels used (Weaver, 1995). The primary focus of these post-traumatic interventions is not only to provide some immediate support and relief from psychological distress, but also to prevent the development of significant posttraumatic psychological symptoms.

Clearly, addressing current problems and the prevention of future ones are desirable and appropriate goals of posttraumatic interventions. Critical incidents can produce significant distress and traumatic events can place some persons at risk for the development of psychiatric problems. Although self-reports of individuals participating in posttraumatic interventions tend to be positive (Robinson & Mitchell, 1993), the evidence on the utility of debriefings is less clear when only randomized controlled trials are examined (Rose & Bisson, 1998). Nevertheless, early posttraumatic interventions have become quite typical in the United States and elsewhere (Everly & Mitchell, 1995). But for the vast majority of persons experiencing traumas, the outcome is likely to be quite good, and therefore the posttraumatic benefits discussed above should also be given consideration along with symptom prevention. It must also be made clear that there is limited information on the processes by which posttraumatic growth occurs and how one might encourage it in the posttraumatic intervention process (for more extensive discussions in both of these domains, readers may want to consult Tedeschi, Park, & Calhoun, 1998 and Calhoun & Tedeschi, 1999).

With these cautionary notes in mind we will offer some suggestions about how issues of posttraumatic growth might be dealt with in the context of early posttraumatic interventions. We will be drawing on our combined experiences as clinical psychologists, the general literature on trauma and its aftermath, and the literature on posttraumatic growth.

General Considerations for Interventions

The brief posttraumatic interventions currently in use tend to follow a clearly prescribed format, with specific phases. The general assumption is that the phases will always be followed in the same sequence and that all phases will, at least ideally, be completed before the debriefing meeting is over (Everly, 1995; Weaver, 1995). Our view is that recommended phases are useful guidelines for leaders, and they may be particularly useful for laypersons without extensive experience beyond training in the debriefing process. However, it may be better for more experienced clinicians to view the recommended phases as a very helpful framework that should be applied as appropriate to specific contexts, with a reasonable amount of flexibility.

In working with individual clients who have been exposed to highly traumatic events, a key component of intervention is to assist the person to recover a sense of safety (Herman, 1992). A similar process is also an important consideration for the brief early posttraumatic interventions designed for groups, such as critical incident debriefings. Not only does the need for a sense of safety apply to any immediate physical threat, but also to the general sense that the posttraumatic intervention itself is "safe." Participants not only need to experience, but leaders must also provide, a context in which those present can accurately perceive that it is "safe" to express themselves and to freely participate (Jenkins, 1996; Weaver, 1995).

It is possible that in some specific contexts, implicit norms for behavior during brief posttraumatic interventions develop which encourage a full and complete report of the horrible components of the event. As more individuals participate in such interventions, a general assumption may begin to be made by both laypersons and professional clinicians, that it is both important and good to "spill it all." It is, of course, crucial for individual participants to feel supported and accepted by the participants in the intervention, particularly when relating aspects of the event that are troublesome to them. However, it may not necessarily be useful for leaders to engage in excessive probing about the details of horror.

Leaders of posttraumatic interventions may inadvertently encourage the group norm that promotes the vivid dwelling on the traumatic elements of the situation and the helplessness and distress of the individual's response. It is important to encourage the group to accept, listen, and to offer empathy and support throughout the intervention, since these elements are highly important to participants (Jenkins, 1996). It seems equally important, however, to also keep a focus on elements of good coping that are articulated or demonstrated by participants (Juhnke & Osborne, 1997). The inadvertent reexposure to traumatic elements may be particularly likely during the phase of the intervention in which participants are encouraged to describe what happened and what their roles were in the events. An excessively rigid adherence to the "phases," and how they are supposed to progress, may unintentionally discourage participants who wish to articulate positive coping strategies.

In order to maintain a posttraumatic growth perspective on interventions, a strategy we recommend is for leaders to *listen for and attend to* (Calhoun & Tedeschi, 1999) possible themes of growth in what participants articulate. However, in the immediate context of the traumatic event, such as would be the case with most preventative posttraumatic interventions, this must be done with great care and clinical skill. *Early on is not a useful time to explicitly encourage either "recovery" or "growth."* The early posttraumatic period is not a time for clinicians or group leaders to begin talking about how the struggle with trauma can be a good thing or to begin an explicit focus on "recovery." As a general rule, this focus on growth or recovery in the immediate posttraumatic time tends to be at best unappreciated and at worst grotesquely insensitive.

However, if participants themselves articulate themes of potential posttraumatic growth, it is appropriate for group leaders to acknowledge and validate them. For example, it is not uncommon for participants to articulate, at least at some point during immediate posttraumatic interventions, a desire to make something good come out of the tragedy. Once a critical incident debriefer is oriented to the possibility of posttraumatic growth, it may be surprising to see how many references are made to this from members of groups being debriefed. We think it is quite appropriate for leaders to help participants to explicitly acknowledge that theme, and perhaps to help the group steer a course in the direction of identifiable potential positive goals.

The suggestions to group leaders who wish to utilize a posttraumatic growth perspective on brief posttraumatic interventions can be summarized with the simplistic phrase—*listen* for posttraumatic growth, *attend* to it, and *point it out*. However, there is a crucial semantic issue that we have consistently argued for (Calhoun & Tedeschi, 1998, 1999; Tedeschi & Calhoun, 1995). It is important to talk about *growth as a result of the struggle* with a difficult event, not a direct consequence of the event itself. Participants may be told that "as you *struggle* to come to terms and cope with what has happened, some of you may find that you are developing in new and effective ways." It is, of course, important to remind participants that horrible events can also take a serious and highly negative toll. Because it may not be appropriate to address issues of growth in the interventions conducted in the immediate aftermath of a critical incident, there may be some utility in brief posttraumatic interventions that provide the opportunity for more than one session (Juhnke & Osborne, 1997). Interventions that include two or three sessions, for example, separated by periods of one week, can offer not only the possibility of helping participants identify coping strategies that have proved helpful, but there also exists the possibility that themes of posttraumatic growth will begin to be articulated.

Even in interventions that have only one session, however, it may be possible to include information about posttraumatic growth in the "teaching" or "education" phase. This phase typically occurs toward the end of the session. Group leaders provide direct psychoeducational instruction in a variety of matters related to coping strategies and further potential consequences of severe stress. In addition to what is already suggested as desirable components of this part of the intervention, leaders may also want to introduce the possibility of posttraumatic growth. To the extent that listening and attending to themes of posttraumatic growth during the session has proved fruitful, then leaders can refer to these as examples of what is being discussed.

For example, in one intervention the participants were workers at a resident facility for severely handicapped adults. A fire had swept through one of the buildings, killing one of the residents. During the session, several members had been highly supportive of the supervisor in charge on the day of the fire, moving their chairs closer, putting their arms around the individual, and providing verbal reassurance that all that was possible had been done. In the psychoeducational phase of the intervention, in discussing the possibility that some people experience some degree of positive change in their struggle with highly stressful situations, the leader pointed to the highly supportive way in which group members had treated the supervisor, as perhaps providing a basis for continued supportive relationships between those people.

When leaders address the teaching/education functions of the intervention, we are suggesting that references to possible positive changes arising from the struggle to cope with the traumatic exposure be explicitly addressed. The leader can say something like the following:

> In addition to the difficulties and added burdens you may experience as a result of this incident, some people report that as they struggle to come to terms with situations like this they can see some good coming from the bad. Some people may experience some shift in their priorities in life, with some things becoming more important to them than before. Other people talk about how they may be a little more compassionate toward other people, sometimes especially people who are suffering somehow; they may feel their hearts going out to them more than before. There may also be the possibility that you may feel a little closer, a little more connected to other people, maybe those that have shared this debriefing experience with you. That might present some opportunities for increasing team support once we leave here today. So, what I am saying is that being forced to struggle with the really tough kinds of situations like the one we have been wrestling with, can not only put you at risk for some negative things, but the struggle to come to terms with events like this may also prompt you to develop in ways that would not have happened otherwise. What happened was *not* a good thing, but maybe there are some good things that can come out of it for some people, at least in some ways.

Following is a brief description of an incident and of some aspects of the brief psychological intervention that followed. The case is illustrative. We have altered many elements to maintain the confidentiality of all involved.

A TRAUMATIC INCIDENT: ROBBERY, HOSTAGE, AND SUICIDE

It began as the robbery of a fast food restaurant. However, it did not go as the robber had planned. A delay in the speed with which the cashier opened the cash register as ordered led the gunman to take a hostage. The police were called by an employee who had escaped in the initial confusion, and who had run to a store next to the restaurant. But other employees remained as hostages of the gunman. A lengthy period of hostage negotiations occurred. In the next several hours, negotiators were able to obtain the release of all the hostages except two. As the standoff extended into the next several hours the police became concerned that the remaining hostages were not going to be released, and there was the enhanced worry caused by the increasing degree of labile and irrational behavior on the part of the criminal. The decision was made to mount an assault. During the operation, the gunman shot himself in the head in front of the remaining hostages.

A posttraumatic intervention was provided for the restaurant personnel who had been working in the store that evening, in accordance with the policies and procedures of the restaurant chain. The employees involved were gathered together at the restaurant the next day. There was a mixture of new employees and veterans, managerial and line workers, young and old. There was also a husband and wife who worked together that night. The usual review of the events was done, together with a report of how events had affected each one during the past 18 hours. In this debriefing, positive messages were given about how well people were coping and how the anxieties that were described were normal reactions, and how these reactions could be understood. As is typical in these situations (Avery, King, Bretherton & Orner, 1999), the group did not request additional meetings, and most felt that they were coping well enough. But, following company policy, the group was told that they would be gathered together again in a few days as a follow-up. The follow-up sessions present a better opportunity for discussion beyond the recounting of events, including the consideration of positive coping and posttraumatic growth.

At the follow-up meeting several days later, most employees had returned to work, although one adolescent girl had not, as her parents felt that it was unsafe for her to work at the store. This person was contacted by telephone, since there was concern that her parents' concern might prevent her from confronting a situation that may evoke some fear, leading to a maintenance of the fear. The rest of the group discussed their ways of coping with a return to work. The debriefer focused on the constructive coping strategies used and put into a normal context the thoughts, emotional reactions, and behaviors that employees had noticed in themselves in the aftermath of the incident. Below is an excerpt that illustrates how this was done:

Debriefer: Linda mentioned that she is watching customers more closely now. Are any of you others doing that? (*Almost all the employees respond affirmatively*).

Debriefer: So, why are you doing this?

Linda: Well, I want to make sure we're not robbed again.

Bob: I'd like to get a head start on the next one.

Kim: Yeah, I'm ready to run like hell!

Linda: You got a pretty good head start this time, Bob! (*Laughter*)

Debriefer: So, you're all looking for ways to protect yourselves and each other.

Linda: Yeah, if we can.

Debriefer: Do you think you can?

Connie: To some extent, but you can't stop all the crazy people who decide they want to rob us.

Debriefer: What do you do about them?

Linda: Well, like Kim said, run like hell! (*Laughter*)

Connie: Yeah, but sometimes you can't. Bob made it out, but you and me and the others couldn't.

Debriefer: Then you're left with trying to cope with the situation. How do you think you did?

Connie: I think we did pretty well. No one got really hurt. Beth was amazing the way she kept talking to the guy, trying to keep him calm. You were great Beth!

Beth: It was weird, I just felt some sort of calmness come over me after I started praying. I felt God was with me, and what I'd do would be OK. You know, I feel bad he killed himself, even though he didn't hurt us, and I'm mad at him for putting us all in danger, he didn't have to do that.

Bob: Hey, better him than us!

Beth: I know, but I still wish it hadn't ended like that.

Linda: Yeah, me, too, but only because I've got this picture in my mind of his head blowing apart. Thanks a lot, fella.

At this point in this conversation, the debriefer has some choices. The choices basically represent a focus on positive or negative elements of the aftermath of the trauma that the employees are mention-

ing. The negative elements include Beth's apparent guilt at not stop-
ping the suicide, Linda's intrusive images of the gunman's suicide, and
the employees' difficulty in protecting themselves and each other from
future attacks. These should not be ignored, but in our approach to
debriefing, we do not make these experiences the focus. We put them
in the context of normal, expected human reactions to the aftermath of
traumatic situations, and then emphasize strength and possibility. First,
to "normalize" the reactions, the debriefer takes a poll.

Debriefer: Has anyone else here had pictures come to mind like Linda has?

Connie: Yeah, but I try to put them out of my mind.

Bob: I wasn't here for that but with all this talk of it, I feel like I'm making my
   own movie of it.

Kim: Yeah, I really don't want to think about that.

Linda: Sure, I saw it, I can remember it, but like Kim said, I try not to think
   about it.

Beth: I'm afraid I'll have nightmares about it, and sometimes it just pops into
   my head.

Debriefer: So all of you have had some experience of these pictures, even
   Bob, who has heard the story but did not see it. This is all quite expected
   in a situation like this–you're all going through something similar. It will
   be unpleasant at times to have these pictures pop up, but I'd like you to
   view this as some unpleasantness, and not something to get worried about.
   Connie, how do you try to put the pictures out of your mind?

Connie: I just try to think about something else instead.

Debriefer: How does that work for you?

Connie: Pretty good, but it's not perfect.

Debriefer: Sure. Connie's way is a good one. Don't try to battle any of the pictures from this incident. Just acknowledge to yourself that this is the
   unpleasantness I mentioned would likely happen for a while, and then
   gently turn your thoughts to something else. Do you think you can do
   that?

Kim: Yeah, but they'll still come back for a while?

Debriefer: Sure. It's a memory you can always have, just like you remember
   other things from your life, good and bad. Now this is part of your life,
   too. OK? (*Assent from various members of the group*)

Debriefer: But you know what else there is to remember from this? (*Here the
   debriefer pauses for effect.*) To me, listening to this group, I'm struck by the
   way you helped each other through this.

Bob: I have to admit I wasn't much help.

Debriefer: Does anyone here begrudge Bob taking off at the beginning of the
   robbery?

Connie: I would have gotten out if I could have.

Beth: And Bob got next door right away to call the police.

Linda: I think Bob helped, too, because he told the cops who was in there and everything–they had details they wouldn't have had.

Debriefer: OK, Bob?

Bob: Yeah, I just didn't want you all thinking I was a wimp.

Debriefer: Instead, it sounds like you played an important role in everyone coming out OK, too. In fact, that was what I was going to say. Each of you did the right thing. Beth, you were able to talk with the guy like Connie said. And all of you were able to calm yourselves and each other enough so as not to unnerve this guy further. You did a great job. Like Connie said, all of you came out unhurt. You can remember that fact, and that you did the right things in very difficult circumstances. It's understandable and normal to be shaken by this, but at the same time, your fears didn't prevent you from doing the right thing.

Linda: That's right. And Beth, I don't think you could have kept that man from killing himself, any more than the rest of us. He did all this out of his own choice. That's a fact, too.

Connie: Yeah, Beth, give yourself a break on that one.

Kim: Beth's always hard on herself.

Debriefer: Hear what they're saying, Beth?

Beth: Yes.

Debriefer: What do you think?

Beth: I guess they're right.

Debriefer: Not too sure?

Beth: Not totally.

Debriefer: This is an issue for you that you may have to take more time to sort out. But it is clear to me that the people who were there with you respect what you did. So don't ever forget that, OK?

Beth: Right, they were there.

Debriefer: Right. And you said you prayed.

Beth: Yeah, and I guess I felt like God was with me.

Debriefer: So, God is probably all right with you too, because he was there, too.

Beth: I hadn't thought of it that way.

Debriefer: This looks like a good strong group to me. And I wouldn't be surprised if you felt even closer to each other after this.

Connie: I think so. We've really been through something together.

Debriefer: Yes, after people go through things like this they sometimes feel stronger in various ways–stronger personally, stronger in their relationships, in their faith, various things. I have to wonder what it has been like for Kim and Bob, our married couple.

Kim: You know, when we went home after this, Bob never looked better! (*Laughter*)

Bob: You looked great to me coming out of this place OK. I'll never forget the police taking you out, and there you were, OK after all. If you had gotten hurt, I don't know that I could ever live with myself, leaving like that.

Kim: Bob, the guy had me right there. There was nothing you could have done. Thank God you got out and got over there. If you'd tried to be some kind of movie hero we might all be dead.

Bob: OK, I hear ya.

Debriefer: So you two feel pretty tight after this?

Bob and Kim: Oh, yeah!

Linda: I went home and hugged my kid that night, you can believe that!

Beth: Exactly!

Debriefer: Things like this make you appreciate things a bit more.

Linda: That's right. It's shaken me up, but maybe in a good way, too.

Debriefer: Is that what you're experiencing too, along with the anxieties?

Beth: I think so. I thank God that He got me through this. He showed I can depend on Him.

Linda: I just wish God would keep the crazies out of here.

Connie: Well, I guess we can handle them if they show up again.

Debriefer: Yes, I think so. You can review with each other how you would handle similar situations in the future, now that you have some experience to go on, where you did very well. And I'd also encourage you to help out Beth and Bob with some of their doubts about themselves in this, since we all know that they did all they could to help. The company wants me to come out and check on employees after these kinds of things to make sure you're doing OK. I see no reason to believe you won't be OK. And I can see that you are handling it in ways that might really benefit you. Like I said, this is part of your life now—a terrible thing, but in some ways a strengthening thing, too. So let's recognize the bad and the good together in all this, OK? You can let me know if you want to talk again, the EAP folks can put you in touch.

Notice that throughout this part of the meeting, the debriefer capitalized on opportunities to highlight the normal and understandable nature of people's reactions, to note examples of strength, and to point toward possibility. We feel that there are few instances of psychological damage that are likely in situations like this, and that we have opportunity to offer basic lessons in psychological health and growth. Although debriefing is supposed to be a preventative measure, it will have more preventative power if the debriefer emphasizes good coping rather than possible symptom development. Furthermore, we cultivate seeds of posttraumatic growth that may be more commonplace than trauma symptoms. Furthermore, this fits with the experiences of people we debrief in the vast majority of circumstances. They experience themselves as being rather healthy, and coping well. Of course, there are variations in this, and when interventions are made after trauma, it is important to take note of those individuals who are having a rougher time. For example, in the situation described above, both Beth and Bob were experiencing some doubt and guilt. But the group was deemed healthy enough to take care of them, once the issues were raised and put before them.

We recognize that highly traumatic events and severely stressful incidents can challenge the coping mechanisms of even the hardiest individuals. These events can also place the individual at significant risk for high levels of distress. Taking a posttraumatic growth perspective on critical incidents does *not* suggest otherwise. It is desirable, however, to see the possibility of posttraumatic growth as an additional possible element to which the leaders of brief preventative posttraumatic interventions should attend. We are suggesting that the addition of posttraumatic growth as a possible consequence of the struggle with traumatic situations, appropriately and significantly expands the potential helpfulness of interventions designed to assist persons exposed to highly traumatic critical incidents.

REFERENCES

Antonovsky, A.: The salutogenic perspective: Toward a new view of health and illness. Advances: *Journal of the Institute for the Advancement of Health, 4:* 47–55, 1987.

Avery, A., King, S., Bretherton, R., and Orner, R.: Deconstructing psychological debriefing and the emergence of calls for evidence-based practice. *Traumatic Stress Points, 13:* 6–8, 1999.

Calhoun, L.G., and Tedeschi, R.G.: Beyond recovery from trauma: Implications for clinical practice and research. *Journal of Social Issues, 54:* 357–371, 1998.

Calhoun, L.G., and Tedeschi, R.G.: *Facilitating posttraumatic growth: A clinician's guide.* Mahwah, NJ: Lawrence Erlbaum Associates Publishers, 1999.

Calhoun, L.G., and Tedeschi, R.G.: Positive aspects of critical life problems: Recollections of grief. *Omega, 20:* 265–272, 1989–90.

Calhoun, L.G., Tedeschi, R.G., and Lincourt, A.: *Life crises and religious beliefs: Changed beliefs or assimilated events?* Paper presented at the meeting of the American Psychological Association, Washington, DC, 1992.

Dunning, C.: Postintervention strategies to reduce police trauma: A paradigm shift. In J. Violanti and D. Paton (Eds.): *Police Trauma.* Springfield, IL, Charles C Thomas, 1999.

Everly, G.S.: The role of the critical incident stress debriefing (CISD) process in disaster counseling. *Journal of Mental Health Counseling, 17:* 278–290, 1995.

Everly, G.S., and Mitchell, J.T.: Prevention of work-related posttraumatic stress: The critical incident stress debriefing process. In L.R. Murphy, J.J. Hurrell, S.L. Sauter, and G.P. Keita (Eds.): *Job Stress Interventions* (pp. 173–183) Washington, DC: American Psychological Association, 1995.

Herman, J.L.: *Trauma and recovery.* New York: Basic Books, 1992.

Janoff-Bulman, R.: *Shattered assumptions.* New York: Free Press, 1992.

Jenkins, S.R.: Social support and debriefing efficacy among emergency medical workers after a mass shooting incident. *Journal of Social Behavior and Personality, 11:* 477–492, 1996.

Juhnke, G. A., and Osborne, W. L.: The solution-focused debriefing group: An integrated postviolence group intervention for adults. *Journal for Specialists in Group Work, 22:* 66–76, 1997.

Lehman, D.R., Davis, C.G., Delongis, A., Wortman, C., Bluck, S., Mandel, D.R., and Ellard, J.H.: Positive and negative life changes following bereavement and their relations to adjustment. *Journal of Social and Clinical Psychology, 12:* 90–112, 1993.

Murphy, L.R., Hurrell, J.J., Sauter, S.L., and Keita, G.P. (Eds.): *Job stress interventions.* Washington, DC: American Psychological Association, 1995.

Norris, F. H.: Epidemiology of trauma: Frequency and impact of different potentially traumatic events on different demographic groups. *Journal of Consulting and Clinical Psychology, 60:* 409–418, 1992.

O'Leary, V.E., Alday, C.L., and Ickovics, J.R.: Models of life change and posttraumatic growth. In R.G. Tedeschi, C.L. Park, and L.G. Calhoun (Eds.) *Posttraumatic growth: Positive changes in the aftermath of crisis* (pp. 127–151). Mahwah, NJ: Lawrence Erlbaum Associates Publishers, 1998.

Robinson, R.C., and Mitchell, J.T.: Evaluation of psychological debriefings. *Journal of Traumatic Stress, 6:* 367–382, 1993.

Rose, S., and Bisson, J.: Brief early psychological interventions following trauma: A systematic review of the literature. *Journal of Traumatic Stress, 11:* 697–710, 1998.

Taylor, S.E., Lichtman, R.R., and Wood, J.V.: Attributions, beliefs in control, and adjustment to breast cancer. *Journal of Personality and Social Psychology, 46:* 489–502, 1984.

Tedeschi, R.G., and Calhoun, L.G.: *Trauma and Transformation—Growing in the aftermath of suffering.* Thousand Oaks, CA: Sage Publications, 1995.

Tedeschi, R.G., Park, C.L., and Calhoun, L.G. (Eds.): *Posttraumatic growth: Positive changes in the aftermath of crisis.* Mahwah, NJ: Lawrence Erlbaum Associates Publishers, 1998.

Weaver, J.D.: *Disasters: Mental health interventions.* Sarasota, FL: Professional Resource Press, 1995.

Wuthnow, R.: *Acts of compassion: Caring for others and helping ourselves.* Princeton, NJ: Princeton University Press, 1991.

Chapter 9

SCRIPTING TRAUMA: THE IMPACT OF PATHOGENIC INTERVENTION

JOHN M. VIOLANTI

INTRODUCTION

IT IS THE ULTIMATE GOAL of mental health professionals to help people deal with adversity in their lives. Have we accomplished this goal with traumatic stress? Have we intervened properly and effectively enough to bring about psychological well-being, or have we made the problem worse? As this chapter title implies, A reliance on pathogenic intervention methods may "script" an individual into traumatic symptoms. By scripting, we mean that pathogenic methods, rigid techniques, and strong group participation can cognitively restructure an individual's perceptions about trauma symptoms. Pathogenesis presupposes the "sick role." In other words, we imply to the person that if they weren't "sick" (i.e., affected by trauma), they wouldn't be at an intervention in the first place.

A second problem with pathogenic approaches is their ready acceptance. Contingents of police agencies, fire fighters, emergency and disaster workers, and others exposed to traumatic incidents are all looking for a "quick fix" to this problem. This is not necessarily wrong, but precisely what is accepted for this "fix" can have an impact on exposed individuals. A pathogenic model that not only assumes trauma symptomatology but also provides an immediate, rigidly defined remedy is thus very attractive. Such models may, however, forsake the individual for reasons of expediency and convenience.

This chapter approaches the process of traumatic stress intervention from the perspective that individuals to a large extent control their own destiny when it comes to dealing with trauma. The individual is thus an *active agent* in the process of healing, along with supportive help of professionals or peers. If we attempt to script individuals into a passive sick role, we adhere too closely to pathogenesis and may well overwhelm the positive strength of the individual.

The chapter first outlines attributes of current popular pathogenic intervention techniques. Second, we discuss how individual adoption of the sick role is facilitated by pathogenic approaches. Third is a discussion of salutogenic approaches to intervention and how individual qualities such as coping abilities, hardiness and resiliency may affect trauma exposure outcomes. Lastly, we discuss the impact of positive individual coping in reducing traumatic stress.

THE PRESENT SCRIPT: PATHOGENIC MODELS OF INTERVENTION

The process of trauma intervention developed in response to an increasing public perception that trauma affects a large number of people. Trauma intervention gathered its largest impetus from emergency service occupations, such as police, fire fighters, and emergency workers, where individuals are chronically exposed to traumatic incidents. These interventions had two purposes: (1) to allow individuals to talk about the traumatic incident; and (2) to facilitate a discussion among participants to educate them about stress reactions, personal coping strategies and counseling resources (see Stuhlmiller & Dunning, Chapter 2). Mitchell (1983) first termed this type of intervention process as "Critical Incident Stress Debriefing" (CISD).

Several studies have been undertaken to substantiate the efficacy of posttrauma intervention. Research has found that police officers, fire fighters, rescue personnel, and emergency medical workers do develop Posttraumatic Stress Disorder as a consequence of duty exposure, but not universally (Violanti, 1996). Notwithstanding, immediate trauma intervention has become the norm under these circumstances.

While some studies find brief trauma intervention to be effective (Mitchell & Bray, 1990; Mitchell & Everly, 1995; Robinson & Mitchell, 1993), others question its efficacy (Raphael, Meldrum, & McFarlane, 1996; Tucker et al., 1998). Other empirical analyses either failed to find evidence of benefit (Kenardy et al., 1996) or concluded that debriefing could have iatrogenic effects (Busuttil & Busuttil, 1995; Carlier et al., 1998). See Carlier and Gersons (Chapter 4) and Gist and Woodall (Chapter 5) for further discussion of this issue.

Widely used intervention models are pathogenic in orientation. It is presupposed that individuals exposed to traumatic incidents develop symptomatology and that group recovery techniques are required to ameliorate those symptoms (Rosenbaum, 1990). Reliance on such assumptions, coupled with strong group cohesion, can cognitively restructure or "script" an individual's perceptions about trauma symptoms. Dunning (1999) refers to this as "affective overload," where cognitions involving imagery, sensory-motor memory, and interpretative sense of meaning held by persons who experienced the event may confabulate and bring such material into their trauma set. While stress may be mitigated by disclosure to another, disclosure in a group where the element of social sharing involves interpretation and feedback does not appear to be as helpful (Stuhlmiller and Dunning, Chapter 2).

Following the Script: The "Sick Role"

The sick role is a social role which one assumes when they perceive that they are not in good health. The concept was first introduced by Parsons (1951) in an effort to explain socialization influence on medical patients. A primary factor determining the extent of sick role adherence is the doctor-patient relationship. As Gartly (1979) has established, the doctor is the expert in medicine and the patient is the novice. Thus, the doctor has a distinct advantage in defining whether or not the patient is sick. Given this advantage, most individuals will strive to be "good patients" (Gartly, 1979). Patients seek to fulfill the sick role by being complacent, trusting, respectful, and confident in the doctor's diagnosis (Maykovich, 1980). In essence, the paradigm of "sick role" is based on illness as acquiescence and the physician as an agent of social control (Gallagher, 1976; Kronenfeld & Glik, 1989). The notion of the sick role has also been applied to mental health (Braginsky, Braginsky,

& Ring, 1969; Goffman, 1971; Segall, 1979). Goffman's (1971) classic "insanity of place" describes the socialization process of becoming labeled and classified as mentally ill.

The use of pathogenic models to intervene in trauma may produce an effect on individuals similar to sick role socialization. Pathogenesis assumes "sickness"; persons are present at sessions because they have been exposed to trauma and are presumed "ill" with trauma symptoms. The mental health professional conducting the intervention is viewed by participants as experts who can cure them, much as the doctor is during medical diagnosis. Persons who attend are urged to fulfill the requirements of the pathogenic intervention (e.g., to cooperate, trust, and respect) much like medical patients (Kronenfield & Glik, 1989). This, in essence, makes them patients who are presumed ill and in need of care. Following the script becomes the way out of professed suffering from traumatic stress.

The sick role has its benefits, both individually and politically. An increasing number of police officers, for example, are being retired on stress disability due to job exposure to traumatic incidents. Such disabilities may be financially lucrative for individuals (Manocchia, Keller, & Ware, 1997). In one state, police officers retired for psychological disability receive two-thirds of their pay for the rest of their lives. Most of these officers may legitimately deserve such disability, but the impact of pathogenic trauma intervention may erroneously place them in such situations.

Politically, pathogenic models can legitimize an organization's efforts to "deal" with trauma among its members. Over the past 15 years, many police agencies have initiated employee assistance programs and teams to help officers exposed to stress and trauma in their work. While many of these programs are worthwhile, they sometimes serve as facades for organizations to demonstrate that they are "doing something" about trauma. The organization may fear liability issues, or may be pressured to fulfill contract demands by unions. Thus, the process comes full circle; officers exposed to trauma are first presumed to be "sick" and the organization proclaims to provide the cure—pathogenic intervention. In this way, both individual and organizational political goals are attended. Most "trauma units" or "shooting teams" in policing are specifically designed to help the officer deal with presupposed trauma. I once heard a police shooting team leader say to an officer: "if you didn't feel anything after you shot that guy, there is something wrong with you. You are not human."

Why do pathogenic models make assumptions that all exposed to trauma are afflicted? Such assumptions may be based on not knowing precisely who is suffering from trauma exposure, or it may the belief that a "shotgun" approach to intervention will in the least help those who are afflicted. But, what of those who were not affected by the traumatic event? Do pathogenic models "talk them into" trauma? These are important questions. Often the individual is not given the benefit of the doubt and assumptions are made that only intervention can solve problems associated with trauma.

A NEW APPROACH: SALUTOGENESIS

The Individual as an Agent of Change

It is important to note that traumatic exposure does not necessarily result in pathogenic outcomes. It may prove to be a positive growth experience for many. In fact, it has long been administrative procedure in law enforcement to rotate as many police officers as possible at a mass casualty scene in order to give as great a number of officers as possible the "training experience." Here, trauma exposure seems to be a well-accepted practice of a source of growth and development (Dunning, 1999).

Scripting does not necessarily have to be detrimental to trauma intervention. If intervenors employ a positive rather than negative perspective persons exposed to trauma can utilize their own personal strengths along with the support of others. In other words, affected individuals can be scripted positively instead of negatively, leading to salutogenic amelioration.

Salutogenesis refers to the individual's ability to not only survive traumatic events but also to achieve greater personal strength, understanding and purpose from the event (Antonovsky, 1987). Antonovsky (1993) first posited that a salutogenic orientation has far wider implications than simply focusing on the pathology of traumatized persons. Suedfeld (1996) refers to this human quality as "invictus," meaning unbeaten or unconquerable. Michenbaum (1995) refers to persons who develop "learned resourcefulness" from stressful situations. Salutogenesis views difficult or stressful life experiences such as trauma as promoting growth in the direction of positive change. Tedeschi and Calhoun (1996) organized growth from trauma into three broad categories of self-perception, improved personal relationships, and a positive philosophy of life. These approaches oppose pathogenesis, which assumes individual helplessness and ignores the individual's capacity for self-exploration and personal growth (Yalom & Lieberman, 1991; Jaffe, 1985).

The Salutogenic Approach recommends that mental health professionals perceive their role as facilitator in a debrief process that occurs informally as the professional participates in organizational processes of trauma recovery. In the remainder of this chapter, we address some individual actions which may help to reduce trauma: coping and vulnerability.

Individual Coping Abilities

Pathogenic models seldom pay tribute to the ability of individuals to cope effectively with trauma or distress. A salutogenic model would instead posit that the perception of positive benefits resulting from traumatic events may be the result of individual coping processes as well as outcomes of intervention (Tedeschi, Park, & Calhoun, 1998). For example, positive reinterpretation of events, positive reframing and event interpretive ability (Carver, Pozo, Harris, Noriega et al., 1993; Rothbaum, Weisz, & Snyder, 1982; Park, Cohen, & Murch, 1996; Lazarus & Folkman, 1984). Individual coping differences may thus account for successful trauma amelioration (Stroebe, Hansson, & Stroebe, 1993). Carver et al., (1993) found that negative coping strategies may impede adjustment of trauma while positive coping may increase positive responses to trauma. In addition, social support may be an important factor in helping individuals to find meaning in a traumatic event (Lyons, 1991; Park et al., 1996).

An Experiment in Coping with High Stress

The present author conducted a study of police recruits situated in an extreme high stress training situation (Violanti, 1993). Results demonstrated that highly distressed recruits utilized effective coping strategies more often than lower distressed recruits. The positive, controlled type of coping used by these recruits indicated that the training experience taught them how to more effectively deal with high stress and handle problems.

The police academy experience represents a time of abrupt resocialization for the recruit. It invokes a strong process designed to change the recruit from civilian to police officer and is similar to basic military indoctrination. An attempt is made by academy trainers to subject police recruits without prejudice to stressors of indoctrination, including academic, physical training and psychological harassment. In essence, the police academy was a situation where stressors were intentionally produced on a uniform basis over an extended period of time. It should be noted that police training employs such a protocol to help the police recruit learn to handle difficult and stressful situations, i.e., to grow as an individual.

The sample consisted of 180 police recruits attending the first week of a four-month basic police training session. The first five weeks of training involved rigorous periods of harassment, debasement, isolation, and loss of identity for the recruit. We considered this period as the most stressful time for recruits. They were separated from their families and subjected to the sudden shock of readjustment into police training.

Coping was assessed by the 66-item Ways of Coping Check List (WCCL), used extensively by Folkman and Lazarus (1986); Folkman et al. (1986), and others. The WCCL determines a broad range of coping and behavioral strategies that people use to manage internal and external demands in a stressful situation. Folkman et al. (1986) reported that their scale measures eight types of coping responses: (1) confrontive coping; (2) distancing; (3) self-control; (4) seeking social support; (5) accepting responsibility; (6) escape-avoidance; (7) planful problem solving; and (8) positive reappraisal. Higher scores indicated an increased use of particular coping methods. Measures of psychological stress and life events were also employed. The task was to determine what coping strategies were employed by highly stressed police recruits.

These results (Table 9.1) demonstrated that highly distressed recruits gained effective ways to cope through the experience of mili-

Table 9.1
A COMPARISON OF COPING STRATEGIES IN POLICE RECRUITS
WITH HIGH AND LOW LEVELS OF DISTRESS

Coping Strategy	Mean Distress Scores*	
	Low Distress	High Distress
Distancing	7.80	8.10
Self-control	8.77	11.18
Sought support	5.49	6.34
Accepted responsibility	3.47	4.98
Positive reappraising	8.06	8.97

* Stress was measured by the CES-D
(Center for Epidemiological Studies Depression Scale, Radloff, 1977)

tary-style police training. Keeping themselves mentally distant, controlling emotion and responses, accepting self-responsibility, and positively reappraising the situation were used more by highly distressed recruits than by lower distressed recruits. In essence, highly stressed recruits grew in their ability to cope with stress through exposure to extreme stress conditions. This was viewed by many recruits as a positive attribute to help them deal with stress in police work. Although we did not know the status of police recruit's personality dimensions prior to training, we did know that police training emphasized problem solving (Violanti, 1993). Recruits may have acquired this skill regardless of their stress levels through training; it may not have been part of their past repertoire of coping skills. The use of positive appraisal may have been the result of a newly acquired ability to solve problems, a perception by recruits that they had grown or changed in some positive way. As one recruit commented "I was a nobody before I came to the academy. This training showed me what I was made of. I feel like I can handle anything now."

This study suggests how individuals under extreme stress conditions can adapt and grow to the task. To some degree, efficacious coping and a positive outlook may be related to individual personality traits such as hardiness and resiliency (Tedeschi & Calhoun, 1996). These are not generally considered in a pathogenic framework. The concept of hardiness was developed to describe individuals who continuously rise to their life challenges and turn stressful experiences into opportunities for personal growth (Kobasa, Maddi, & Kahn, 1982). Hardiness also represents the ability of an individual to face difficult conditions with absolute courage (Williams, Weibe, & Smith, 1992; Bartone, Ursano, Wright, & Ingraham, 1989; Funk, 1992). Kobasa et al. (1982) describe hardiness as significantly influencing how people cope with stressful events. Resiliency, as defined by Bartone et al. (1989), involves the capability to recover after a stressful encounter and to make quick adjustments through coping. Both hardiness and resiliency are described in greater detail in other chapters throughout this book.

CONCLUSION

This chapter introduced the concept of scripting trauma, which refers to the effect produced by pathogenic intervention models that assume symtomatology due to trauma exposure. Such methods, with rigid protocols and lack of follow-up can cognitively restructure an individual's perceptions about trauma symptoms. Lacking in pathogenic approaches is the utilization of individual strengths to deal with trauma. Indeed, the participant in a pathogenic trauma intervention may not be "sick," and may possess resources such as coping, hardiness and resiliency to such an extent that they will successfully deal with the traumatic event. The inner strength of every human being may still be beyond our scientific comprehension. We must continue to explore this untapped resource that can make even the most tragic personal event one of positive and enduring growth.

Individual coping is an essential part of recovery from any stressful life event. Trauma intervention protocols should consider incorporating transactional models of coping in their systems. Transactionism views psychological distress as resulting from the interaction of many factors, including individual appraisal of the situation (Aldwin, 1994). The individual's ability to cognitively "fit" coping to an appraisal of the traumatic event should not be underestimated (Conway & Terry, 1992; Vitaliano et al., 1990). In sum, trauma, individual appraisal, coping, and psychological well-being all occur in a dynamic transactional relationship (Lazarus & Folkman, 1984). This is contrary to the static nature of pathogenesis.

The majority of those exposed to traumatic events recover without external intervention. While some individuals may experience severe reactions, it is important for intervenors to recognize that individuals have their own script for dealing with life adversities. If such professionals continue to preach preordained trauma, people may continue to believe them. Individuals should be allowed to make their own appraisal of just how "sick" they are when exposed to trauma.

Moving Toward a Paradigm Shift

Kuhn (1970) has stated that counterinstances in themselves are not sufficient to cause a paradigm to be discarded. This is true because what is legitimized as scientific fact is largely dictated by the paradigm itself, and all paradigms outlaw some observations that would be recognized by others. This was referred to by Kuhn (1970) as the "assimilative" function of a paradigm; more likely to be adjusted than discarded. A paradigm will be declared invalid only if an alternate candidate is available and accepted to take its place.

If our analysis in this chapter is legitimate, perhaps we have met Kuhn's conditions for a paradigm shift. We have attempted to demonstrate in this paper the problems of present trauma intervention paradigms and the existence of one alternative paradigm: Salutogenesis. In terms of Kuhn's (1970) structure, we have, in the least, made apparent the desirability of such a paradigm shift. For any existing paradigm to be maintained, it must continue to satisfy not only the rigors of science, but also that of common sense. Neither should be disregarded.

REFERENCES

Aldwin, C.M.: *Stress, coping, and development: An integrative perspective.* New York: Guilford Press, 1994.

Antonovsky, A.: *Unraveling the mystery of health: How people manage stress and stay well.* San Francisco: Jossey-Bass Publishers, 1987.

Antonovsky, A.: The implications of salutogenesis: An outsider's view. In A. Turnbull, J. Patterson, S. Behr, D. Murphy et al. (Eds.): *Cognitive coping, families, and disability.* Baltimore, MD: Paul H. Brookes, 1993.

Bartone, P., Ursano, A.R., Wright, K., and Ingraham, L.: The impact of a military air disaster on the health of assistance workers: A prospective study. *Journal of Nervous and Mental Disease, 777:* 317–328, 1989.

Bisson, J.I., and Deahl, M.P.: Psychological debriefing and prevention of post traumatic stress: More research is needed. *British Journal of Psychiatry, 165:* 717–720, 1994.

Braginski, B.M., Braginski, D.D., and Ring K.: *Methods of madness: The mental hospital as a last resort.* New York: Holt, Rinehart and Winston, 1969.

Busuttil, A., and Busuttil, W.: Psychological debriefing. *British Journal of Psychiatry, 166:* 676–677, 1995.

Carlier, I.V.E., Lamberts, R.D., Van Uchelen, A.J., and Gersons, B.P.R.: Disaster related posttraumatic stress in police officers: A field study of the impact of debriefing. *Stress Medicine, 14:* 143–148, 1998.

Carver, C.S., Pozo, C., Harris, S.D., Noriega, V., Scheir, M.F., Robinson, D.S., et al.: How coping mediate the effect of optimism on distress: A study of women with early stage breast cancer. *Journal of Personality and Social Psychology, 65:* 375–390, 1993.

Conway, V.J., and Terry, D.J.: Appraised controllability as a moderator of the effectiveness of different coping strategies: A test of goodness of fit hypothesis. *Australian Journal of Psychology, 44:* 1–7, 1992.

Deahl, M.P., and Bisson, J.I.: Dealing with disasters: Does psychological debriefing work? *Journal of Accident and Emergency Medicine, 12:* 255–258, 1995.

Dunning C.: Postintervention strategies to reduce police trauma: A paradigm shift. In J.M. Violanti and D. Paton (Eds.): *Police trauma: Psychological aftermath of civilian combat.* Springfield, IL: Charles C Thomas, 1999.

Dyregrov, A.: The process of psychological debriefings. *Journal of Traumatic Stress, 10:* 589–605, 1997.

Folkman, S., and Lazarus, R.: Stress process and depressive symptomatology. *Journal of Abnormal Psychology, 95:* 107–113, 1986.

Folkman, S., Lazarus, R., Gruen, R., and Delongis, A.: Appraisal, coping, health status, and psychological symptoms. *Journal of Personality and Social Psychology, 50:* 571–579, 1986.

Funk, S.C.: Hardiness: A review of theory and research. *Health Psychology, 11:* 335–345. 1992.

Gallagher, E.B.: Lines of reconstruction and extension in the Parsonian sociology of illness. *Social Science and Medicine, 10:* 207–218, 1976.

Gartly, J.E.: *Patients, Physicians, and Illness: A Sourcebook in Behavioral Science and Health* (3rd ed.). New York, McMillan, 1979.

Goffman, E.: *Relations in Public.* New York: Harper, 1971.

Horowitz, M., Wilner, N., and Alverez, W.: Impact of event scale: A measure of subjective stress. *Psychosomatic Medicine, 41:* 209–218, 1979.

Jaffe, D.T.: Self-renewal: Personal transformation following extreme trauma. *Journal of Humanistic Psychology, 25:* 99–124, 1985.

Kenardy, J.A., Webster, R.A., Lewin, T.J., Carr, V.J., Hazell, P.L., and Carter G.L.: Stress debriefings and patterns of recovery following a natural disaster. *Journal of Traumatic Stress, 9:* 37–49, 1996.

Kobasa, S., Maddi, S., and Cahn, S.: Hardiness and health: A prospective study. *Journal of Personality and Social Psychology, 42:* 168–177, 1982.

Kronenfield, J.J., and Glik, D.C.: *Well roles: An approach to reincorporate role theory into medical sociology.* Association paper, American Sociological Association, 1989.

Kuhn, T.S.: *The Structure of Scientific Revolution* (2nd ed.). Chicago, IL: University of Chicago Press, 1970.

Lazarus, R.A., and Folkman, S.: *Stress, appraisal, and coping.* New York: Springer, 1984.

Lyons, J. A.: Strategies for assessing the potential for positive readjustment following trauma. *Journal of Traumatic Stress, 4:* 93–112, 1991.

Manocchia, M., Keller, S., and Ware, J., Jr.: *The sick role as moderator between employment status and health outcomes.* Association paper, American Sociological Association, 1997.

Maykovich, M.K.: *Medical sociology.* Sherman Oaks, CA: Alfred Publishing, 1980.

Meichenbaum, D.: *Stress inoculation training.* New York: Pergamon Press, 1985.

Mitchell, J.T.: When disaster strikes: The critical incident stress debriefing process. *Journal of Emergency Medical Services, 8:* 35–39, 1983.

Mitchell J.T., and Bray, G.: *Emergency service stress.* Englewood Cliffs, NJ: Prentice-Hall, 1990.

Mitchell, J.T., and Everly, G.S.: *Critical incident stress debriefing: An operations manual for the prevention of traumatic stress among emergency service workers.* Ellicott City, MD: Chevron, 1995.

Park, C.L., Cohen, L.H., and Murch, R.L.: Assessment and prediction of stress related growth. *Journal of Personality, 64:* 71–105, 1996.

Parsons, T.: *The social system.* Glencoe: Free Press, 1951.

Radloff, L.S.: The CES-D Scale: a self-report depression scale for research in the general population. *Applied Psychological Measurement, 1:* 385–401, 1977.

Raphael, B., Meldrum, L., and McFarlane, A.C.: Does debriefing after psychological trauma work? Time for randomized control trials. *British Journal of Psychiatry, 310:* 1479–1480, 1996.

Robinson, R.C., and Mitchell, J.T.: Evaluation of psychological debriefings. *Journal of Traumatic Stress, 6:* 367–382, 1993.

Rosenbaum, M.: *Learned resourcefulness: On coping skills, self-control, and adaptive behavior.* New York: Springer Publishing, 1990.

Rothbaum, F., Weicz, J.R., and Snyder, S.S.: Changing the world and changing the self: A two process model of perceived control. *Journal of Personality and Social Psychology, 42:* 5–37, 1982.

Segall, A.: The sick role concept: Understanding illness behavior. *Journal of Health and Social Behavior, 17:* 162–169, 1976.

Stroebe, M.S., Hansson, R.O., and Stoebe, W.: Contemporary themes and controversies in bereavement research. In M.S. Stroebe, W. Stroebe, and R.O. Hanssen (Eds.): *Handbook of bereavement.* New York: Cambridge University Press, 1993, pp. 457–471.

Suedfeld, P.: Homo invictus: The indomitable species. *Canadian Psychology, 38:* 164–173, 1997.

Tedeschi R., and Calhoun, L.: Posttraumatic growth inventory: Measuring the positive legacy of trauma. *Journal of Traumatic Stress, 9:* 455–471, 1996.

Tedeschi, R., Park, C., and Calhoun, L. (Eds.): *Posttraumatic growth: Positive change in the aftermath of crisis.* New York: Lawrence Erlbaum, 1998.

Tucker, P., Pfefferbaum, B., Vincent, R., Boehler, S., and Nixon, S.J.: Oklahoma City: Disaster challenges mental health and medical administrators. *Journal of Behavioral Health Service and Research, 25:* 93–99, 1998.

Violanti, J.M.: What does high stress training teach recruits? An analysis of coping. *Journal of Criminal Justice, 21:* 411–417, 1993.

Violanti, J.M.: Trauma stress and police work. In D. Paton and J.M. Violanti (Eds.):. *Traumatic stress in critical occupations: Recognition, consequences, and treatment.* Springfield, IL: Charles C Thomas, 1996.

Vitaliano, P.P., DeWolfe, D.J., Maiuro, R.D., Russo, J., and Katon, W.: Appraised changebility of a stressor of the relationship between coping and depression: A test of the hypothesis of fit. *Journal of Personality and Social Psychology, 59:* 582–592, 1990.

Williams, P., Wiebe, D., and Smith, T.: Coping processes as mediators of the relationship between hardiness and health. *Journal of Behavioral Medicine, 15:* 237–255, 1997.

Yalom, I.D., and Lieberman, M.A.: Bereavement and heightened existential awareness. *Psychiatry, 54:* 334–345, 1991.

Chapter 10

THE FUTURE IS ALWAYS BRIGHTER: TEMPORAL ORIENTATION AND ADJUSTMENT TO TRAUMA

Malcolm D. MacLeod

INTRODUCTION

IN THE AFTERMATH OF A TRAUMATIC EVENT, how often have we heard ourselves say that we think someone is *"coping well"?* For much of the time, we are making relative judgments that we think a traumatized person is coping better than we reckon most people would, or better than we imagine we would if we had experienced a similar traumatic episode. In some cases, the consequences of the trauma may be so severe and beyond our normal experiences that the fact that the person appears to be able to continue with any form of activity merits our admiration. Few of us, however, give any thought to what we actually mean by "coping." For lay people, coping is most often equated with behavioral outcome, i.e., how successful a person is perceived to be in resuming normal life following a traumatic episode. For psychologists, however, "coping" refers to the activities that are intentionally undertaken to tolerate, minimize or eradicate actual or perceived stressful or threatening effects of negative events (Lazarus & Folkman, 1984; Carver, Scheier, & Weintraub, 1989). These can range from the positive reinterpretation of the traumatic event, denial, and seeking social support to seeking assistance, taking direct action, and planning.

Coping effectiveness can be constrained by anger and frustration, intrusive ideation, emotional numbing, depression and anxiety (Collins, Taylor, & Skogan, 1990; Frazier, 1990; MacLeod, Carson, & Prescott, 1996; Winkel, Denkers, & Vrij, 1994). Similarly, the consequences of trauma which undermine previously cherished beliefs can have profound effects on coping (Janoff-Bulman, 1985; McCann & Pearlman, 1990). As a result, victims of trauma can often appear cognitively preoccupied, especially with issues concerned with how the incident had happened, why it had happened to them in particular, and the severity or extent of the emotional and practical consequences of the trauma (MacLeod et al., 1996). The cognitive processes by which people ascribe blame have been directly implicated in coping. Tennen and Affleck (1990), for example, argued that the act of blaming someone else can restrict the range of available coping strategies by alienating significant others and undermining self-efficacy beliefs. Those who appear to adapt best are those who can access a range of coping strategies, permitting greater flexibility in dealing with the emotional and practical consequences of the trauma (Silver & Wortman, 1980).

Focusing research on coping mechanisms alone, however, is unlikely to further our understanding of *how* people actually achieve psychological adjustment following trauma. We need to go beyond the study of those intentional activities undertaken by the trauma victim and consider the impact of habitual or automatic processes that may underlie recovery (cf. MacLeod et al., 1999; Graham, Dibben, & MacLeod, 1999). For individuals who have just experienced a traumatic event, or those for whom trauma is an occupational hazard (e.g., emergency service personnel), understanding the complex relationship between social cognition processes and psychological well-being may facilitate not only adjustment (MacLeod & Paton, 1999a) but promote resilience to trauma (Holman & Silver, 1998).

This chapter reviews recent advances in social cognition and evaluates their implications for the process of psychological adjustment following traumatic experience. A conceptual framework based around the theme of temporal orientation is developed and used to evaluate the implications of social cognition processes for developing effectiveness of trauma interventions.

SOCIAL COGNITION AND
RECOVERY FROM TRAUMA

Given a primary interest in the psychological health of people following trauma rather than the extent of behavioral change *per se,* we
need to consider models that are more applicable. The most dominant
of these have focused on the associations between attributions and psychological adjustment (e.g., Janoff-Bulman, 1985, 1992; Shaver, 1985;
Tennen & Affleck, 1990). These models are typically concerned with
people's explanations of negative events and/or the apportioning of
blame for their occurrence. They assume that the way in which people
construct reality has relevance for their health and well-being. Janoff-
Bulman's influential work (1979, 1982), for example, asserts that behavioral self-blame attributions facilitate adjustment. Her basic thesis is that
blaming the cause of a negative event on some aspect of one's behavior allows one to reassert control over the likelihood of a similar event
occurring in the future, allowing one to regain a sense of control over
one's life which, in turn, is associated with better psychological adjustment (Thompson et al., 1993). Making characterological self-blame
attributions (i.e., those concerning aspects of one's personality that are
immutable), in contrast, should be associated with poorer adjustment as
these do not afford any sense of control. Timko and Janoff-Bulman
(1985) also found that other-blame was associated with lower levels of
self-esteem presumably because it implies that one had been unable to
prevent the situation having occurred which, in turn, serves to undermine beliefs about one's abilities and perceived invulnerability. This is
consistent with the observation that participation in formal recovery
interventions (e.g., debriefings) may be interpreted as an unfavorable
source of information about one's own abilities to cope with trauma,
thereby threatening self-esteem (Coyne, Ellard, & Smith, 1990; Gross,
Wallston & Piliavin, 1980).

Some studies, however, have indicated that self-blame attributions
(both behavioral and characterological) are related to poor psychological adjustment (Edward & MacLeod, 1996; Frazier, 1990; Meyer &
Taylor, 1986) and that other-blame attributions facilitate adjustment.
These findings are consistent with predictions based on Abramson,
Seligman and Teasdale's (1978) reformulated model of learned helplessness where external attributions for bad outcomes should buffer

self-esteem and therefore be associated with better recovery. Shaver (1985) has similarly argued that attributing the cause of a negative event to external factors such as chance or fate will enhance or protect an individual's self-esteem.

More recently, Janoff-Bulman (1992) refined her argument so that behavioral self-blame attributions are unlikely to be related to adjustment when an individual has also made characterological self-blame attributions. In other words, any benefit of blaming one's behavior for a traumatic event is likely to be undone if some aspect of one's personality is also implicated. The problem for this qualification is that people often experience difficulties in distinguishing between the two kinds of self-blame (Meyer & Taylor, 1986). Indeed, it may be very difficult to blame one's behavior without implicating some aspect of one's personality (Downey, Silver, & Wortman, 1990; Frazier, 1990; Frazier & Schauben, 1994). Thus, the value of a model which predicts better psychological adjustment on the basis of behavioral self-blame attributions alone is questionable (MacLeod, 1999). Another fundamental problem that is often overlooked when considering the role of attributions in adjustment is that attributions made following a traumatic episode may be largely driven by our psychological distress (Malcarne, Compas, Epping-Jordan, & Howell, 1995). We cannot assume that attributions accurately reflect cognitive processing (Nisbett & Wilson, 1977).

The relationship between perceived control and adjustment has come under similar scrutiny in recent years. Perceived control has proved an important concept in the adjustment and recovery literature as it provides one of the principal mechanisms by which attributions are thought to play a causal role. However, a belief in control over a particular situation does not necessarily confer adjustment. If one believes that one can exert control over a situation and then fails, this may exacerbate distress (Burger, 1989; Thompson, Cheek, & Graham, 1988) although, in some contexts, any sense of control may be beneficial even when control beliefs are subsequently disconfirmed (Thompson et al., 1993).

Carver and Scheier (1990, 1994), however, consider an alternative explanation for the apparent link between perceived control and psychological adjustment. They argue that while people may consider the effects of external factors and feelings of personal control in arriving at an expected outcome, it is whether the outcome is expected that predicts emotional reactions. Thus, it is possible that how an outcome is achieved (e.g., through perceptions of personal control) may be less important than whether it actually occurs. More recently, Carver (1997) has compounded his criticism of perceived control by arguing that locus of control measures have been typically confounded with outcome probability, and specifically our expectancies about the occurrence of future events. Consequently, he warns about the danger of assuming that perceived control plays a fundamental role in psychological adjustment and that other factors (albeit closely related to control beliefs) may prove to have greater predictive power (Wallston, 1992). Such arguments have prompted some researchers to consider what these factors might be (see MacLeod, 1999).

TEMPORAL ORIENTATION AS A CONCEPTUAL FRAMEWORK

In a field of research where there is no overarching theoretical model or where there are doubts about the explanatory value of existing models (e.g., attributional and perceived control models), it is useful to have some way of organizing the available empirical evidence. The following framework is based upon the theme of temporal orientation. Importantly, such a framework allows us to identify and consider relationships between social and cognitive factors that have, so far, been largely neglected.

So why focus on temporal orientation? In one sense it is not an entirely new concept. Psychologists have argued for decades about the importance of temporal factors for coping effectively with traumatic events and, in particular, the importance of maintaining a future perspective for mental health and well-being (e.g., Nuttin, 1985; Kelly, 1955). Additionally, some have argued that we need to be able to integrate our past and present experiences with our future expectations if we are to adjust successfully to trauma (e.g., Fraser, 1966; Kelly, 1955; Lewin, 1942). Given this, victims of trauma face a major potential problem. In trying to make sense of the event by integrating it into their fundamental beliefs about how the world works and how it relates to them, they run the risk of getting "stuck" in the past (Holman & Silver, 1998; Silver, Boon, & Stones, 1983). People can become so preoccupied with past events that it affects both their interpretation of past events and their interpretation of current events.

In the short-term, focusing on the past may actually help us to cope more effectively with a traumatic experience by helping us to make sense of the traumatic episode (Horowitz, 1986; Silver et al., 1983). By focusing on the past and mentally simulating the negative event we can "work through" or integrate our traumatic experiences into our existing schemata (Epstein, 1991; Janoff-Bulman, 1992; Silver et al., 1983). In the long-term, however, this initially adaptive temporal focus can become maladaptive by maintaining, or even amplifying, negative affect associated with the original event (Baum, Cohen, & Hall, 1993; Silver et al., 1983; Holman & Silver, 1998). Having a future focus, in contrast, has been associated with good psychological adjustment (Tedeschi & Calhoun, 1995).

Adopting a temporal orientation approach may also help us to understand some of the apparent inconsistencies in the attributional literature, rather than looking at attributional processes in their own right. What might prove important for psychological adjustment is the extent to which one is engaged in thinking about the past rather than the content of the attribution per se. The fact that attributions are sometimes associated with good adjustment and at other times with poor adjustment may have more to do with factors such as the amount of time elapsed since the trauma, or the mutability of the perceived cause of the incident, rather than any inherent property of the attribution (e.g., whether it affords a sense of control or not). There may be a critical window within which attributional activity (be it cause, blame, or responsibility) performs an adaptive role but beyond a certain point it serves only to maintain psychological distress. Focusing on events that are perceived as uncontrollable and having a high likelihood of recurrence is also likely to maintain psychological distress (Carson & MacLeod, 1997).

Of course, despite the intuitive appeal of such an argument it remains unsatisfactory from an empirical point of view as it is essentially post hoc, i.e., we have no formal test of the model. However, there exists a substantial body of psychological research that points to not only the importance of temporal factors in psychological adjustment (i.e., time elapsed since the trauma) but also the possible mechanisms by which people become cognitively preoccupied with the past.

It is to a discussion of this research, and its implications for future research and the effectiveness of interventions following trauma, that this chapter now turns.

Temporal Disintegration

It is well-documented that experiencing a traumatic event can disrupt sequential thinking (Melges, 1982). One explanation for this involves temporal orientation and, in particular, the tendency for trauma victims to focus their thoughts on what has happened. Zimbardo (1994) argued that temporal orientation is an important organizing principle and as such has a powerful effect on our lives through the way we think, feel and behave. By focusing on the past, therefore, we run the risk of distorting how we process information and particularly the temporal element associated with the events that affect our lives.

This line of argument has recently been developed by Holman and Silver (1998) who examined the possibility that individuals who experience the greatest temporal disintegration following trauma will be more focused on the past and have higher levels of psychological distress. They conducted a prospective study (Study 3) of people who had experienced fire storms in southern California (some of whom had lost their homes in the fires). They found that individuals who were predominantly past-oriented 6 months after the fire storms, were significantly more distressed six months later than those who were predominantly either present or future oriented. Individuals who experienced the highest degree of temporal disintegration in the immediate aftermath of the fires were also significantly more focused on the past six months later and had the highest levels of distress one year after the fires (controlling for initial distress, age, gender, loss of home, degree of exposure to the fire, degree of ongoing stress, and rumination). Interestingly, Holman and Silver's findings also point to the possible inoculating effects of previous exposure to acute trauma. While those exposed to chronic trauma prior to the fires showed high levels of temporal disintegration, people who reported acute trauma experiences prior to the fires showed lower levels of temporal disintegration.

Holman and Silver also presented evidence to suggest that temporal orientation can be associated with different psychological outcomes depending upon the recency of the trauma. For example, for individuals from fire-stricken communities (Study 3), present temporal orientation was found to be positively associated with distress whereas for individuals who had been victims of childhood incest, present temporal orientation was negatively associated with distress. For the latter, present orientation may signify that the past is objectively and subjectively over and hence they are no longer reliving the negative experience in their present lives (Holman & Silver, 1998). For those in fire-stricken communities, in contrast, the relationship between present orientation and distress may reflect the fact that many were still contending with the ongoing stress of cleaning up and rebuilding. Holman and Silver also indicated that there was a relationship between severity of loss and level of temporal disintegration. Specifically, people who had lost their homes in the fires reported much higher levels of temporal disintegration in the immediate aftermath than those who did not lose their homes.

Holman and Silver's innovative study also suggested that individuals who perceived a threat to their identities through loss of personal belongings (e.g., irreplaceable family heirlooms) were most at risk of immediate temporal disintegration. Although the measure of social identity employed was relatively unsophisticated in that victims of the fires were categorized into those who took predominantly memorability items with them (high identifiers) versus those who took expensive material goods (low identifiers), it nevertheless suggests an issue worthy of further investigation. Loss of, or alteration to, identity may be an important contributor to the level of psychological distress experienced. For much of our lives, we tend not to think of ourselves as vulnerable, or belonging to devalued groups in society such as "ill people," "rape victims," etc. Experiencing a traumatic event may fundamentally rock our beliefs about our identity and, in doing so, may prolong distress.

Intrusive Thoughts and Thought Suppression

Having established a relationship between temporal orientation and psychological adjustment, how does a trauma victim develop a past temporal orientation? One possibility (as discussed above) is through attributional processes that focus on the antecedents of the trauma. However, other cognitive processes may also contribute to a past temporal perspective. A well-recognized consequence of trauma is intrusive recollections (Nolen-Hoeksema & Morrow, 1991; Shore, Tatum, & Vollmer, 1986; Tait & Silver, 1989). While these intrusive thoughts can be upsetting, they may also serve an adaptive function by helping our cognitive system to assimilate traumatic experiences with existing cognitive schemata to reconcile our traumatic experiences with our beliefs about how the world works and how we relate to it, helping to resume normal cognitive functioning (Horowitz, 1986). Thus, intrusive thoughts can, to some extent, be seen as part of the normal adaptive process.

King and Pennebaker (1995), however, point out that intrusive thoughts may also play a role in developing and sustaining a past temporal orientation by keeping memories and thoughts about the traumatic event alive in one's consciousness. For some trauma victims, intrusive thoughts result in their continuing to think about the event and its consequences many years after the traumatic event originally occurred (McCann & Pearlman, 1990). Holman and Silver (1998) argue that individuals who experience persistent intrusions from the past may get drawn into a negative cycle in which the intrusive memories access negative feelings associated with the original traumatic episode, which, in turn, drives the tendency to focus predominantly on the past. Specifically, Holman and Silver argue that thinking about the trauma and the activation of either trauma-related schemata or cues may trigger an emotionally-laden memory which produces confusion between the past trauma and the current situation (see also Nolen-Hoeksema, Morrow, & Fredrickson, 1993). Nolen-Hoeksema and Morrow (1991) also argued that focusing on the past can amplify negative affect associated with the original trauma, result in individuals becoming stuck in the past, affect their ability to deal with current problems, and lead to further distress.

So what happens when we try not to think about our traumatic experiences? Can we simply block them out or suppress them and thus avoid these kinds of problems? Wegner, Quillian, and Houston (1996) have explored this issue and have found that thought suppression may actually cause disordering in memory for an episode. Presumably such disordering to temporal processing could also affect an individual's ability to cope with current demands. Thus, although one would anticipate that suppressing one's thoughts about a trauma would help an individual temporarily to function in the present, it may actually have the opposite effect. Indeed, trying to suppress a particular memory may lead to a search for the very thing that the person is trying to forget (Wegner, 1992). Wegner (1994) demonstrated that suppressed thoughts are not only difficult to keep out of mind, but when people are asked to think about a target thought after initially trying to suppress that thought, they are more likely to think about the suppressed thought than people who never suppressed the thought in the first place. Thus, thought suppression may actually create a monitoring process that ironically increases the automatic activation of the thought it is supposed to suppress which, in turn, may lead to repeated and uncontrollable intrusions of unwanted thoughts and associated emotions. The harder we try to push away unwanted thoughts, the more likely it seems that we are to think about them (Gold & Wegner, 1995).

Wegner et al. (1996) also make the point that researchers who have commented on the apparent fragmentation and loss of memory following a traumatic event have tended to attribute these phenomena to the effects of emotion during encoding. Yet, research on the effects of emotion during encoding fail to support this interpretation (e.g., Christianson, 1992; Loftus & Burns, 1982). Indeed, emotion can enhance certain aspects of memory for an event (e.g., Christianson & Loftus, 1990; Yuille & Cutshall, 1989; Woolnough & MacLeod, 1999). Wegner et al.'s (1996) study suggests an interesting alternative. Fragmentation and loss of memory is more likely due to attempts to suppress memories about the traumatic event.

Rumination Processes and Counterfactuals

Another process that may contribute to a past temporal orientation in trauma victims is rumination (i.e., the mental rerunning of the event, its antecedents and consequences). This differs from intrusive thoughts in the sense that we choose to engage in this kind of thinking, believing that it will help us to gain an insight into our problems and emotions (Lyubomirsky & Nolen-Hoeksema, 1993). As with intrusive thoughts, rumination is also considered to facilitate coping in some individuals (Horowitz, 1986) by helping to integrate traumatic experiences with preexisting belief systems. Indeed, many people seem to wish to avoid distracting themselves from thinking about their trauma because they believe it would interfere with their efforts to understand themselves. Unfortunately, rumination processes may also serve to exacerbate depressogenic thinking and undermine coping (Aspinwall & Taylor, 1997: Lyubomirsky & Nolen-Hoeksema, 1993). By continuing to focus on the past, individuals can become stuck in a self-perpetuating cycle of rumination that may be ultimately detrimental to psychological adjustment (Nolen-Hoeksema, 1987). Of course, other factors may also contribute to depression by maintaining or refreshing negative affect associated with the original traumatic event such as feelings of revenge (Kahler & MacLeod, 1996; Weinberg, 1994) and particular patterns of attributional analysis (Davis, Lehman, Silver, Wortman & Ellard, 1996).

A closely related temporal process to rumination is counterfactual thinking: the process by which people mentally simulate the events leading up to the outcome with a view to mentally undoing them. Mentally undoing an event represents a state of continual upward comparison between reality and a better hypothetical alternative in which the negative outcome does not occur. When people create hypothetically better scenarios, their actual outcomes appear especially poor by comparison. Mentally undoing an event may amplify negative affect over "what might have been" and therefore suggests that events that are easier to undo are more distressing because they are likely to leave one thinking that the event was avoidable. Davis, Lehman, Wortman, Silver & Thompson (1995) examined whether undoing the outcome is dependent upon the extent to which the events leading up to the outcome are perceived as being mutable or changeable. Where events are seen as immutable one is likely to accept the reality of the occurrence. However, if an incident in the sequence of events is perceived as highly mutable then that incident is likely to be shifted to its alternative in a mental simulation, thereby undoing the event.

Davis et al.'s (1996) first study found that individuals who were currently engaged in undoing the event reported greater psychological distress than did those who reported never attempting to undo the event or who reported undoing only in the past. There was also a significant correlation between frequency of undoing in the past month and respondents' current level of distress. This significant correlation held even when other factors such as ruminating about the event in the past month and about the deceased in the past month had been partialled out. Conversely, when frequency of undoing thoughts was partialled out, the correlation between ruminations and distress was no longer significant. Thus, the association between undoing and distress does not seem simply to be due to a general tendency to ruminate about the event or the deceased.

Their second study was longitudinal and based on data collected from parents who had lost a child to SIDS (Sudden Infant Death Syndrome) interviewed approximately three weeks and 18 months after the baby's death. Parents were vindicated of any blame or responsibility for the death having happened by health officials. For these reasons, there was no obvious causal event for parents to undo and no known objective reason to self-blame. Yet, Davis et al. found that 76% of their sample reported undoing the baby's death at three weeks postloss. By 18 months, this had dropped to 42%. Again they found that more undoing was associated with greater distress and that undoing at three weeks post death was predictive of undoing 18 months postloss. This is consistent with the idea that highly distressed people come to undo more frequently, thereby perpetuating their distress.

So why do people engage in this undoing process? One possibility is that undoing may be an attempt by people to gain some sense of psychological control over or understanding of uncontrollable, senseless events and avoid similar events happening to us in the future. However, where future control is not attainable, counterfactual thinking may lead some people to get stuck in the past and develop a past temporal orientation that affects their perception of past and present events thereby reducing their ability to adapt effectively to the demands of the trauma. In addition, counterfactual thoughts may increase feelings of guilt and self-blame for not having avoided the incident in the first place.

Roese's (1997) review, however, suggests an alternative view, arguing that counterfactual thoughts are an important component of healthy functioning (e.g., Landman, 1993, 1995). In those cases where counterfactuals have been linked to continued distress it may be not so much that counterfactuals are inherently harmful but rather that counterfactual ruminations are. Roese points out that depressed individuals have difficulty suppressing negative thoughts and that a general failure of inhibitory processes might account for the unleashing of vicious circles of counterfactual thinking which, in turn, result in negative affect. Of course, from our earlier discussion, one could also suggest that depressed people may well be trying to suppress negative thoughts but that the act of suppression ironically results in the hyperaccessibility of those things they are trying to forget. Roese argues that counterfactual thinking that is not shut down normally but spins repeatedly into unhealthy ruminations may occur in some individuals and that this represents a breakdown in the normally functional process of activation and inhibition rather than an inherent negative property of counterfactuals. Thus, counterfactuals may facilitate adjustment by helping individuals to focus on the cause of the incident and to focus on what is normal, and plan how to avoid such incidents in the future.

Making Social Comparisons with Ourselves in the Past

One way in which victims attempt to restore feelings of control and/or meaning is by comparing themselves with others who are worse off than they are through making downward social comparisons. This explanation emanates from social comparison theory (Festinger, 1954) which argues that, in the absence of physical or objective standards, people look to others to evaluate themselves and establish the kinds of behavior which are appropriate in given situations. Festinger, however, also realized that people don't always seek objective information and that social comparisons are sometimes made in self-defense. When a person's self-esteem is at stake, especially after experiencing a traumatic event, there may be some benefit in making downward comparisons with those who are less fortunate (Wills, 1981). For people with low self-esteem, downward comparisons can lead to positive effect and increase self-esteem (Aspinwall & Taylor, 1993; Gibbons, 1986; Hakmiller, 1966; Taylor, 1983). Upward comparisons (i.e., comparing oneself to others whose outcomes or abilities are slightly better), in contrast, tend to be associated with negative effect and low self-esteem (Salovey & Rodin, 1984; Brickman & Bulman, 1977; Morse & Gergen, 1970). However, this may be too simplistic a picture. The effective responses associated with comparison processes may not be dependent upon the direction of the social comparison (Buunk, Collins, Taylor, Dakof, van Yperen, 1990; Testa & Major, 1988) as much as context (Taylor & Lobel, 1989) and personality characteristics (van der Zee, Oldersma, Buunk, & Bos, 1998). Recent research also suggests that upward comparisons can be ego deflating and self-enhancing (e.g., Ybema and Buunk, 1995).

When making comparisons with ourselves we introduce another factor. Typically such comparisons not only include a directional component (i.e., upward or downward) but also a temporal component (i.e., making comparisons with ourselves either in the past or what we could be like in the future). In the case of criminal victimization, it may be that the experience leaves you feeling more vulnerable and fearful than before, if it involves activities in which that person is no longer able to engage. Such comparisons are of an upward nature in that one is comparing poorer conditions with better ones. These comparisons, however, also involve comparisons over time (i.e., comparing current problems with a carefree, problem-free, better past). Thus, making upward comparisons with oneself over time may be associated with negative effect because the temporal focus is in the past (see Graham et al., in press). Making upward comparisons with other people, in contrast, (especially those who have recovered from similar traumatic incidents) may be adaptive not simply in providing role models to emulate but also because such comparisons are forward-looking and may constitute an important part of future planning.

Is Temporal Perspective Important?

This chapter has outlined a temporal orientation framework to provide structure for the vast number of psychological studies in this field. While further research would be required to test this model, there exists good evidence to suggest that temporal orientation is important for psychological adjustment. Temporal orientation has measurable consequences. The degree of temporal disintegration appears to be related to perceived severity of the traumatic incident, and is predictive of psychological adjustment. This temporal perspective model also draws attention to the fact that intrusive thoughts, ruminations, temporal orientation and counterfactuals have all been considered to be part of the normal adjustment process—at least up to a point. There may be a critical window in which they play an adaptive role but beyond this they contribute to a past temporal orientation and poor adaptation via the effective interpretation of current events, and the limiting of available coping/planning strategies. This line of argument is consistent with the predictions made by many stage models of psychological adjustment (e.g., Pennebaker & Harber, 1993). The notion that the amount of time elapsed since the trauma tends to be associated with different processes and different outcomes has important ramifications for future research and for the development of appropriate and effective interventions.

WHAT DOES THIS MEAN FOR CURRENT INTERVENTIONS?

One of the difficulties of suggesting any alternative to debriefing is the pervasiveness of "sick-role" culture in our society, i.e., the extent to which we, as individuals, tend to give up responsibility for our own health and well-being and devolve responsibility to health-care professionals. Such a strategy may be entirely appropriate in certain circumstances (e.g., surgical or drug interventions following a heart attack or breast cancer). In the case of recovery from trauma, debriefing may help those who do not have the social or psychological repertoire to cope and help people come to terms with a negative event. However, the orientation of debriefing protocols may stimulate exactly those kinds of cognitive processes that one would wish to avoid (e.g., the development of a past temporal orientation which is significantly related to poor adjustment). Debriefing procedures typically assume that all traumatized individuals no longer have any agency for their own recovery. In doing so, there is a tendency to forget that people often have considerable psychological reserves of their own to deal with the aftermath of traumatic events and that they may have a need to try to regain control over their own lives rather than being directed by others. Perhaps we should focus more on assessing whether individuals are continuing to focus on the past at a time when such cognitions are maladaptive and develop our interventions accordingly. While it could be argued that the absence of any opportunity to talk through one's experience of trauma may hinder recovery (e.g., Lepore, Silver, Wortman, & Wayment, 1996; Pennebaker & Harber, 1993), debriefing may initiate those processes which increase the risk of developing a past temporal focus long after it is adaptive.

Thus, while some kinds of interventions following trauma may facilitate adjustment, others may unwittingly exacerbate the symptoms they are designed to eradicate or reduce. One of the reasons for this is a lack of a dominant theoretical approach. Indeed, in order to understand what kind of intervention would be most appropriate and when it should be implemented, we need a detailed understanding of the psychological processes that underlie reactions and adjustment to trauma (see MacLeod & Paton, 1999b). Otherwise, the interventions we administer are arguably no better than those superstitious rituals performed by shamen on the ill. As we improve our understanding of the social cognition processes by which people become stuck in the past, we will be in a better position to develop effective ways of helping people deal with their traumatic experiences.

REFERENCES

Abramson, L.Y., Seligman, M.E.P., and Teasdale, J.D.: Learned helplessness in humans: Critique and reformulation. *Journal of Abnormal Psychology, 87:* 49–74, 1978.

Aspinwall, L.G., and Taylor, S.E.: The effects of social comparison direction, threat, and self-esteem on affect, self-evaluation, and expected success. *Journal of Personality, 64:* 708–722, 1993.

Aspinwall, L.G., and Taylor, S.E.: A stitch in time: Self-regulation and proactive coping. *Psychological Bulletin, 121:* 417–436, 1997.

Baum, A., Cohen, L., and Hall, M.: Control and intrusive memories as possible determinants of chronic stress. *Psychosomatic Medicine, 55:* 274–286, 1993.

Brickman, P., and Bulman, R.: Pleasure and pain in social comparison. In J. Suls and R.L. Miller (Eds.): *Social comparison processes: Theoretical and empirical perspectives.* New York: Hemisphere, 1997.

Buunk, B.P., Collins, R., Taylor, S., Dakof, G., and van Yperen, N.: The affective consequences of social comparisons: Either direction has its ups and downs. *Journal of Personality and Social Psychology, 59:* 1238–1249, 1990.

Burger, J.M.: Negative reactions to increases in perceived personal control. *Journal of Personality and Social Psychology, 56:* 246–256, 1989.

Carson, L., and MacLeod, M.D.: Explanations about crime and psychological distress in ethnic minority and white victims of crime: A qualitative exploration. *Journal of Community and Applied Social Psychology, 7:* 361–375, 1997.

Carver, C.S.: The internal-external scale confounds internal locus of control with expectancies of positive outcomes. *Personality and Social Psychology Bulletin, 23:* 580–585, 1997.

Carver, C.S., and Scheier, M.F.: Principles of self-regulation: Action and emotion. In E.T. Higgins and R.M. Sorrentino (Eds.): *Handbook of motivation and cognition: Foundations of social behaviour.* New York: Guilford, 1990.

Carver, C.S., and Scheier, M.F.: Optimism and health-related cognition: What variables actually matter? *Psychology and Health, 9:* 191–195, 1994.

Carver, C.S., Scheier, M.F., and Weintraub, J.K.: Assessing coping strategies: A theoretically based approach. *Journal of Personality and Social Psychology, 56:* 267–283, 1989.

Christianson, S.: Emotional stress and eyewitness memory: A critical review. *Psychological Bulletin, 112:* 284–309, 1992.

Christianson, S., and Loftus, E.F.: Some characteristics of people's traumatic memories. *Bulletin of the Psychonomic Society, 28:* 195–198, 1990.

Collins, R.L., Taylor, S.E., and Skogan, L.A.: A better world or shattered vision? Changes in life perspectives following victimization. *Social Cognition, 8:* 263–285, 1990.

Coyne, J.C., Ellard, J.H., and Smith, D.A.F.: Social support, interdependence, and the dilemmas of helping. In B.R. Sarason, I.G. Sarason, and C.R. Pierce (Eds.): *Social support: An interactional view.* New York: Wiley, 1990.

Davis, C.G., Lehman, D.R., Silver, R.C., Wortman, C.B., and Ellard, J.H.: Self-blame following a traumatic event: the role of perceived avoidability. *Personality and Social Psychology Bulletin, 22:* 557–567, 1996.

Davis, C.G., Lehman, D.R., Wortman, C.B., Silver, R.C., and Thompson, S.C.: The undoing of traumatic life events. *Personality and Social Psychological Bulletin, 21:* 109–124, 1995.

Downey, G., Silver, R.C., and Wortman, C.B.: Reconsidering the attribution-adjustment relation following a major negative event: Coping with the loss of a child. *Journal of Personality and Social Psychology, 59:* 925–940, 1990.

Edward, K.E., and MacLeod, M.D.: *Blame, beliefs and recovery: An examination of factors affecting victim recovery from sexual and non-sexual crimes.* Paper presented at the VI European Conference on Psychology and Law, Siena, 1996.

Epstein, S.: The self-concept, the traumatic neurosis, and the structure of personality. In D. Ozer, J.M. Healy, and A.J. Stewart (Eds.): *Perspectives of personality.* London: Jessica Kingsley, 1991.

Festinger, L.: A theory of social comparison processes. *Human Relations, 7:* 117–140, 1954.

Fraser, J.T.: *The voice of time: A cooperative survey of man's views of time as expressed by the sciences and by the humanities.* New York: George Braziller, 1966.

Frazier, P. A.: Victim attributions and post-rape trauma. *Journal of Personality and Social Psychology, 59:* 298–304, 1990.

Frazier, P.A., and Schauben, L.: Causal attributions and recovery from rape and other stressful life events. *Journal of Social and Clinical Psychology, 13:* 1–14, 1994.

Gibbons, F. X.: Social comparison and depression: Company's effect on misery. *Journal of Personality and Social Psychology, 51:* 140–148, 1986.

Gold, D.B., and Wegner, D.M.: Origins of ruminative thought: Trauma, incompleteness, nondisclosure, and suppression. *Journal of Applied Social Psychology, 25:* 1245–1261, 1995.

Graham, E., Dibben, C., and MacLeod, M.D.: The "pulling up" and "pulling down" effects of relative deprivation on limiting long-term illness. Manuscript submitted for publication, 1999.

Graham, E., MacLeod, M.D., Johnston, M., Dibben, C., and Morgan, I.: Individual deprivation, neighborhood, and recovery from illness. Buckingham: Open University Press, in press.

Gross, A.E., Wallston, B.S., and Pilliavin, I.M.: The help recipient's perspective. In D.H. Smith and J. McCalay (Eds.): *Participation in social and political activities.* San Francisco: Josey Bass, 1980.

Hakmiller, K.L.: Threat as a determinant of downward comparison. *Journal of Experimental Social Psychology, (Suppl. 1):* 32, 39, 1966.

Holman, E.A., and Silver, R.C.: Getting "stuck" in the past: Temporal orientation and coping with trauma. *Journal of Personality and Social Psychology, 74:* 1146–1163, 1998.

Horowitz, M.J.: *Stress response syndromes.* Northvale, NJ: Aronson, 1986.

Janoff-Bulman, R.: Characterological versus behavioural self-blame: Inquiries into depression and rape. *Journal of Personality and Social Psychology, 37:* 1798–1809, 1979.

Janoff-Bulman, R.: Esteem and control bases of blame: 'Adaptive' strategies for victims versus observers. *Journal of Personality, 50:* 180–192, 1982.

Janoff-Bulman, R.: The aftermath of victimization: Rebuilding shattered assumptions. In C.R. Figley (Ed.): *Trauma and its wake.* New York: Brunner/Mazel, 1985.

Janoff-Bulman, R.: *Shattered assumptions: Towards a new psychology of trauma.* New York: Free Press, 1992.

Kahler, A.S., and MacLeod, M.D.: Blame, revenge and the bereavement process. Paper presented at the XXVI International Congress of Psychology, Ottawa. *International Journal of Psychology, 31:* 3174, 1996.

Kelly, G.A.: *The psychology of personal constructs.* New York: Norton, 1955.

King, L.A., and Pennebaker, J.W.: Thinking about goals, glue, and the meaning of life. In R.S. Wyer, (Ed.): *Advances in social cognition: Ruminative thoughts, 9:* Hillsdale, NJ: Erlbaum, 1995, pp. 97–106.

Landman, J.: *Regret: The persistence of the possible.* New York: Oxford University Press, 1993.

Landman, J.: Through a glass darkly: Worldviews, counterfactual thought, and emotion. In N.J. Roese and J.M. Olson (Eds.): *What might have been: The social psychology of counterfactual thinking.* Mahwah, NJ: Erlbaum, 1995.

Lazarus, R.S., and Folkman, S.: *Stress, appraisal, and coping.* New York: Springer, 1984.

Lepore, S.J., Silver, R.C., Wortman, C.B., and Wayment, H.A.: Social constraints, intrusive thoughts, and depressive symptoms among bereaved mothers. *Journal of Personality and Social Psychology, 70:* 271–282, 1996.

Lewin, K.: Time perspective and morale. In G. Watson (Ed.): *Civilian morale.* New York: Houghton Mifflin, 1942.

Loftus, E.F., and Burns, T.E.: Mental shock can produce retrograde amnesia. *Memory and Cognition, 10:* 318–323, 1982.

Lyubomirsky, S., and Nolen-Hoeksema, S.: Self perpetuating properties of dysphoric rumination. *Journal of Personality and Social Psychology, 65:* 339–349, 1993.

MacLeod, M. D.: Why did it happen to me? Social cognition processes in adjustment and recovery from criminal victimization and illness. *Current Psychology, 18:* 18–31, 1999.

MacLeod, M.D., Carson, L., and Prescott, R.G.W.: *Listening to victims: Victimisation episodes and the criminal justice system in Scotland.* Edinburgh: HMSO, 1996.

MacLeod, M.D., Graham, E., Johnston, M., Dibben, C., and Morgan, I.: How does relative deprivation affect health. *ESRC Health Variations Newsletter, 3:* 12–14, 1999.

MacLeod, M.D., and Paton, D.: Victims, violent crime, and the criminal justice system: Developing an integrated model of recovery. *Legal and Criminological Psychology.4:* 203–220, 1999a.

MacLeod, M.D., and Paton, D.: Police officers and violent crime: Social psychological perspectives on impact and recovery. In J. Violanti and D. Paton (Eds.): *Police trauma: Psychological aftermath of civilian combat.* Springfield, IL: Charles C Thomas, 1999b.

Malcarne, V.L., Compas, B.E., Epping-Jordan, J.E., and Howell, D.C.: Cognitive factors in adjustment to cancer: Attributions of self-blame and perceptions of control. *Journal of Behavioral Medicine, 18:* 401–417, 1995.

McCann, I., and Pearlman, L.: *Psychological trauma and the adult survivor.* New York: Brunner/Mazel, 1990.

Melges, F.T.: *Time and the inner future: A temporal approach to psychiatric disorders.* New York: Wiley, 1982.

Meyer, C. B., and Taylor, S. E.: Adjustment to rape. *Journal of Personality and Social Psychology, 50:* 1226–1234, 1986.

Morse, S., and Gergen, K.J.: Social comparison, self-consistency, and the concept of self. *Journal of Personality and Social Psychology, 16:* 148–156, 1970.

Nisbett, R.E., and Wilson, T.D.: Telling more than we can know: Verbal reports on mental processes. *Psychological Review, 84:* 231–259, 1977.

Nolen-Hoeksema, S.: Sex differences in unipolar depression: Evidence and theory. *Psychological Bulletin, 101:* 259–282, 1987.

Nolen-Hoeksema, S., and Morrow, J.: A prospective study of depression and posttraumatic stress symptoms after a natural disaster; the 1989 Loma Prieta earthquake. *Journal of Personality and Social Psychology, 61:* 115–121, 1991.

Nolen-Hoeksema, S., Morrow, J., and Fredrickson, B.L.: Response styles and the duration of episodes of depressed mood. *Journal of Abnormal Psychology, 102:* 20–28, 1993.

Nuttin, J.: *Future time perspective and motivation: Theory and research method.* Hillsdale, NJ: Erlbaum, 1985.

Pennebaker, J.W., and Harber, K.D.: A social stage model of collective coping: The Loma Prieta Earthquake and the Persian Gulf War. *Journal of Social Issues, 49:* 125–145, 1993.

Roese, N.J.: Counterfactual thinking. *Psychological Bulletin, 121:* 133–148, 1997.

Salovey, P., and Rodin, J.: Some antecedents and consequences of social comparison jealousy. *Journal of Personality and Social Psychology, 47:* 780–792, 1984.

Shaver, H.G.: *The attribution of blame: Causality, responsibility, and blameworthiness.* New York: Springer-Verlag, 1985.

Shore, J.H., Tatum, E.T., and Vollmer, W.M.: Psychiatric reactions to disaster: The Mount St. Helens experience. *American Journal of Psychiatry, 143:* 590–595, 1986.

Silver, R.L., Boon, C., and Stones, M.H.: Searching for meaning in misfortune: Making sense of incest. *Journal of Social Issues, 39:* 81–102, 1983.

Silver, R., and Wortman, C.: Coping with undesirable life events. In J. Garber and M. Seligman (Eds.): *Human Helplessness.* New York: Academic Press, 1980.

Tait, R., and Silver, R.C.: Coming to terms with major negative life events. In J.S. Thurman and J.A. Bargh (Eds): *Unintended thought.* New York: Guildford Press, 1989.

Taylor, S.E.: Adjustment to threatening events: A theory of cognitive adaptation. *American Psychologist, 38:* 1161–1173, 1983.

Taylor, S.E., and Lobel, M.: Social comparison activity under threat: Downward evaluations and upward contacts. *Psychological Review, 96:* 569–575, 1989.

Tedeschi, R.G., and Calhoun, L.G.: *Trauma and transformation.* Thousand Oaks, CA: Sage, 1995.

Tennen, H., and Affleck, G.: Blaming others for threatening events. *Psychological Bulletin, 108:* 209–232, 1990.

Testa, M., and Major, B.: The impact of social comparison after failure: the moderating effects of perceived control. *Basic and Applied Social Psychology, 44:* 672–682, 1990.

Thompson, S.C., Cheek, P.R., and Graham, M.A.: The other side of perceived control: Disadvantages and negative effects. In S. Spacapan and S. Oskamp (Eds.): *The Social Psychology of Health.* Beverley Hills, CA: Sage, 1988.

Thompson, S.C., Sobolew-Shubin, A., Galbraith, M., Schwankovsky, L., and Cruzen, D.: Maintaining perceptions of control: Finding perceived control in low-control circumstances. *Journal of Personality and Social Psychology, 64:* 293–304, 1993.

Timko, C., and Janoff-Bulman, R.: Attribution, vulnerability and psychological adjustment: The case of breast cancer. *Health Psychology, 4:* 521–546, 1985.

van der Zee, K.I., Oldersma, F., Buunk, B.P., and Bos, D.: Social comparison preferences among cancer patients as related to neuroticism and social comparison orientation. *Journal of Personality and Social Psychology, 75:* 801–810, 1998.

Wallston, K.A.: Hocus-pocus, the focus isn't strictly on locus: Rotter's social learning theory modified for health. *Cognitive Therapy and Research, 16:* 183–199, 1992.

Wegner, D.M.: You can't always think what you want: Problems in the suppression of unwanted thoughts. In M. Zanna (Ed.): *Advances in Experimental Social Psychology, vol. 25.* San Diego, CA: Academic Press, 1992.

Wegner, D.M.: *White bears and other unwanted thoughts.* New York: Guilford, 1994.

Wegner, D.M., Quillian, F., and Houston, C.E.: Memories out of order: Thought suppression and the disturbance of sequence memory. *Journal of Personality and Social Psychology, 71:* 680–691, 1996.

Weinberg, N.: Self-blame, other-blame and desire for revenge. Factors in recovery from bereavement. *Death Studies, 18:* 583–593, 1994.

Wills, T.A.: Downward comparison principles in social psychology. *Psychological Bulletin, 90:* 245–271, 1981.

Winkel, F.W., Denkers, A., and Vrij, A.: The effects of attributions on crime victims' psychological readjustment. *Genetic, Social and General Psychology Monographs, 120:* 147–168, 1994.

Woolnough, P., and MacLeod, M.D.: The camera never lies: An exploratory assessment of eyewitness memory for actions using CCTV recordings of actual crimes. Manuscript submitted for publication, 1999.

Ybema, J.F., and Buunk, B.P.: Affective responses to social comparison: A study among disabled individuals. *British Journal of Social Psychology, 34:* 279–292, 1995.

Yuille, J.C., and Cutshall, J.L.: Analysis of the statements of victims, witnesses, and suspects. In J.C. Yuille (Ed.): *Credibility assessment.* Dordrecht, The Netherlands: Kluwer Press, 1989.

Zimbardo, P.G.: *Whose time it is, I think I know–Research on time perspectives.* Symposium, 102nd Annual Convention of the American Psychological Association, Los Angeles, CA, 1994.

Chapter 11

WORK-RELATED TRAUMATIC STRESS: RISK, VULNERABILITY, AND RESILIENCE

Douglas Paton, Leigh Smith, John M. Violanti, & Liisa Eränen

INTRODUCTION

THE RISK OF EXPOSURE, and increasingly multiple exposure, to potentially traumatic events is substantial for those performing in, for example, emergency services, law enforcement and disaster relief roles. While the focus, in this context, has typically been on the relationship between this exposure and the development of personal distress and organizational (e.g., performance losses, and litigation costs) losses, the contributions to this text have emphasized the need to expand the range of outcomes anticipated and to accommodate the fact that these outcomes need not be mutually exclusive. As Calhoun and Tedeschi (Chapter 8) point out, although growth following trauma is commonly reported, it is not inevitable, and its occurrence does not necessarily free an individual from experiencing the negative consequences of traumatic events. Similar views were expressed by Aldwin, Levenson, & Spiro (1994) and Moran (1999). Nor is it just a matter of considering growth or distress. Other outcomes and stress phenomena can also be anticipated and must be accounted for.

For example, while it is conceivable to anticipate that repetitive exposure to unresolved trauma episodes could result in progressively more complicated reactions (Williams, 1993), the possibility of exposure to "traumatic" events constituting a growth experience represents an alternative outcome. Event and organizational characteristics such as a strong sense of team identity, perception of a job well done, and heightened appreciation of life and colleagues can influence the meaning attributed to a traumatic experience and increase the likelihood of positive resolution and posttraumatic growth (Alexander & Wells, 1991; Andersen, Christensen, & Petersen, 1991; Moran, 1999; Tedeschi & Calhoun, 1996). In this context, it may be the return to routine work that is the stressor. Hartsough and Myers (1985) described the latter as the "letdown phase," in recognition of the fact that returning to work after a period of emotionally intense, but professionally rewarding, work could constitute a more significant stressor than the traumatic event. Under these circumstances, systematic reintegration strategies would represent the most appropriate form of support resource and would be vital to help sustain any benefits accruing from working in the traumatic context. It has also been suggested that expectations about positive reactions, while representing a valuable coping resource under most circumstances, may increase vulnerability when emergency workers cannot do anything to save lives or prevent destruction (Moran, 1999).

The possibility of factors which protect individuals under some circumstances acting to increase risk status under others cannot be ignored. For example, the phenomenon of risk addiction describes how members of high-risk groups (e.g., military, law enforcement) can become addicted to violence, excitement and trauma, have difficulty functioning effectively without it, and experience problems reviewing or accepting their traumatic experiences (Paton, Violanti, & Schmuckler, 1999). While evidence to inform this issue is sparse, the possibility of resilience factors and/or growth experiences fueling this outcome, over time, is worth exploring. In other words, the very personal and environmental factors that promote resilience and growth could act to the detriment of the individual at other times (see also Moran, 1999). Similarly, while intended to reduce risk, interventions such as new safety practices or training (intended to reduce vulnerability or enhance resilience) can, ironically, have the opposite effect. For example, risk homeostasis (e.g., Adams, 1995) describes how a perceived increase in safety can reduce the risk attributed to a hazard, increase risk behavior and render individuals more vulnerable to negative stress effects.

The addition of a temporal dimension introduces further outcomes that must be accounted for. For example, disengagement from high-risk work can constitute a hazard in the form of "residual trauma" (Violanti, 1996). While it may depend on the nature, frequency and meaning attributed to prior trauma experiences, residual trauma occurs not from exposure to a traumatic event, but rather from the loss of the support networks and organizational culture that represented protective or resilience resources during active service. The loss of these resources, and difficulty establishing new support systems, can heighten vulnerability (Violanti, 1996). In this context, the development of disengagement and retirement planning would be beneficial, as would the development of programs designed to develop support resources for those separating from active duty.

To accommodate the diversity of these observations, it would be useful to have in place some overarching framework that, rather than prescribing outcome expectations, accommodates a range of possibilities, good and bad. In this chapter we consider the utility of a risk management model for this purpose.

The concept of risk describes the assessment of the frequency of occurrence and magnitude of consequences associated with hazard (stressor) activity (Hood & Jones, 1996). The advantage of this approach over some contemporary conceptualizations of traumatic stress is that risk does not automatically imply the occurrence of pathological or negative outcomes. Hood and Jones point out that risk management typically involves some mixture of anticipation ("looking forward") and resilience ("bouncing back"), so conferring upon risk management models the potential to encapsulate perspectives that cover growth and distress. Risk management models also provide a different perspective on explaining the adoption of pathologically-orientated CISM models described by Stuhlmiller and Dunning (Chapter 2) and Gist and Woodall (Chapter 5) using the concept of social amplification of risk (Kasperson, 1992; Smallman & Weir, 1999). While the original conception of this model emphasized negative impacts, it also has the potential to amplify and transmit positive effects (Smallman & Weir, 1999).

While additional development work is required, the potentially less prescriptive risk concept provides a more flexible framework for the conceptualization and analysis of stress phenomena, affords opportunities to consider a range of outcomes, and facilitates thinking about traumatic stress mitigation strategies in terms of either enhancing resilience and/or reducing vulnerability. Adding a temporal dimension (see also MacLeod, Chapter 10) to this model can help appreciate how a given factor can heighten resilience at one time, but increase vulnerability at another time or under different circumstances. What is clear is that the issues canvassed here would not be amenable to resolution using programs such CISM. A risk management model, when developed for this express purpose, has considerable potential for understanding and managing traumatic stress phenomena. As a starting point, it is appropriate to examine the components of this model and their implications for understanding and managing work-related traumatic stress.

Conceptualizations of risk generally include vulnerability as a determinant of differences in individual susceptibility to negative hazard effects. Blaikie et al. (1994) defined vulnerability as the combination of characteristics of a person or group in terms of their capacity to anticipate, cope with, resist, and recover from hazard impacts that threaten their life, well-being and livelihood. Using this definition, the term "vulnerability" does not imply the adoption of a pathogenic framework. Indeed, as used here it contains elements (e.g., "cope with," "resist") consistent with the concept of resilience described throughout this book. Notwithstanding, capturing the wealth of resources that could be used to adjust to traumatic experience, and developing comprehensive models of stress processes, suggests that resilience be included as a discrete category within risk management models. Resilience describes an active process of self-righting, learned resourcefulness and growth; the ability to function psychologically at a level far greater than expected given the individual's capabilities and previous experiences (Dunning, 1999).

A STATISTICAL MODEL OF VULNERABILITY AND RESILIENCE

Consistent with risk management models, Violanti (1990) described a statistical model describing how vulnerability interacts with traumatic events to demonstrate how exposure alone cannot account for the complex relationship between psychological distress and traumatic events. There are many persons so exposed who do not suffer psychological consequences and yet others who experience extreme reactions, with vulnerability acting to moderate effects.

The best strategy for a model would be to assess vulnerability on a personal level. However, due to the complex interaction of individual differences, environmental influences, and socialization factors, it is difficult to obtain an individual indicator of vulnerability. The best available measure would be a vulnerability coefficient, estimated as a constant across a group of individuals. Such coefficients can be statistically applied within and between groups at risk of trauma exposure.

While typically focusing on the interaction between hazards and vulnerability, it is prudent, for reasons outlined above, to introduce the construct of resilience as a discrete factor within a risk management model. We can anticipate that environmental and constitutional factors affect the potential for change (growth or distress). These interact with the combined effects of structural and personal resilience and vulnerability factors to determine the outcome of any set of event characteristics (Paton, Violanti, & Smith, in prep).

Once developed, such a model will facilitate a shift in the research and intervention focus from a pathological orientation to one which acknowledges outcomes ranging from growth to distress. Pursuing this line has other terminological implications. Contemporary risk management models typically use the term hazard to denote the phenomenon capable of causing harm. While this term could be used here, its connotations of negative outcome or harm detract from the objective of refocusing attention away from constructs that may reinforce pathological orientations and toward those that embrace the possibility of other outcomes, particularly those involving growth and resilience. The adoption of the term "event characteristic" could serve to maintain neutrality in the model. There is another reason why the adoption of this term may be more appropriate.

While organizational hazard and risk assessment typically focus on possible exposure to industrial (e.g., fire), natural (e.g., earthquake), and environmental (e.g., toxic waste) hazards, this level of analysis is insufficiently detailed for psychological risk analysis (Davies & Walters, 1998; Paton, 1997a). The latter requires identifying the event characteristics which threaten or promote psychological integrity. These include, for example, threat nature and duration, performance expectations and opportunities, perceived control, sense of community, suspension of bureaucracy, resource adequacy, support practices, responsibility, and management practices (Hartsough & Myers, 1985; Moran & Colless, 1995; Paton, 1996; 1997b). These event characteristics interact with personal resilience and vulnerability characteristics to influence, rather than prescribe, the probability of experiencing growth or distress. More detailed analysis of event characteristics, and valid and reliable means for their measurement and assessment, is required.

Developing and applying this model requires the identification of the event, resilience and vulnerability characteristics that influence outcomes ranging from growth to distress. Dunning (1999) describes resilience as comprising three components: dispositional, cognitive, and environmental. Dispositional resilience reflects how personal characteristics (e.g., hardiness) affect adjustment. This concept is amenable to application in organizational contexts as a consequence of the salient role of selection and assessment in organizational activities. The cognitive component is concerned with the individual's sense of coherence and meaning. In organizational contexts, training and development strategies represent means for facilitating a capability to impose coherence and meaning on atypical and extreme experiences. The final element, an environment that fosters and sustains resilience, can be cultivated through organizational design and management development strategies that create practices, procedures and a culture which mitigates adverse consequences and maximizes potential for recovery and posttraumatic growth. Organizational factors have also been implicated as event characteristics (hazards) (Hartsough & Myers, 1985; Moran & Colless, 1995). Although stressor characteristics and individual differences have been studied extensively in traumatic stress research, organizational factors have not enjoyed similar prominence. As a starting point in this discussion, it is important to ask whether the organizational environment represents a salient determinant of traumatic stress reactions and whether, and how, it influences recovery. We illustrate the role of organizational factors in this context by reference to two recent studies.

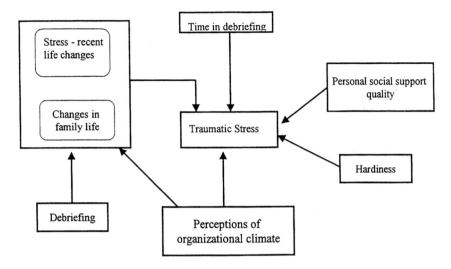

Figure 11.1. Factors influencing traumatic stress in Estonia rescue workers

WORK-RELATED TRAUMATIC STRESS

Eränen, Millar, & Paton, 1999 examined factors affecting trauma symptoms in passenger ferry employees six months after their involvement in rescue work following the sinking of the Estonia ferry. This study examined the role of organizational climate (Kalimo, Olkkonen, & Toppinan, 1993), hardiness (Dispositional Resilience Scale–Bartone et al., 1989), social support (Raphael et al., 1989), changes in family life (Eränen et al., 1999), and life change (Holmes & Rahe, 1967) on symptomatology. It also examined the perceived usefulness and effectiveness of debriefing (Marmar et al., 1993), and, because some 51% of those involved received debriefing and 49% did not, a comparison of a debriefed and a non-debriefed group was also possible.

Regression analyses revealed that "perceptions of organizational climate" was the most important predictor of symptomatology (see Figure 11.1), followed by "recent life change," "time spent in debriefing," "social support quantity," "changes in family life since the disaster," and "hardiness." Perceptions of organizational climate had both a direct effect on symptomatology and an indirect effect through both "changes in family life" and "recent life change."

On all measures, those who received debriefing recorded higher symptomatology. A further statistical procedure was performed to examine causal relationships between variables (Figure 11.1), specifically those associated with debriefing. Debriefing did exert an indirect effect on trauma symptoms and is not, therefore, expected to be a major contributor to reducing adverse psychological effects following disaster. The direct effect of time in debriefing on symptoms implies that those needing more than two hours debriefing should have been targeted for more intensive counseling since they reported higher symptom levels. Debriefing did have a direct relationship with social support quality and, in turn, influenced perceptions of beneficial changes in family life since the disaster. This relationship suggests that debriefing helps develop social skills and enhances the quality of social relationships, allowing better utilization of available support resources (particularly within the family). While more work is required to examine this possibility, if this inference is correct, then the assessment and development of social skills and family relationships have a role to play in trauma mitigation (see also Scotti et al., 1995; Wraith, 1994). Taken together, these data highlight the important role played by organizational characteristics in the recovery process. They also indicate that organizational characteristics influence recovery both directly and indirectly through the quality of family relationships and life stress.

Paton, Smith, Ramsay, & Akande (1999) adopted a different approach to examining the organizational influence of traumatic reactivity by exploring the psychometric structure of responses to traumatic events using the Impact of Event Scale (IES–Horowitz et al., 1979). If a scale is accessing a latent construct the structural relations between items should hold irrespective of, for the example, professional or organizational membership. Using this approach Paton et al. (1999) examined the structural dimensions of traumatic reactivity across organizations (e.g., human service and emergency service organizations), professions (e.g., fire fighters versus social workers) and countries (e.g., by comparing Scottish and Australian fire fighters). Multidimensional scaling was used to examine structural relationships to determine if the organizational environment influenced the nature of traumatic stress reactions. It was hypothesized that if the environment does not influence response, a high level of structural homogeneity would be observed across the populations sampled. A two-dimensional solution (Figure 11.2) reveals considerable heterogeneity in structural relations. The hypothesis was thus not supported. These data

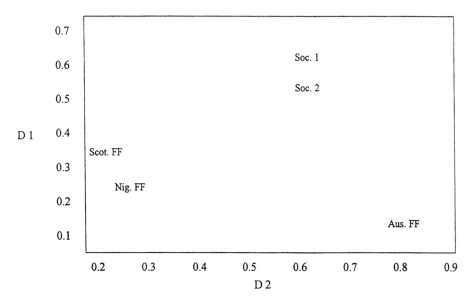

Figure 11.2. Heterogeneity in interorganizational structural relationships using the Impact of Event scale. Adapted from Paton, Smith, Ramsay, and Akande (1999). FF denotes fire fighter groups (Scot. = Scottish, Nig. = Nigerian, Aus. = Australian. Soc. denotes a Social Service agency (1=1993 survey, 2=1995 survey. D1: Action-Thought dimension and D2: Intrusion-Avoidance dimension.

reinforce the view that the organizational environment influences traumatic stress reactions in high-risk professions and that professional, organizational and cultural factors influence the underlying traumatic stress construct that serves as a basis for the interpretation of specific experiences. That this construct appears to have a learned component signals the possibility that the interpretive schemata that facilitate a sense of coherence and impose meaning on experience can be developed and are influenced by the organizational environment.

Taken together, these studies illustrate the important role played by organizational contexts in traumatic stress process and suggests that organizational intervention can be used to prevent/minimize reactivity prior to exposure rather than waiting until after the event. Given the likely diversity in organizational characteristics, highly prescriptive, generalized and invariant postevent stress management interventions will be inadequate as a means of managing reactivity. Intervention models such as CISM, while conducted for work groups, focus on the relationships between a person or group and a traumatic incident and do not provide opportunity to elicit an understanding of work environment influences on reactions (which can only be done after detailed organizational analysis over time). Nor do they provide mechanisms for rectifying problems at organizational or cultural levels. However, given that work-related traumatic stress reactions occur within an organizational context and are often directly related to job performance or professional role the environmental element becomes particularly important. Consequently, an intervention that focuses only on the symptomatic correlates of a work experience is tackling only part of the problem. Having identified the organizational environment as a salient variable, the next step in the process involves identifying organizational characteristics with a potential to influence outcome.

Dispositional Vulnerability and Resilience: Organizational Assessment

The often pronounced differences in reactions documented within the trauma literature has heightened awareness of the role of individual differences as determinants of reactivity. With respect to vulnerability characteristics, Scotti, Beach, Northrop, Rode, and Forsyth (1995) identified three categories. Biological vulnerability factors include genetically-based predispositions (e.g., heightened autonomic and physiological reactivity) and changes in physiological reactivity as a consequence of prior traumatic exposure. Their second category, historical antecedents, included learning history, socioeconomic status, experience of child abuse, and preexisting psychopathology. The final category, psychological vulnerability, described learned behavior including avoidance of threat situations, social skills deficits leading to problems obtaining and utilizing social support, hypervigilance of threat-relevant cues, inadequate problem-solving behavior, domestic violence and divorce, and drug and alcohol abuse. Vulnerability can also be influenced by the persons history of traumatic experience prior to their employment (Paton, 1999). Important issues here are the nature, frequency, timing and extent of resolution of such experiences. Transient factors such as health status (e.g., colds, flu), fatigue (e.g., if called to manage a disaster at the end of a days work), and psychological fitness (e.g., occupational stress, personal concerns), can increase stress vulnerability.

Individuals can also differ in regard to their resilience characteristics. As the contents of this book demonstrate (see Stuhlmiller & Dunning, Chapter 2; Bartone, Chapter 7), traits such as hardiness can constitute stress protective factors. Lyons (1991) review of the literature covering individual differences in posttrauma coping identified level of control over cognitive reexperience, perceived meaning, behavioral self-blame, attributional style, and hardiness as possible mediating factors. Other factors such as emotional stability, decisiveness, controlled risk-taking, self-awareness, tolerance for ambiguity, and self-efficacy may facilitate resilience (Flin, 1996; Paton, 1989, 1997). There is a clear need to identify resilience and vulnerability characteristics and to develop the psychometric instruments with which they can be assessed (Paton & Smith, 1999).

In addition to facilitating understanding of the stress process, knowledge of the relationship between dispositional characteristics and outcome has other implications (Paton, 1997a; 1999). For example, vulnerability data can be used to identify groups (e.g., older staff, ethnic minorities, single parents, staff with young children) likely to present special needs following their involvement in a traumatic incident. On another level, vulnerability and resilience data can be used to, for example, anticipate staff needs, select resilient staff for business continuity roles, and/or for prioritizing postevent support provision and monitoring.

Cognitive Resilience: Coherence, Meaning, and Training

The organizational strategy most amenable to facilitating a sense of meaning and coherence on atypical and emotionally threatening events is training. Training represents a trauma mitigation strategy that works by reducing the perception of traumatic demands as stressors and assisting personnel to impose meaning upon their experience, so reducing psychological morbidity, enhancing performance capability and hastening the recovery of those affected (Alexander & Wells, 1991; Driskell & Salas, 1996; Paton, 1994, see also Violanti, Chapter 9).

Resilience can be enhanced by adopting an all-hazards approach to facilitate technical and psychological preparedness and to develop an adaptable response capability (Paton, Flin, & Violanti, 1999). In addition to knowledge and skill development, training should address how the traumatic incident context influences performance and well-being (Paton, 1994). According to this model training designed to facilitate resilience requires two inputs. One involves the detailed analysis of emergency response roles, tasks, and responsibilities to define the skills and knowledge required to protect well-being. The second involves considering how the operating environment can render operational procedures and expectations inadequate or inappropriate to the needs of the situation.

The characteristics of the routine operating environment (e.g., clear role/task expectations, hierarchical reporting and command structures) are incorporated into the psychological frameworks (schemata) that guide response and become implicit, or "taken for granted," facets of routine operations. However, their importance as determinants of well-being and performance effectiveness may go unrealized until faced with atypical operational demands (e.g., scale of infrastructure disruption, multiagency operating environments, rapid role change) which challenge these assumptions (Flin, 1996; Paton, 1994). This signals a need to develop procedures, and expectations that accurately reflect the operating context in which expertise is applied. This model also illustrates the interaction between cognitive and environmental determinants of resilience and the importance of developing a systems perspective for analysis and intervention.

The relative infrequence of traumatic events means that developing the capability to impose coherence and meaning on such experiences requires the use of simulations that model the demands, competencies and contextual factors likely to be encountered in emergencies. Simulations afford opportunities for individuals to review plans, develop technical and management skills, practice their use under realistic circumstances, receive feedback on their performance, increase awareness of stress reactions, and facilitate rehearsal of strategies to minimize stress reactions (Paton et al., 1999; Moran, 1999; see also Violanti, Chapter 9).

While training can reduce reactivity and hasten recovery, the latter takes time, differs from person to person, and occurs within an organizational environment that represents a resource that can, depending upon its characteristics, act as either a vulnerability or as a resilience factor. In addition to its systems and procedures, managerial personnel can exercise a significant influence on the manner in which events are perceived, and on recovery. Further, managers are well placed to manage recovery over time and to adapt support and organizational procedures to accommodate individual differences. It is to a discussion of some of these factors that this chapter now turns.

Environmental Resilience: Organizational Characteristics and Managerial Behavior

Traumatic stress reactions are influenced by organizational characteristics (e.g., management style, reporting procedures) and bureaucratic flexibility (Alexander & Wells, 1991; Doepal, 1991; Dunning, 1994; Eränen et al., 1999; Paton et al., 1999; Powell, 1991). Bureaucratic systems can, through persistent use of established procedures when responding to crisis demands, internal conflicts regarding responsibility, and a desire to protect the organization from criticism or blame act as a vulnerability factor, complicate staff recovery, and increase absenteeism, performance, treatment and compensation costs (Doepal, 1991; Powell, 1991; Stephens, Long, & Miller, 1997).

To sustain staff, and constitute a resilience resource, management procedures designed specifically to manage response and recovery (both for staff and productivity) and organizational ownership of the crisis and its implications (Paton, 1997 a,b; Paton, Johnston, & Houghton, 1998) are essential. Moreover, these activities may be required over a period of several months. Training of senior management and considerable organizational development may be required to plan and implement systems designed to support staff rather than (pre-existing) bureaucratic imperatives.

Managerial behavior and attitudes represents another potential environmental vulnerability factor. Managers have a key role to play in both response and recovery, but often lack the capability and/or willingness to realize their potential in this context (Alexander & Wells, 1991; Dunning, 1994; Paton, 1997a; Paton & Violanti 1996; Violanti & Paton, 1999). For example, a cultural predisposition to suppress emotional disclosure, contempt for those displaying emotions, or focusing on attributing blame can undermine support provision (Dunning, 1994). Managerial activities which minimize the significance of reactions or feelings inhibit recovery and extend performance deficits. Consequently, developing managerial capability represents a worthwhile and cost-effective organizational mitigation strategy. Developing managerial capability as a resilience factor involves training covering, for example: participative and supportive management style; acknowledging and accepting staff needs; identifying and meeting staff needs; communication; planning and contingent plan implementation skills; delegation; managing uncertainty and ambiguity; and managing recovery and the return to productive functioning (Paton, 1997b).

Managerial behavior likely to sustain resilience includes their acting as role models (e.g., acknowledging their own feelings) and providing feedback to staff (Alexander & Wells, 1991; Duckworth, 1986; Dunning, 1994; Paton, 1997b). This behavior also demonstrates how staff can reconcile the personal impact of the event with the process of returning to work, and provides a framework for the positive resolution of their experience. The latter can be facilitated by assisting staff to identify the strengths that helped them deal with the traumatic event or using the experience to discuss how future incidents could be dealt with more effectively. Managers can also promote recovery by supplying accurate information about what happened, what may happen (e.g., trials, inquiries), providing opportunities to discuss experiences, attend funerals and memorial services, and helping staff return to work.

Returning to work and getting back into normal routines is therapeutic. This helps personnel put their experience into perspective, helps them regain a sense of perceived control, and facilitates access to support networks. However, managing the gradual return and reintegration into work requires careful planning and judgement. Managers should ensure that staff do not take on too much too soon and, because cognitive capacities may be temporarily diminished, remind them to take care when, for example, driving or making complex decisions.

At a more general level, organizational analyses can help define the climate of relationships between managers and staff and determine its implications for support and recovery (Paton, 1997 a,b). In the longer term, such analyses can contribute to organizational development programs through, for example, identifying response constraints within organizational systems (e.g., lack of policy and procedures for managing workplace assault or deaths, inadequate reintegration and recovery procedures and capabilities). This information can be used both to promote future response effectiveness and to develop and maintain a supportive organizational climate.

While not representing an exhaustive list by any means, it is clear that the organizational environment represents a rich resource for post-trauma research and intervention planning. More work in this area is clearly required and, consistent with the thesis of this book, this must focus on the potential of individual and organizational attributes and practices to act as resilience and vulnerability factors.

CONCLUSION

Given the influence of organizational characteristics on the nature, intensity and duration of traumatic stress symptoms, it is important to accommodate their role in mitigation and recovery planning. Crucial issues here include examining the conceptual validity of the "work trauma" construct, the identification of salient dispositional and environmental variables, and defining the mechanisms responsible for growth and distress outcomes. It was proposed here that a risk management model would represent an appropriate framework for organizing the complex relationships between variables that can, over time or in different circumstances, constitute both vulnerability and resilience factors and provide a framework capable of explaining the diverse outcomes recorded in the work trauma literature. Once salient variables are identified, it will be vital to be able to assess them using instruments with known and sound psychometric properties. Since the nature and implications of the relationships between these factors can change over time, multiwave longitudinal designs, and methods capable of the analysis of change data will be required (Paton & Smith, 1999). This chapter described assessment, training, organizational design strategies that are consistent with, and provide a means of operationalizing, the resilience paradigm outlined by Dunning (1999). This paradigm focuses attention on mitigating traumatic stress risk and facilitating recovery and growth in individuals for whom work-related traumatic stress is, or becomes, an occupational reality.

REFERENCES

Adams, J.: *Risk*. London: UCL Press, 1995.

Aldwin, C.M., Levenson, M.R., and Spiro, III, A.: Vulnerability and resilience to combat exposure: Can stress have lifelong effects? *Psychology and Aging, 9:* 34–44, 1994.

Alexander, D.A., and Wells, A.: Reactions of police officers to body handling after a major disaster: A before and after comparison. *British Journal of Psychiatry, 159:* 517–555, 1991.

Andersen, H.S., Christensen, A.K., and Petersen, G.O.: Posttraumatic stress reactions amongst rescue workers after a major rail accident. *Anxiety Research, 4:* 245–251, 1991.

Bartone, P.T., Ursano, R.J., Wright, K.M., and Ingraham, L.H. (1989). The impact of a military air disaster on the health of assistance workers. *The Journal of Nervous and Mental Disease, 177:* 317–328, 1989.

Blaikie, P., Cannon, T., Davis, I, and Wisner, B.: *At risk: Natural hazards, people's vulnerability and disaster*. London: Routledge, 1994.

Davies, H., and Walters, M.: Do all crises have to become disasters? Risk and risk mitigation. *Disaster Prevention and Management, 7:* 396–400, 1998.

Doepal, D.: Crisis management: The psychological dimension. *Industrial Crisis Quarterly, 5:* 177–188, 1991.

Driskell, J., and Salas, E.: *Stress and Human Performance*. Hillsdale, NJ: Lawrence Erlbaum, 1996.

Duckworth, D.: Psychological problems arising from disaster work. *Stress Medicine, 2:* 315–323, 1986.

Dunning, C.: Trauma and countertransference in the workplace. In J.P. Wilson and J.D. Lindy (Eds.): *Countertransference in the treatment of PTSD*. New York: Guildford Press, 1994.

Dunning, C.: Postintervention strategies to reduce police trauma: A paradigm shift. In J.M. Violanti, & D. Paton (Eds.): *Police trauma: Psychological aftermath of civilian combat*. Springfield, IL: Charles C Thomas, 1999.

Eränen, L., Millar, M., and Paton, D.: *Organizational recovery from disaster: Traumatic response within voluntary disaster workers*. Paper presented at the International Society for Stress Studies Conference, Istanbul, Turkey, June, 1999.

Eränen, L., Paavola, J., and Kajanne, A.: Psykologinen jälkipuiuti ja travmaattisten muistojen jäscutyminen kertomuksiksi. *Suomen Lääkärilehti, 7:* 1999.

Flin, R.: *Sitting in the hot seat: Leaders and teams for critical incident management*. Chichester: Wiley, 1996.

Hartsough, D.M., and Myers, D.G.: *Disaster work and mental health: Prevention and control of stress among workers*. U.S. Department of Health and Human Services, 1985.

Holmes, T., and Rahe, R.: The social readjustment rating scale. *Journal of Psychosomatic Research, 11:* 213–218, 1967.

Hood, C., and Jones, D.K.C.: *Accident and design: Contemporary debates in risk management*. London: UCL Press, 1996.

Horowitz, M., Wilner, M., and Alvarez, W.: Impact of event scale: A measure of subjective stress. *Psychosomatic Medicine, 41:* 209–218, 1979.

Kalimo, R., Olkkonen, M., and Toppinen, S.: Ihminen kehittyvassa tuotannossa: I and II. *Tyo ja ihminen: Tyomparistotutkmuksen aikakauskirja, lisanumero 4/93 & 5/93:* 1993.

Kasperson, R.E.: The social amplification of risk: Progress in developing an integrative framework. In S. Krimsky and D. Golding (Eds.): *Social Theories of Risk.* London: Praeger, 1992.

Lyons, J.A.: Strategies for assessing the potential for positive adjustment following trauma. *Journal of Traumatic Stress, 4:* 93–111, 1991.

Marmar, C.R., Weiss, D.S., Metzler, T.J., Ronfeldt, H.M., and Foreman, C.: Stress responses of emergency services personnel to the Loma Prieta Earthquake Interstate 880 freeway collapse and control traumatic incidents. *Journal of Traumatic Stress, 9:* 63–86, 1996.

Moran, C.C.: Recruits' prediction of positive reactions in disaster and emergency work. *Disaster Prevention and Management, 8:* 177–183, 1999.

Moran, C.C., and Colless, E.: Positive reactions following emergency and disaster responses. *Disaster Prevention and Management, 4:* 55–60, 1995.

Paton, D.: Disasters and helpers: Psychological dynamics and implications for counseling. *Counseling Psychology Quarterly, 2:* 303–321, 1989.

Paton, D.: Training disaster workers: Promoting well-being and operational effectiveness. *Disaster Prevention and Management, 5:* 10–16, 1996.

Paton, D.: Managing work-related psychological trauma: An organizational psychology of response and recovery. *Australian Psychologist, 32:* 46–55, 1997a.

Paton, D.: *Dealing with traumatic incidents in the workplace.* (3rd ed.) Queensland, Australia: Gull Publishing, 1997b.

Paton, D.: Disaster business continuity: Promoting staff capability. *Disaster Prevention and Management, 8:* 127–133, 1999.

Paton, D., Flin, R., and Violanti, J.: Incident response and recovery management. In J.M. Violanti and D. Paton (Eds): *Police trauma: Psychological aftermath of civilian combat.* Springfield, IL: Charles C Thomas, 1999.

Paton, D.; Johnston, D., and Houghton, B.: Organizational responses to a volcanic eruption. *Disaster Prevention and Management, 7:* 5–13, 1998.

Paton, D., and Smith, L.M.: Assessment, conceptual and methodological issues in researching traumatic stress in police officers. In J.M. Violanti and D. Paton (Eds.): *Police trauma: Psychological aftermath of civilian combat.* Springfield, IL: Charles C Thomas, 1999.

Paton, D., Smith, L.M. Ramsay, R., and Akande, D.: A structural reassessment of the Impact of Event Scale: The influence of occupational and cultural contexts. In R. Gist and B. Lubin (Eds.): *Response to disaster: Psychosocial, community and ecological approaches.* Philadelphia: Taylor & Francis, 1999.

Paton, D. and Violanti, J.: *Traumatic stress in critical occupations: Recognition, consequences and treatment.* Springfield, IL: Charles C Thomas, 1996.

Paton, D., Violanti, J., and Schmuckler, E.: Chronic exposure to risk and trauma: Addiction and separation issues in police officers. In J.M. Violanti and D. Paton (Eds.): *Police trauma: Psychological aftermath of civilian combat*. Springfield, IL: Charles C Thomas, 1999.

Powell, T.C.: Shaken, but alive: Organizational behaviour in the wake of catastrophic events. *Industrial Crisis Quarterly, 5:* 271–291, 1991.

Raphael, B., Lundin, T., and Weisaeth, L.: A research method for the study of psychological and psychiatric aspects of disaster. *Acta Psychiatrica Scandinavica, supplement 353, Vol. 80:* 1989.

Scotti, J.R., Beach, B.K., Northrop, L.M.E., Rode, C.A., and Forsyth, J.P.: The psychological impact of accidental injury. In J.R. Freedy and S.E. Hobfoll (Eds.): *Traumatic stress: From theory to practice*. New York: Plenum Press, 1995.

Smallman, C., and Weir, D.: Communication and cultural distortion during crises. *Disaster Prevention and Management, 8:* 33–41, 1999.

Stephens, C., Long, N., and Miller, I.: The impact of trauma and social support on posttraumatic stress disorder: A study of New Zealand police officers. *Journal of Criminal Justice, 25:* 303–314, 1997.

Tedeschi R., and Calhoun, L: Posttraumatic growth inventory: Measuring the positive legacy of trauma. *Journal of Traumatic Stress, 9:* 455–471, 1996.

Violanti, J.M. (1990). Posttrauma vulnerability: A proposed model. In J.W. Reese, J.M. Horn, and C. Dunning (Eds.): *Critical Incidents in Policing*. U.S. Government Printing Office, Washington, DC, 1990.

Violanti, J.: Residuals of occupational trauma: Separation from police duty. In D. Paton and J. Violanti (Eds.): *Traumatic stress in critical occupations: Recognition, consequences and treatment*. Springfield, IL: Charles C Thomas, 1996.

Violanti, J.M. and Paton, D.: *Police trauma: Psychological aftermath of civilian combat*. Springfield, IL: Charles C Thomas, 1999.

Williams, T.: Trauma in the workplace. In J.P. Wilson and B. Raphael (Eds.): *International Handbook of Traumatic Stress Syndromes*. New York: Plenum Press, 1993.

Wraith, R.: The impact of major events on children. In R. Watts and D.J. de la Horne (Eds.): *Coping with trauma*. Brisbane: Australian Academic Press, 1994.

Chapter 12

POSTTRAUMA STRESS INTERVENTION:
PURSUING THE ALTERNATIVES

Douglas Paton, John M. Violanti and Chris Dunning

DISASTERS AND TRAUMATIC incidents will continue to be part of the human experience for the foreseeable future. Moreover, several professions, most notably law enforcement, fire and rescue, and the military, may have to deal with their effects repeatedly throughout their careers and, consequently, risk experiencing traumatic stress reactions. In this context, the need for intervention to manage traumatic stress is self-evident.

In the past, the practice has been to provide posttrauma intervention with the intention of managing the anticipated pathological reactions that were assumed to be an inevitable consequence of exposure to some critical or traumatic incident. As the contents of this text testify, however, the experience of such incidents can be interpreted positively by, and may constitute a stimulus for personal and professional growth in, those so involved. Consequently, assumptions of automatic pathology may be premature and misleading.

There is a need to rethink our approach to intervention and to focus on developing those capable of assisting individuals and groups to utilize natural coping and resilience mechanisms to facilitate positive outcomes. This represents a departure both in the prevailing goals of contemporary trauma intervention and its timing in relation to the events under consideration. We will revisit this issue later in this concluding chapter. First, we must acknowledge the fact that posttrauma intervention may still be required, albeit by a smaller proportion of those involved than existing models and paradigms. There is, however, little evidence to support the continued use of existing approaches.

During the past 15–20 years, posttrauma intervention in work-related contexts has been dominated by Critical Incident Stress Debriefing/Management (CISM) (Mitchell, 1983; Mitchell & Everly, 1997). However, despite its long history and popularity as a posttrauma intervention, the contributions to this text collectively propose a need for alternatives to such pathogenic methods. Many of the authors have presented theoretical, procedural and conceptual critiques of pathogenic models and offered explanation for the observed relationship between these models and possible iatrogenic effects in some of those exposed to this intervention. More importantly, these authors also presented several alternative protocols for the management of posttrauma reactions.

The continued, and growing, risk to diverse occupational and community groups of exposure to traumatic events and adversity highlights the importance of having in place posttrauma interventions that are theoretically and ecologically sound. With respect to the latter, differences between groups with respect to organizational structures and procedures, professional philosophy, goals, experience, personal histories and the nature of a given experience illustrate the complex web of factors that will interact with the traumatic event to influence the nature and intensity of reactions (Violanti & Paton, 1999). Consequently, intervention must be tailored to the needs and circumstances of those they are intended to assist. The contributors to this text have illustrated the existence of such procedures and provided direction for their future development, particularly with respect to ensuring a capability to meet the needs of diverse groups. In the context of diversity, the inadequacy of idiosyncratic, uniformly delivered procedures to exercise their intended effect is understandable. Similarly, diversity must be accommodated within any research agenda.

This book goes beyond alternative posttrauma interventions. While it is essential to have in place interventions capable of meeting the needs of those who do experience posttraumatic stress, it is important that we do not focus exclusively on pathological outcomes, nor should we wait until exposure has occurred before intervening.

The contributors to this text have uniformly argued for traumatic experience and disaster exposure to be recognized for their potential to contribute to positive outcomes and growth. Pursuing this paradigm shift (Dunning, 1999) also requires that we consider alternative and more neutral labels to describe the focal "critical" or "traumatic" incidents and that we develop alternative ways of conceptualizing traumatic stress processes and interventions.

The realization of the importance of, and benefits accruing from, the adoption of a salutogenic paradigm is coming from diverse perspectives. In this text, we have seen it emerging from psychological, sociological, psychiatric, nursing, military, law enforcement, and fire and rescue service perspectives. If we add to this professional diversity the breadth and depth of theoretical and empirically evaluated work that is emerging to support its adoption, it appears that salutogenesis has come of age. Taken together, the contents of this text have demonstrated that natural coping and resilience mechanisms can constitute powerful protective and recovery resources that are capable of channeling adversity into a vehicle for growth rather than distress.

We must, however, do more than attract attention to the fact that alternatives exist. We must also direct our efforts to developing strategies and interventions capable of maximizing resilience and facilitating growth. As Stuhlmiller and Dunning, Gist and Woodall, Perrin-Klingler, MacLeod, and Calhoun and Tedeschi have demonstrated, this challenge has been accepted and considerable inroads have already been made towards realizing this potential. In their respective chapters, Bartone, Violanti, and Paton, Smith, Violanti and Eranen provided theoretical and empirical demonstrations of the role of hardiness, coping and inoculation training as resilience resources and their capability for assisting employees to realize growth outcomes. Calhoun and Tedeschi illustrated how the debriefing process could be refocused to facilitate the attainment of growth outcomes. We still, however, have some way to go, both with respect to encouraging organizational adoption of alternative posttrauma interventions and salutogenic mitigation strategies and having rigorous and systematic research with which to fully understand salutogenic processes and outcomes.

These issues are certainly not only of "theoretical" value. They are highly significant at practical levels. To not rigorously pursue this line of thinking and action would constitute a significant disservice to those we seek to assist. Of particular importance is the fact that adoption of a salutogenic paradigm clarifies the possibility of intervening in ways that can mitigate traumatic stress, and possibly, in some cases, eliminate the risk of experiencing negative consequences. Of greater significance, though, are the possibilities that this way of thinking opens up for developing and implementing strategies that maximize the potential for growth in those who face exposure to adversity.

Pursuing salutogenic goals will require not just a new way of thinking about an old problem. As Stuhlmiller and Dunning and Gist and Woodall pointed out, the popularity of pathogenic models can be attributed to their low cost and ease of administration. Pursuing a salutogenic alternative will require organizational and attitudinal change and a high level of commitment to the protection of mental health. Resistance to its adoption could be anticipated from an organizational perception of these alternatives, particularly those involving wholesale change, being more costly than the pathogenic protocols they replace. However, costs of implementing intervention alternatives described here must be weighed against the costs associated with continuing to provide services that may contribute to mental health problems and ultimately contribute to the performance, compensation and litigation costs that organizations are trying to avoid. Even if not done for purely altruistic reasons, there thus exist several economic grounds for pursuing the salutogenic alternatives. Another reason for the popularity of CISM was its simplicity. We have seen here that this simplicity was acquired at the expense of being able to cater for the needs of diverse groups and their respective experiences. As Gist and Woodall pointed out, there are no simple solutions to this problem, but there are solutions.

Realizing the benefits of a salutogenic approach has significant research implications. The contributions to this text have emphasized the need to develop theories and models capable of accommodating individual and organizational diversity, the complexity of traumatic stress processes, and the fact that exposure to adversity can have several consequences, both positive and negative. This, in turn, has implications for the manner in which precipitating events and reactions are defined, the way in which the antecedents and context are conceptualized, the measurement instruments and research methodology required, and the interventions developed and used. With respect to the events themselves, perhaps we should start to think of them as forms of adversity rather than describing them as "traumatic" events. Attention must also be directed towards the other constructs and variables that will constitute the fabric of understanding.

Bartone commented on the need for refining the hardiness construct, similarly, in their respective chapters, Paton, Smith, Violanti and Eranen, Gist and Woodall, Violanti, and MacLeod, identified a wide range of personal, cognitive, and environmental factors that have been implicated as vulnerability or resilience factors. Identifying those that are salient, the conditions under which they attain this status, and defining the mechanisms by which they influence well-being represents a major goal for future research in this area. Pursuing this objective raises some important conceptual, measurement and methodological issues.

For example, it remains to be determined whether "vulnerability" and "resilience" represent discrete or continuous constructs, or possibly a mixture of both. This issue has considerable significance in the context of modeling traumatic stress processes. We also need to devote more attention to defining the salient variables, developing rigorous means for their measurement, and modeling the processes by which they exercise their influence. Further, the contributions to this text have consistently emphasized how traumatic stress processes are dynamic. Consequently, research and evaluation methodology must be capable of dealing with the modeling and analysis of change (Paton & Smith, 1999).

In conclusion, this book has demonstrated the need for alternatives to the prevailing model of posttrauma intervention and described several such alternatives. It is important that posttrauma intervention is driven less by dogma and pecuniary interest and more by rigorous research and evaluation. The contributions to this text have repeatedly demonstrated how theoretically and ecologically sound intervention can facilitate recovery and growth in those who have faced adversity.

A second goal of this book was to focus attention on alternative ways of thinking about patterns of interaction between people and adversity. Collectively, the contents of this book have advocated the adoption of a salutogenic paradigm for conceptualizing, researching designing and delivering effective trauma intervention. The adoption of a salutogenic offers opportunities to intervene to mitigate traumatic stress reactions, to develop resilience, and to provide the individual and organizational resources necessary to sustain resilience and facilitate growth outcomes in those who encounter adversity.

Much of our focus was on alternative ways of thinking about patterns of interaction between people and adversity. The adoption of a salutogenic paradigm has been advocated for conceptualizing, researching designing, and delivering effective trauma intervention. This paradigm offers opportunities to effectively intervene into traumatic stress reactions, and provide resources necessary to sustain resilience and facilitate growth in persons affected. It is important that we recognize the evolutionary nature of trauma intervention and not fall into the complacency status of present pathogenic approaches.

REFERENCES

Dunning, C.: Post-intervention strategies to reduce police trauma: A paradigm shift. In J.M. Violanti, and D. Paton, (Eds.): *Police trauma: Psychological aftermath of civilian combat.* Springfield, IL: Charles C Thomas, 1999.

Mitchell, J. T.: When disaster strikes : The critical incident stress debriefing process. *Journal of Emergency Medical Services, 8:* 36–39, 1983.

Mitchell, J. T., and Everly, G. S., Jr.: The scientific evidence for critical incident stress management. *Journal of Emergency Medical Services, 22:* 86–93, 1997.

Paton, D., and Smith, L.M.: Assessment, conceptual and methodological issues in researching traumatic stress in police officers. In J.M. Violanti, and D. Paton (Eds.): *Police trauma: Psychological aftermath of civilian combat.* Springfield, IL: Charles C Thomas, 1999.

Violanti, J.M., and Paton, D.: *Police trauma: Psychological aftermath of civilian combat.* Springfield, IL: Charles C Thomas, 1999.

AUTHOR INDEX

SUBJECT INDEX